ISBN 978-1-330-55369-5
PIBN 10077772

1 MONTH OF
FREE
READING

at

www.ForgottenBooks.com

By purchasing this book you are eligible for one month membership to ForgottenBooks.com, giving you unlimited access to our entire collection of over 1,000,000 titles via our web site and mobile apps.

To claim your free month visit: www.forgottenbooks.com/free77772

English
Français
Deutsche
Italiano
Español
Português

www.forgottenbooks.com

Mythology Photography **Fiction**
Fishing Christianity **Art** Cooking
Essays Buddhism Freemasonry
Medicine **Biology** Music **Ancient
Egypt** Evolution Carpentry Physics
Dance Geology **Mathematics** Fitness
Shakespeare **Folklore** Yoga Marketing
Confidence Immortality Biographies
Poetry **Psychology** Witchcraft
Electronics Chemistry History **Law**
Accounting **Philosophy** Anthropology
Alchemy Drama Quantum Mechanics
Atheism Sexual Health **Ancient History**
Entrepreneurship Languages Sport
Paleontology Needlework Islam
Metaphysics Investment Archaeology
Parenting Statistics Criminology
Motivational

HUGH LANE.

From the portrait by J. S. Sargent.

HUGH LANE'S LIFE AND ACHIEVEMENT, WITH SOME ACCOUNT OF THE DUBLIN GALLERIES. BY LADY GREGORY

WITH ILLUSTRATIONS

54,329

LONDON

JOHN MURRAY, ALBEMARLE STREET, W. 1

1921

TIVE

TO ALEC MARTIN, HUGH'S FRIEND AND MINE

L'ART DE DONNER UN MUSÉE

(From *Le Figaro*, March 20, 1908.)

"Voilà une belle merveille de faire bonne chère avec bien de l'argent ! C'est la chose la plus aisée du monde . . ., mais pour agir en habile homme, il faut parler de faire bonne chére avec peu d'argent ! "

De même pourrait-on dire, à l'exemple de Valère : " Voilà une belle merveille de créer un musée avec quelques millions. Tout le monde y pourrait réussir . . . (et encore ! . . .), mais créer, sans fortune, sans appui d'aucune sorte, et avec pour uniqucs armes une volonté tenace et un passionné amour du beau, un musée complet, riche en belles œuvres, un musée envié des Etats les plus prospères et des cités les plus orgueilleuses, puis donner à une ville qu'on aime ce trésor rassemblé avec tant d'efforts et de sollicitude :—voilà qui est agir mieux encore qu'en habile homme."

Cette comparaison nous venait à l'esprit en recevant le catalogue illustré de ce nouveau musée d'art moderne de Dublin, qui vient de s'ouvrir pour la plus grande gloire de son créateur et donateur, M. Hugh Lane.

Singulier et attrayant personnage que celui-là, et type qui ne court pas les rues. Il est fait pour

tendre la main à travers mers et continents à
M. de Tschudi, de qui notre correspondant,
M. Charles Bonnefon, disait l'autre jour l'œuvre
et annonçait le repos momentané. Seulement, si
M. de Tschudi a créé à la Galerie nationale de
Berlin une section d'art moderne très remarquable,
et cela avec le concours d'amis très riches—ce
qui ne diminue pas son mérite,—Hugh Lane, lui,
a créé un musée tout entier à Dublin, sans le
secours de personne. Comment s'y est-il pris ?
Voici :

M. Hugh Lane a fréquenté assidûment les
expositions parisiennes et les ventes londoniennes
chez Christie. Ce furent ses deux sources d'ali-
mentation. Avec une très petite mise de fonds,
qui fut promptement absorbée, il achetait quelques
toiles. Il en revendait la majeure partie, gardait
celles qu'il destinait à son futur musée, s'endettait
et s'enrichissait (si cela peut s'appeler ainsi),
successivement. Au fur et à mesure de ces
opérations, le noyau du musée se formait. C'est
ainsi qu'un grand nombre de peintures lui passèr-
ent par les mains et qu'un nombre plus restreint
d'œuvres choisies fut gardé jalousement.

On nous contait ce trait delicieux. A un
voyage à Paris, il lui restait quelques centaines
de francs ; il convoitait deux dessins de Puvis de
Chavannes qui valaient cette somme. Le mar-
chand à qui il les achète le connaissant bien et
s'intéressant à lui propose de lui faire crédit.
" Mais non, répond notre Lane. Il me reste mon
billet de retour et deux shillings six pence ; c'est
bien assez pour m'arranger jusqu'à Londres."
Et il emporte ses dessins.

C'est ainsi que se privant de tout, n'ayant pas de home, vivant presque comme un *tramp*, mais un *tramp* qui remuerait sans cesse des centaines et des centaines de mille francs, M. Hugh Lane, Irlandais amoureux d'art, a la joie d'avoir doté sa ville natale d'un musée d'art moderne que maintenant lui envie Londres. Quelle victoire pour l'Irlande !

Et ce n'est pas un musée de second ordre, croyez-le bien, que possède Dublin. On y voit entre autres une douzaine de Corots, dont une admirable et très importante figure de femme, et une ravissante et rarissime *Vue de Marseille ;* des aquarelles de Barye ; des dessins de Millet ; des peintures de Theodore Rousseau, de Daumier, de Courbet, de Monticelli, de Fantin-Latour, de Gérôme (l'éclectisme, vous le voyez, est encore une vertu de ce passionné) ; l'admirable *Femme à la toilette* de Puvis de Chavannes ; deux Manets d'une grande importance : le *Portrait d'Eva Gonzalès* et le *Concert Besselièvre ;* des œuvres de Rodin, de Legros, de Monet, de Renoir. Les écoles étrangères ont de très beaux représentants. Enfin, une très belle place est faite aux écoles britanniques, et une collection des célébrités irlandaises par les meilleurs peintres irlandais contemporains complète ce musée créé par un pauvre.

M. Hugh Lane a donné une belle leçon et un bel exemple à des gens que nous nommerions bien si nous avions le moindre espoir de leur voir suivre cet exemple et profiter de cette leçon.

ARSÈNE ALEXANDRE.

CONTENTS

LIST OF ILLUSTRATIONS

Hugh Lane was born November 9th, 1875.

1893. Taken into Colnaghi's Gallery in Pall Mall.

1898. Takes a room and begins dealing at 2, Pall Mall Place.

1902. Organises Exhibition of Old Masters in Dublin.

1904. Organises Exhibition of Irish Artists at the Guildhall.

1905. Exhibits Staats Forbes Collection in Dublin.

1906. Municipal Gallery in Harcourt Street opened.

Is presented with his portrait painted by Sargent "in recognition of his unselfish and untiring efforts to establish a Gallery of Modern Art for Ireland."

1908. Organises Irish Art Gallery at Franco-British Exhibition.

1909. Knighted.

Goes to Johannesburg to organise Picture Gallery founded by Lady Phillips.

1912. Makes collection of pictures for gallery at Cape Town founded and presented by Mr. Michaelis.

1914. Appointed Director of the National Gallery of Ireland.

1915. Gives £10,000 to Red Cross sale for Mr. Sargent's canvas.

Lost with the *Lusitania*, aged thirty-nine.

HUGH LANE'S LIFE AND ACHIEVEMENT

CHAPTER I

THE CHAIN OF CAUSES

WHEN I sometimes said to Hugh that two lives had been spoiled, been squandered, for his making, I said it half in jest. And yet in pondering as to where he came from, what his roots were, how that daring imagination and amazing fulfilment found its place in the line of a county family of Galway, a professional family of Cork, it sometimes seems to me that I did not exaggerate, that the sacrifice was necessary, that a clash between opposing natures had been needed to create such a fiery current, that the force which enabled him to accomplish in his shortened life so much that will endure, could have come from no other well-head than that romantic unhappy marriage, that ill-mated parentage.

His mother, my sister Adelaide Persse, was among the elders of my mother's many children when I was but a child. Elizabeth was the clever one of the family ; Gertrude the musical, the popular one; Adelaide the beauty. She had been named at her christening after the then Queen Dowager "because she was such a good woman." I don't know that our Adelaide was in those days good out of the common, but she was queenly as poets and painters of the Renaissance have taught us to imagine queens; the head well carried, the oval face well moulded, the stature sufficient: the dark, beautiful eyes were at tragic moments indignant, but their expression changed to happy content when she was with children or occupied with the handiwork or embroidery she loved. Henry James once asked me of a girl in whose marriage we had a common interest, "Is she a mother or a wife? Every woman is more of one than the other." I think Adelaide was by nature a mother, yielding to and loving the weakness and waywardness of a child, rather than a wife easily yielding to the yoke. And in those days the submission ordered by St. Paul was a part of religion—even a wife's control of her own money was denied by law at the time of her marriage settlements—and this denial had in it the seed of later trouble. With all her kindliness she was a somewhat stern judge of herself and those dear to her. I have sometimes meditated on the marriages possible to her, or made by her sisters, and wondered if she could have been satisfied in any, and I have always seen where the struggle would have come. She had the strength of will and obstinacy that one recognised long after in Hugh's tenacity, in what I have called "his hard patience." Though to the end of her life she could not understand and even resented his lavish giving outside his own family or the recognised poor, I find it akin to an open-handedness that never left her even in lean days, a desire "to satisfy the hungry, to banish every hardship, to save every sorrowful man"; only where she thought to satisfy with bread and meat, he was for building a temple in Jerusalem. She was shy and unresponsive, from a lack of self-confidence, in the society where she was so much admired, and never really loved it; and towards the end of her twenties she turned to religion in our sudden Evangelical way. From that time she, who had rustled the brightest silks over the largest crinoline, passionately wished to work for the souls and bodies of the poor. Her mind dwelt on ragged schools and refuges and hospitals; in these days she would, I think, have become a trained nurse, but such an escape from home barriers had not come into fashion in the seventies, at least not in our neighbourhood. She was for another season one of the beauties of the Viceregal Court, and the letters read at the breakfast table told of new fashions—I have some memory of a puzzling "rose and apple-green peplum"—and of compliments paid her, and great acquaintances. Hugh was amused one day when driving with him in London I pointed out the bronze heroic statue of one of his mother's old partners. Those of us who were still within the enclosure of the schoolroom had dreams of our beautiful sister being led back some day from that fairyland by some wonderful Marquis of Carabas. It was a shock when on her return from that last brilliant season it was discovered rather than confessed that she intended to marry a divinity student of Trinity College, six years her junior, without money or certain prospects beyond those in the Church. I remember the day well. It was as if there had been a death in the house. We knew nothing of his family—quite a good old professional one. " Who is he ? He may be the son of an *attorney !* " we whispered in horror. So he was, but our ideas of attorneys have widened since then ; I think we had taken them from Miss Edgeworth's novels. Our old nurse, half a century in the family, had a yet worse possibility in mind and was heard muttering, " I don't like those sort of names, Lane and Street and Field. They are apt to be given to foundlings."

The family authorities would not at first hear of the marriage, but after a while consented it should take place at the end of three years, during which the two lovers who had so far found but little chance of learning anything about each other, were not to meet or even to write more than, I think, once in a twelvemonth. At the end of two years the marriage took place.

I have called it a romantic one because each of the lovers was less in love with the other than with an illusion, an idea. The man had been dazzled by the sight of this lovely woman made much of and admired in a society, whether in country houses or Dublin Castle, he was not familiar with, and which was probably glorified by hearsay, but in which he was confident he could play a successful part. He was ambitious, and if there was something of forwardness, why should we blame the hope of advancement ?

Yet it was this self-confidence, this certainty of his own power to please, to gain his way, that I remember looking on with much disfavour in common with my family, even after I had been freed by my own happy marriage from many family traditions. But I know now that this very quality, this assurance, was needed in Hugh's making to balance his mother's shyness and sensitive pride. Without it I cannot imagine his quick success. I remember telling Sir Frederic Burton, the gentle Director of the Trafalgar Square National Gallery, of one of Hugh's early rapid dealings, and his answer, " I have never in all my life been able to have the same courage in my own opinion as that young man." In his later work it turned to an indomitable energy, the faith that breaks obstacles down.

But as to Mr. Lane, whether from slight or sufficient reason, Adelaide's friends and kindred would have none of him, the glorified life was still out of reach ; he had to see her in those first years of marriage with but the background of a curate's lodging in a smoky English town. He had another disillusionment—he had possessed some sentiment, some turn for poetry and literature. Had they spent even a few weeks together he would have found that she who never pretended, who as a child had given us a family word, " I hate *hypocry*," had no taste in these things. She told me long after that once in that long engagement she had sent him in place of the forbidden letter a copy of some poem, a religious one, she thought might please him, and it was not till a few days after their marriage she discovered he had all the time supposed her to be its author. She said, "It was a great disappointment to him; things never went very well with us after that." Yet she had a larger share than his own, had he known it, of the imagination that builds up a city of dreams.

The other night, being alone, I took up a book, the "Life of Felicia Skene." There is a portrait in it of her niece Zoe, who was later Mrs. Thomson, wife of the Archbishop of York; and as I looked at the charming sympathetic face some memory came back to me. I remembered that Adelaide and her husband had soon after their marriage been guests of that Archbishop for a night or two for some congress or gathering of Churchmen, and that his wife, their hostess, had asked Adelaide for a photograph, and had written thanking her for the portrait but saying it did not do justice to her beauty. It had seemed an unusual grace on so short an acquaintance from the wife of an Archbishop to a curate's wife; so I was interested in reading that Zoë Skene had herself belonged to a country where there is respect for beauty, that is Greece; and it was with an actual bodily pang the thought came that Hugh was out of reach of hearing what would have so much delighted him in that windrift of memory.

I remember also in the account of that visit that Adelaide, accustomed as were all the county families of that time to a certain tradition of travelling, wrote as an event worth putting down that they had come back in a second-class railway carriage and had not liked it, because they found themselves travelling with, and recognised by, some servants who had waited at the Archbishop's feast. But a little later they were finding third-class companions pleasanter, market-women with vegetables and flowers.

It was not until after the open breach between her and her husband that she spoke even to her sisters of her own disappointment. The ragged schools, the personal devotion to the poor, were pushed farther away than before by child-bearing (and the first child died); by the change from easy luxury to the narrow cares of a home that had upon it the critical eyes of churchworkers; to an entertaining she imagined a harder task than washing a beggar's feet. When advancement came and she was a well-to-do rector's wife, other troubles arose. If she was stern to herself, she did not flatter his somewhat self-indulgent ways, and there were others to flatter. At last there was a formal separation. A more worldly-wise woman would have for the children's sake kept the home unbroken, but where jealousy comes in wisdom takes its leave, and will do so until there comes a change in human nature.

Mr. Lane had inherited unexpectedly a house and small estate near the southern coast of Ireland, and it was there Hugh was born, the only one of their children who was born in Ireland. It was almost within sight of this house that thirty-nine years later the *Lusitania* went down.

His childhood was passed unhappily; he never had good health; he could not, like his stronger brothers, go away to school; he was not only

left among the bickerings but was a cause of them.
His father was harsh to him, his mother took his
part. It may have been this lack of ease in a
well-to-do home that gave him later a contempt
for comfort, and made him hard to himself in
matters of what he thought luxury. He was
always a delicate child; his mother used constantly to write asking for game or fowl, " a bird
of some kind " for him, and when she brought
him to stay at our houses would press on him all
that was most tempting. His more robust
brothers resented this and bore him a grudge,
and such treatment might have made him selfish
or dainty about food, but he never was one or
the other. He was a very small eater, did not
indeed take enough to nourish his tall body.
When Mancini was in Dublin and Hugh was
paying his bills I am confident there was no
stinting, and that though he sometimes longed
for the macaroni of Naples, his meals provided
by Hugh were sufficient; for I, punctual by
nature, had often enough to await my painter,
who would come in late from his lunch with the
complacent content of a cat that had been in
the dairy. But Hugh, arriving hurriedly to see
how the work went on, would, keeping to his own
lean living, as often as not bring his own lunch in
his pocket, two hard biscuits protecting a slice
of cheese. My own meals were simple enough
in that occupied Dublin time, but I would have
on my table in the evening some provision of cold
fowl or eggs or game, for there were no eating-
houses open after theatre time, and Yeats and
Synge and Fay, or some other artist, would find

comfort in that simple meal; but Hugh, should he come in, would take nothing but fruit or a little cake, nor would he touch wine.

Although there is a memory of his wanting to bathe at Jersey as a child when there was danger in a high tide and stormy sea, he used to shrink from rough play, finding more content in the greenhouse plants that were his care, or the dressing up of dolls in such brilliant coloured silken scraps as came his way, or in decorating parish feasts or Christmas trees, drawn by some lure of yet unattainable beauty. Even then, as I have heard him say, even in the nursery, he had in his mind the intention to make some day a wonderful gallery of pictures that became later the passionate purpose of his life.

Once or twice as a child he had been brought by his mother to visit at our family houses. I remember that my husband liked the handsome delicate boy; others of us were impatient that he did not care for the sports of other boys, as his sunny-haired elder brother and a whole generation of nephews had done, overjoyed with the handling of a ferret and a gun. Those visits were to Hugh a great romance and excitement; he loved to look at pictures and ornaments, finger family miniatures and jewels and the like; it seemed as if he had been starved by the want of distinction, of tradition, in his changing homes. He wrote to me long after, in 1913, in a fit of depression:—"My early romantic notion of Ireland was got in my childhood in Galway, and I am now so completely disillusioned that I don't want to be reminded of those early happy days."

Yet as we see by his will and his codicil, it was to Ireland his heart turned at the last.

I think his escape from school life may have been a benefit, for his mother brought her children away to Paris, and then settled with them for a while in Jersey. She read Dickens to them, and put them in the way of learning French, and that knowledge of French served him better in his business than classics or mathematics would have done. She insisted also on mannerly ways. I remember Hugh saying he liked *The Bogie Men* better than any of my comedies, that it seemed as if founded on his own bringing up. "For," he said, "when we were children my mother used to tease us by saying, if we did anything against good manners, 'Your cousins the Beauchamps would not behave like that,' but when, afterwards, we met and played with the Beauchamps we didn't see that they were very different to ourselves." And that is likely, for poor Gertrude's children were wild merry girls enough.

She had him taught also something of music, so following unconsciously the way of Plato and those Greeks who would not send a child to the gymnasium until he had learned to play upon the lyre. Then later, his childhood passed, and when they had drifted back to Plymouth, opportunity came as is its way to the mind that is all unconsciously prepared for it, and where it may in a moment "work thoughts into desires, desires to resolutions." A lady who made a poor living by cleaning and restoring paintings, and to whom his mother had been kind, taught her art to the boy.

CHAPTER II

His inclination towards pictures thus fostered, and that vision of making a great collection still in his mind, he determined to find work through which he could increase the knowledge he coveted. And his eighteenth birthday being near, when his father's help towards his support would cease, it was necessary he should begin to earn a living. I went to consult an old friend, Sir Charles Robinson, the Keeper of the Queen's pictures, and through his advice and introduction Mr. Martin Colnaghi offered him employment for a year, giving him twenty shillings a week and an indefinite position in his gallery. Hugh was overjoyed when the offer came. His mother was also pleased. She had faith in him and had written to her mother before his work had even begun, "In a few years Hugh will be making his thousands." He hurried to London sooner than he need lest one day's learning should escape him, and he wrote in high spirits of the first meeting with Mr. Colnaghi and that they were "in sympathy in preferring the old painters to the new." But disappointment came, I think, to each of them. He was given a clerk's work to do, and Colnaghi grumbled at his bad handwriting.

He made it easier to read by the simple plan of making it more upright, but he had always an awkwardness in holding a pen because of an old accident to his hand in some rough play in his childhood. It was soon plain that Colnaghi did not much like him, it may be he thought as some of the dealers were used to say later, "Lane's not a dealer, he is a damned amateur." He met him with me one evening at a Royal Academy Reception—no great feather one would think in any of our caps—and railed at him the next day as an upstart. He showed no inclination to help him to knowledge, he would not even speak to him about the pictures that came and went; his consultations with his manager were always behind closed doors. Yet in a way he trusted him. I found Hugh in the gallery one morning alone and lonely, very glad to see me, and I remember that Sir Arthur Birch, who was with me, coming from the well-manned machinery of the Bank of England, was astonished at the sight of this whole costly collection in the sole charge of that young boy. With pictures so near at hand it would have been hard to keep him penned up in an office. And if his master grudged him knowledge he soon made use of his patrician appearance and courtesy, setting him to show pictures to possible buyers. But a part of this work was the moving and shifting of many stacked frames, a heavy task enough for his slight body. He had a friend living in the country but not far from London, a clergyman who had been curate to his father and who made him welcome whenever he was free to come. His widow, who joined in that welcome hospitality, tells me that Hugh used to arrive very tired, and asked only to sit still through those Saturdays and Sundays, or to be taken out for a drive; although in another year, when he was in the Marlborough Gallery, where his business was to sit all day in the office, he would be glad to stretch his long limbs by walks, sometimes of sixteen and seventeen miles; or later again, when he had done with apprenticeship, he would take delight in working in their garden, planting roses, making pleasure grounds, roaming in search of flowery branches to carry back to London, " always some for Lady Drogheda," one of his most kind and constant friends.

Yet I think in that first year in London he was happier than ever before, beginning to feel his powers and to lay his foundations. No doubt he learned a great deal there concerning the technicalities of painting; yet no length of living in galleries could ever have given him that certainty of insight, that recognition, that is outside and beyond knowledge, that is a gift brought into the world at birth, any more than living in stables and paddocks will make a man without the right instinct divine at a glimpse in a scraggy three-year-old the future winner of a Queen's Plate. That is a gift that goes sometimes with the other, as those who knew my husband still remember. But though Hugh liked hunting, and his " gymnasium " in each possible year was a few weeks riding after the hounds, his was the one highly-developed power of judging the sign of the painter's hand long after that hand was turned to dust.

C

He lived on very little in those first London days. I don't know what his mother added to Colnaghi's wage. I was for part of that time in London, and might better have given to him the money I was using for the schooling of one of his brothers, who fell into ill health later and died young. Had that help gone into Hugh's pocket it might have hastened his approach to fortune, but I do not think it would have softened his bed or given him a more plentiful table. He always grudged shillings, almost pence, spent on the nourishment of his body. When he urged me to some embellishment of life that I could not reach to, he would say, "I would do it if I had to live on bread and scrape," and I would answer, "Yes, you might, but my bread and scrape wouldn't help much unless all my guests and dependents would join in renouncing any better dish." I remember we, his relations, laughed because on his first visit to Italy he wrote that after the delay of a few hours at Basle on the way back he was so moneyless that he had not even a soldo left for the porter "*who was carrying a picture I had bought during the wait.*" He had been obliged to give him his umbrella in place of money, and was, as I lately heard, very much afraid that the delighted porter would find out before the train started that one of its ribs was broken. Even at Lindsay House, when he was giving with both hands, he denied himself personal pleasures. He always kept his love of music, he liked to play to himself when tired or worried, and I found him sad one day because the piano he used had been sent for by the old friend who had lent it to him ; but he would not buy or hire another.

I don't know if it was my fault that I did not come nearer to him in those Colnaghi days. He seemed, as I thought, to hanker after coronets and fashion, and I was over-prompt to recognise some tang of his father. In his later years, when mellowing humour and unselfish work and the wit he turned so readily against himself had simplified his nature, he was gracious, dignified, and direct. Of all the ways in which I miss him, perhaps I miss him most as one I laughed with. And in later days if he was glad to have friends in high places it was because they could perchance help to carry out his dream, or help some artist whose work he would make known. I remember saying when I saw a photograph of the opening of the Johannesburg Exhibition in which he is seen talking earnestly to the Duke of Connaught, " I am sure Hugh is advising the Duke to have his portrait painted by Kelly."

But I grieve that in those early days I was but just an adequate aunt ; and when, from his first tiny warehouse, he sent me with some grateful words a Poussin I had liked, a portrait of Homer, of Raftery, of the wandering poet of the ages, I felt I was overpaid.

It was little wonder if he was heavy-hearted as well as tired for a while. It seemed as if he would gain but little knowledge in that first London year. But " God never closed a door but set one open " ; there was good help at hand. The manager of the sale room, Mr. Caroline, had taken a liking to him from the first and a friendship began which only ended with Hugh's death. He shared with him all the knowledge he had gathered, and he who knew the secrets of the trade must have understood also some of the secrets of the painters, he must have had skill as well as science. Hugh told me on one of those days—his delight was so great he had to whisper it to me or to the rushes— of a wonderful thing that had just come to pass. Caroline, amusing himself with his paints, had made a copy of a Franz Hals, had played with it, altering, working over it, giving it an appearance of antiquity, till Hugh declared it would deceive even the knowledgeable men at Christie's or Foster's, and urged him to send it, as an audacious pleasantry, to a sale. And Caroline, while still declaring no one could be deceived by it, consented. On the evening of the sale Colnaghi came in, followed by a porter carrying in his arms the imitation Franz Hals. Caroline turned pale ; he believed his master had discovered and had come to upbraid him with his folly, or accuse him of his fraud. But he was yet more aghast when he knew by Colnaghi's elated look and then by his boast, that he believed he had bought for a small sum an original masterpiece. For two days, while the picture stood in Colnaghi's room, he was miserable, not daring to confess, feeling a traitor in being silent. But at the end of the two days it had vanished, and henceforth there was silence in the gallery about what I think we may still call a masterpiece.

When at the end of the year he left Colnaghi's he had saved enough from his narrow means to carry on his education by going to Holland and Belgium for a while. He wrote in little note-books descriptions of pictures and a strict account of what he spent, these items tumbling over each other as in a description of Rubens' " Descent from the Cross "—where he has written a note on " the kneeling figure in blue-grey, perfect in colour," and adds, " I am here demanded two cents for using a chair." Indeed he had to be careful of his little savings. At Cologne, "having existed all day on nothing but a cup of coffee and roll this morning, and two penny gingerbreads for lunch," he has a beefsteak for dinner and writes, " I paid one mark 50pf., for it, potatoes and bread, in a two-franc piece, getting no change as they don't use Belgium money here. I carried my bag from the station. It is so heavy that no ordinary foreigner could support it. I couldn't lift it if it wasn't that I am so afraid of running short as is likely if I stay in Germany much longer, as they seem to charge a mark—a shilling—here for what we can get for a franc at Brussels." At Amsterdam he is tempted to pay four shillings to go to the Opera to hear *Faust;* " I did not realise in the hurry I was giving so much and was mad when I counted up. I am now ruined, I have only £3 to last the remaining two weeks." He makes up his expenses each day as at Amsterdam :—

Six Museum . . 2s. 1d.	(of this he writes : " I was consoled by finding the pic-
Bun. Cocoa . . 4d.	tures very fine.")
Palace . . . . 10d.	
Steamer . . . . 5d.	
Dinner . . . 1s. 8d.	
Biscuits . . . . 2d.	

Another day :—

Bed. Tea. Breakfast, tip . . 2s. 9½d.
Bun. Pear . . . . 3½d.

Then :—" Spent altogether £55 on a holiday.
£20 borrowed."

But whatever he had to go short of in food or
comfort, he never left any town until he had seen
every collection of pictures good and bad. He
would change his plans and stay even in dis-
comfort until he had made this thorough study
and search, for although endued with that amazing
perception he was determined thus to add exact
knowledge to his bag of tools. He had to pay out
some of his carefully counted francs or marks now
and then when he " had a ladder brought in to
examine the pictures better."

That was a habit which he never lost. In the
last summer I was with him we went one Sunday
afternoon to a great London house. Our hostess
had taken me to see garden and children, and when
we came back we looked in vain for her husband
and Hugh. Through the open door of a distant
reception-room I saw the end of a ladder and I
said, " That is where Hugh is to be found." And
there he was, high up on the ladder which was
being held by the butler, while he explained to
the owner the value of a picture that hung near
the ceiling. He had noticed it when at a ball
there, and had wondered why so great a treasure
should have been put so far out of sight.

In 1896 he went as manager for a year to
Mr. Turner at the Marlborough Gallery in Pall
Mall, where it is remembered " he only lived for

pictures," and that his great ambition was to become the Director of one of our National Galleries, as indeed he did in the end. There was some dispute on his leaving—I remember being called in to mediate—but it was carried to the Courts. Hugh was not satisfied with his lawyer's statement there, and asked leave to plead for himself, and the Judge at first refused, believing him from his appearance to be a minor, but let him have his way when assured he had come of age; and pleading his own cause, he won. He told Mrs. Grosvenor that he was sometimes sent from this gallery to the country to look for bargains and " One day was going back rather gloomily to the train with his third-class ticket, his net empty, cold and disappointed, when passing by a bicycle shop he caught sight of some pictures and went in. There he bought one for a song and carried it off to London. It was of considerable value, and he went up in credit with the firm." But he used to say that one seldom found anything in those sort of bric-a-brac shops, the best chances were at the small picture dealers, and of course sometimes at the great sales.

CHAPTER III

MAKING A FORTUNE

HAVING thus attained to knowledge, the next step towards his purpose was the attainment of wealth.

In February, 1898, he took a ground-floor front room at No. 2, Pall Mall Place, and began his regular dealing. He arranged his pictures—they had been here and there in charge of friends—in the little room, and waited for customers. But laughing cousins came more frequently and would play games around him, or, running out, turn the key in the door. There was one great disappointment. The Lord Mayor of that day had some inclination towards picture buying, and one of my nephews, to give a helping hand to Hugh, asked him to look in at the little gallery. He did call there but knocked in vain, for Hugh, who could not then afford to keep a custodian, had been carried off to some merrymaking, that was I think but a tea-drinking, against his will as he declared. He was very sad and very sore, for he had waited through many days when no one had crossed his threshold. And after all he was but twenty-three and had known little of the joys of boyhood.

He owned at that time a very beautiful landscape by Wilson. I had asked an art critic of my acquaintance to look in on Hugh sometimes and, if he had opportunity, to befriend him. And it happened that when I met him at two or three houses about that time, he would say, "That nephew of yours is a clever young fellow, but he asks a ridiculous price for his pictures—£300 for that Wilson!" I told Hugh of this, but he did not seem disturbed. One day later I noticed that it had vanished. "It is sold to your critic," Hugh said. "For how much?" and we both laughed when he said, "For £300." I think his mother had first seen and told him of that Wilson landscape, but its price was then beyond anything he could give. And I think it was the first picture he bought when through a sudden chance it became possible for him to reckon his sovereigns by hundreds in place of tens.

As it happened I had never heard him tell the story of that sudden enrichment, but Yeats had told it to me long ago, saying that Hugh had been astonished at his having come upon its date through astrology. So I asked him to tell it again the other day at Coole, going to my typewriter to take down his words as he talked. He said:—

"Yes, I once did his horoscope. He probably knew the hour of his birth as well as the day, and I suppose that nobody now has the hour, so I could only recalculate it in a very general sense. I remember that in what is called the progressed horoscope, his sun, for nine or ten years, had the conjunction Jupiter. I took the beginning of this as the beginning of a long stream of good luck, and then found the time of year when that luck was likely to become apparent to him, by pointing out in what month Mars made an aspect of the sun the cause of energy and enterprise. I told him also that he could not count upon his luck lasting more than a certain number of years longer ; and there's a story going round that I hit on the year of his death as the close of that period, but I think that unlikely. I can easily know when the Jupiterian influence ceased, by turning to the ephemiris, if someone would tell me merely the day and year of his birth, but I would not have foretold the ending of his luck in any sudden way unless I saw some other aspect, which I did not. I would have expected a gradual lessening, and I had only done a very cursory horoscope.

" My recollection is that I hit the actual month in which he made his first great success. It was then he told me this story as far as I can recollect, but everything except the story is vague to me. He was very poor, as what little money he had went towards the purchase of pictures ; he had to use the greatest economy even with food. Picture sales were his greatest excitement, and he heard of an important one somewhere in the country. When the day of it came round he spent all he had on his railway ticket. When he got out at the station he found that he had a walk of many miles to the house, and at the house found when he had arrived that he had mistaken the week. After a long conversation with a suspicious housekeeper he was allowed in, and recognised amongst the pictures the handiwork of Franz Hals, an unknown masterpiece. On his return he tried to borrow two hundred pounds from his mother, but was refused with indignation, and no one else would trust him. Again he saved enough for his ticket and when the right day of the sale came round walked once again from the station to the house. There were many Hooked noses in the sale room, and it was plain that they too had discovered the Franz Hals. Perhaps, after all, there was an unnoticed signature. Presently a Hook nose came over to him and said, ' Do you want that picture ? ' and out of pure bravado or because he did not know what else to say, he replied, ' Of course I do ! ' The Hook nose joined the other Hooks at the end of the room, and they. began to whisper together. Suddenly it struck him, ' They know that I have been in Colnaghi's. They think I am a rich young man put there to learn my trade.' Presently this particular Hook returned and said, ' You will not bid against us ? ' and he, not having a penny to bid against anybody, replied, ' Of course not.' ' The meeting,' said the Hook, ' will be at the Red Lion.' (I have forgotten the real name of the Public House—it is perhaps as well.) Presently a picture of no importance was put up by the auctioneer and one of the Hooks said in a careless voice, ' I will give you £10 for that picture if I may have the picture next it for the same price.' There was no other bidder, and the Franz Hals went to its new owner for £10. Hugh assured me that when he went to the Red Lion he had no idea what was going to happen. All went to an upper chamber and sitting round a big table every Hook took out a pencil and a piece of paper. He also did the same and waited. Presently somebody bid £20, then somebody bid £30. The man who had bid £20 walked out.

Then somebody bid £40 and the man who had
bid thirty walked out.   Gradually he realised that
they were auctioning the picture among themselves, and that the timid or those who could not
trust their expert knowledge, were only bidding
small sums, for it might not be a Franz Hals after
all.   He watched bid after bid and presently made
his own bid.   He had bid the picture up to £900
without a penny in his pocket, and then said, ' I
cannot go any farther.'   One of the two remaining
Hooks bought it with a sigh of relief for, I think,
£950.   For some days Hugh heard no more.   He
knew he was to receive a substantial sum, and he
guessed it would be somehow in proportion to
his bid, but he did not know how much it would be.
Then came a letter inviting him to lunch with
one Z—— (who was known generally as ' the
gentlemanly dealer ').   The door was opened by
the dealer's son, and Hugh, who now knew
exactly what had happened, said, 'I have come
about the knock-out.'   ' Please,' said the young
man, ' do not use that word.   My father has a
great dislike to that word.   We will call it the
K.O.'   Under his plate at lunch he found a cheque
for several hundred pounds, I forget how many.
In a year he had turned that money into £10,000.
And though he had only robbed the wolves, he
felt some remorse over the whole transaction, and
assured me that he had never attended any more
meetings in any Red Lion.''

He had another lucky day about that time.
He had gone to Plymouth to see his mother, and,
as was his custom, he ransacked every shop in the
town that might hold a treasure to his mind.

In an auctioneer's rooms he saw a Dutch picture and recognised its painter's hand. He made an offer for it, but just as the bargain was being closed, the dealer was called away, and took or came back for the picture. Hugh was waiting for him, was looking out of the window, when he saw it being put into a cab and carried off by, to his astonishment, his old friend Mr. Caroline! He dashed out, but the cab was gone out of sight. The dealer did not know where the buyer had gone, or his name. He had shown him the picture, and told him a customer in another room wanted it, and had sold it for £40.

Hugh rushed off to the station, then from station to station, from hotel to hotel, till at last he found Mr. Caroline. He, on hearing the story, agreed that Hugh had the first claim, and gave it up to him for the price he had paid. It was by Cuyp, and Hugh sold it afterwards for £1000.

A friend, an artist, tells me the story of another purchase: " One morning he entered my studio, carrying in his hand a picture without a frame. He cast the picture to one side and threw himself on my sofa and said he was very ill, and looked ghastly. I was very much concerned and urged him to see a doctor, while he told me at some length how exhausted he was, giving the history of his symptoms. At last we came to a standstill, having no more to say on either side, and then I looked at the picture. At the first glance I saw in it a probable Rembrandt and said so; and there was Lane, standing at my back, gay and alert and obviously quite recovered. I never saw him look better. He recounted to me how he had just been staying at the Z's and had seen this picture hanging over the door ; his host told him that it had been accounted a Rembrandt but that they saw that the attribution was ridiculous, and so had hung it in that dark corner over the door. He answered that an old picture is always interesting, and taking it down went to work, removing by rubbing with his finger the coating of dust and varnish, and as the process went on he kept advancing his monetary estimate. He said, ' It is worth a hundred pounds—two hundred—three hundred,' etc. To which the good-natured couple always replied, ' Then you can have it for nothing, since you've discovered it.' As a fact he finally paid them one thousand pounds, which must have been rather an agreeable surprise. I think that a sense of drama was one of his characteristics, and that this little farce of sickness he played on me was all done in order to heighten my surprise and his enjoyment of it. That Rembrandt remained for a long time in my studio. Its subject a very old woman, but though it was only a sketch, the way in which the painter had modelled the lighted side of her face was a miracle of skill and knowledge, and a constant delight to me."

I have never heard where this picture went, or what it brought him. I only know those who sold it can have felt no discontent, for no cloud ever came upon their friendship. But his bargains were for the most part in the auction rooms.

Once when he arrived in Paris on his way home from some journey he had not enough money either to stay there or to pay his fare home. But before the morning was over he had discovered and bought a picture—one supposes upon credit—and before evening had filled his empty pocket by its sale.

Mr. James Duncan, talking of his swift certainty of recognition, told me of having seen him buy a picture at Christie's, a Velasquez that the dealers scorned. "It was very much painted over and very dirty, but he made up his mind at once. He said, 'I can't afford it, I'm in low water just now—but I *must* have it.' It was knocked down to him for something under £200. He took it home and cleaned it, there was no doubt it was genuine. He sold it afterwards to Durand Ruel for some thousands."

I met the other day an acquaintance just back from the Cape. He had been there when Hugh arrived, and had been with him and Lady Phillips when they visited the old Art Gallery in Cape Town. There was a picture hung high in a dark place, it was attributed to Both in the catalogue. But Hugh at the first glance said, "It looks more like Vanderneer." They got a ladder and took it down, and there was Vanderneer's signature.

Another friend (Mrs. Hinde) says of that mysterious power, that certainty, "It was a sixth sense. As we motored through a town he would recognise the handiwork of some painter old or new in a shop window, as we passed, and would stop the car and bring it out to show us, and he was never wrong."

He was yet in his early twenties when he had conquered Fortune, was of the Alchemists' Guild.

I think he might have said even then, as he once said to me later, when an offer of ten thousand a year had been made to him if he would consent to become buyer for a famous house, " It would be a very poor year in which I couldn't make ten thousand pounds."

CHAPTER IV

THE RETURN TO IRELAND

I THINK it may yet have been in the balance when and where he would begin his life work, and that he was inclined to drift for a while. And this is no great wonder, for his mind needed freedom and his body ease and sustenance, a lessening of the tension of those hard and frugal years. He was sociable by nature, and was but discovering his power of enjoyment; he had made many friends in England and liked staying at houses where he found new surroundings and made new acquaintances.

In 1900 he wrote asking if he might come on a visit to Coole. I had meant to invite him a little later to meet those merry cousins who had been held up to him as examples, and with whom he had played as a child, but I would not refuse him, and he came at his own time. It is likely he had come to Ireland with no settled purpose beyond a wish to revisit places of which he held a happy and romantic memory.

But a great change had come about in Ireland since his mother had made her curtsey at the Viceregal Court, and the great estate owners had been despots, if often good-natured ones, over homesteads and villages whose inhabitants they

D

could have turned out at will. Just after my marriage in 1880 the land war had broken out, as I have written elsewhere, "tenant struggling to gain a lasting possession for his children, landlord to keep that which had been given in trust to him for his; each ready in his anger to turn the heritage of the other to desolation." During its ten most violent years habits had of necessity been changed. Some of the county families had shut up their houses, some had grown poor; dinners such as had gathered neighbours from many miles around during our big Roxborough shooting parties had ceased, for the roads were not safe after dark; hunting was meddled with here and there, the days of easy and idle hospitality had passed away. Then came the overthrow of Parnell by English Liberals, and the breaking up of the Nationalist Party, and his death.

Some of us landowners, forgetting with what certainty "changes follow time," thought to see the old days return. Others, but these were rare, bade the new day welcome and found in it a new quickening of life. For with the passing away of Parnell's long dominance, his necessary discipline, there had come a setting loose of the mind, of the imagination, that had for so long dwelt upon some battle at Westminster or upon some disputed farm. Action and reaction, each was for good—the hard narrowness of conflict, the widening of peace—in its time. For as someone has written, "Where the password is 'March' and not 'Develop,' a body of men to be a serviceable instrument must consent to act as one.

Nothing more fatal can be done for a country, though for an army it is a simple measure of wisdom." When Douglas Hyde disclosed through the Gaelic League the poetry and beauty and tradition still living in the Irish tongue, he gave to the freed imagination a new region to explore. Our neighbour, Edward Martyn, had dedicated a part of his fortune to bringing into Church music a more perfect form. Yeats, even before the creation of our Theatre, had been urging by word and example a more intense achievement, a more stern self-discipline among writers who must no longer be forgiven doggerel for Ireland's sake, but for her sake must find an expression as perfect as that of the world's poets who endure. These, the awakenings of enthusiasm for matters of the mind, were among the new forces around us.

Hugh was unaware of these changes, and when he came to stay with me he was, I think, puzzled to find among his fellow guests at Coole men whose names he had not yet heard, Yeats and Hyde, and for another, O'Brien Butler, the gentle accomplished musical composer, whose tragic end was also to come in the *Lusitania*. He must have felt he was among workers, but had not yet taken his own oar in the galley. He was a little outside the party, a little bored by it; and though in after days he would deny having said to the wife of one of them, that I, his aunt, had "lost her position in the county by entertaining people like your husband," it is likely the epigram was well imagined, and a fair enough summing up of his thoughts. He was quite courteous, rather disappointed, and not sorry to leave. He went on to see

other friends, and then I heard of him in Dublin,
"in the best Castle set." I asked Yeats the other
day if he remembered that visit, and he said,
"Yes, it was the first time I met Lane, and it is
very vivid to me because I disliked him. He
was full of his still recent success, he talked much
of the great houses where he had been, his own
ambitions seemed worldly. I think that he spoke
of taking some country house and becoming a
country gentleman, as though he would forget
as quickly as possible how he had made his money.
When he came down to dinner in the evening, a
small rose in the buttonhole of his evening coat
made him look overdressed. His smooth, handsome face, his movements, gave me no evidence
of his intelligence. When we spoke of modern
painters and modern writers he was ignorant.
In my impatience I thought of his knowledge of
old pictures as a mere trade knowledge, and no
true expression of an intellect. One day I was
helping you to hang some sketches by that painter
I was trying to admire against my own judgment
—but instead of any intelligible criticism he said,
'Very little they'd fetch at a sale at Christie's.'
I don't think you felt entirely sympathetic
either. I know that I was unable to hide a slight
hostility.

"A few months later he seemed changed not
only in mind, but in body. He had returned to
his old ambition of a great gallery in Dublin.
The great houses where he had visited, the people
he had met, were now but means to that end.
His face and his bodily movements seemed to have
changed, they had a curious precision. He had

become exceedingly unworldly, contemptuous even of the old lures and perhaps less anxious to please, less agreeable. From that moment to the last time I saw him he was like a man who knew he had but a few years to live, and who raged against every obstacle to his purpose, saying often what was harsh or unkind where that purpose was involved. I remember discussing him with Charles Ricketts one night, and Charles Ricketts saying to me, 'Everybody who is doing anything for the world is very disagreeable. The agreeable people are those for whom the world is doing something.' We had both just seen him after the buffet from some Dublin or London opposition."

A New York newspaper of 1914 tells of Hugh Lane having said, when asked advice as to forming a gallery, "I believe in having a national portrait gallery, and inviting public men to sit for their portraits; for so many celebrated men have not been painted or modelled while living." It had been with this idea he began his work in Ireland.

One day in London in 1901 I heard that he had come twice to look for me. When he came a third time he said he had just come from Dublin where he had seen an exhibition of paintings by Nathaniel Hone and J. B. Yeats. It was Miss Purser who had formed and arranged this exhibi-tion of her fellow artists' work, and it had good results. Hugh had never seen any of Hone's paintings till then, and he was much excited— "ran about Dublin talking of them and wanted to buy the whole collection." He did buy a part of it then or later, for he made a gift of pictures by

him not only to Harcourt Street, but to the
Scottish National Gallery and to the Luxemburg.

As to Mr. Yeats' portraits, he found them so
interesting that he determined to bring him back
to Dublin.   It was for that he wanted my help.

I said in a letter to W. B. Y., "Hugh Lane wants
to get your father to paint twenty distinguished
Irish or partly Irish people, Wyndham, Redmond,
Hyde, etc., for him to give to the picture gallery.
He would only want head and shoulders, and
would take all the trouble of bringing him sitters
and would look after them. . . . I have written
to your father.   It would probably make him
fashionable, and he would enjoy meeting various
types."

For Mr. J. B. Yeats, the artist, had drifted
away from Ireland and had spent many years
at Bedford Park, and in 1898 he had drifted back
to Dublin hoping to find work.   But after a little
while he had written to me, disheartened, " I hope
to return to London shortly.   It is difficult to
get portraits to do.   In Dublin curiously they have
an appetite for posthumous portraits done from
photos—a ghoulish and horrible industry, corrupt-
ing to him that does it and to him on whose walls
the monstrosity is hung.   I myself have done
many.   The dining halls at the King's Inns have
many of these horrors flaunting in ghastly mockery
beside portraits done straight from the living
sitter, and some of these done in the days of
Queen Elizabeth."

And again :—"I am doing nothing, kept here
in a state of unrest—portraits, phantom portraits
appearing and disappearing."   Even helpful A. E.,

when I asked for counsel, wrote, " The artists here with one or two exceptions live by teaching, and Dublin can't support more than one portrait painter—now it is Walter Osborne. The rest would starve if they did not teach or eke out their income in other ways, or had independent means like Hone and some others." So to occupy Mr. Yeats for a little while, I had asked him to make some pencil drawings for me of " my best country-men," his own two sons and Douglas Hyde, Edward Martyn, Horace Plunkett, Synge, A. E., Standish O'Grady (John Shawe Taylor came later, and one of Hugh, long bespoken, never came to me). Then he was asked to paint a portrait subscribed for by friends of Standish O'Grady, that " Fenian Unionist " as I am credited with calling him, who had carried the heroic ideas of the Red Branch into the economic questions of the day. A. E. writes to me of that portrait, now in the Municipal Gallery, and certainly one of those that had interested Hugh Lane, " It is very striking, grim though, like some terrible warrior of ancient days. It should have this legend attached to it, ' O'Grady—his Financial period '; that would explain the grim look. Poor Mr. Yeats painted him under difficulties. He was always starting up to walk about the room. The world could not contain his spirit when the financial question incarnated itself in him. It is a path leading to the stars he sees, not the recovery of paltry pence. His absence in Kilkenny will certainly be a loss to Dublin, but the gods move their pieces with skill, and O'Grady is one of their best."

And then the artist himself writes :—" The

sketch of Russell is considered good and I think
or rather hope Willie's is good.   I am not so sure
as regards Douglas Hyde.   He was an impatient
sitter, having come off a long railway journey
and about to undertake another.   Although a
sketch takes so short a time in the doing, there is
nothing more difficult to make a success with.
By right one should stalk one's subject so as to
catch him at the right moment and with the right
gesture.   A sketch is far better, reveals more of
a man portrayed than the best photograph, since
it gives not merely the facts but a comment."

I knew Hugh's offer would be welcome to him
and was able to send on his answer with a note:
" You will see he is really delighted. . . . I think
you should begin with trying to get Wyndham,
Horace Plunkett, and Redmond, this would make
it safe for both Unionists and politicians to follow.
Of course you won't please everybody.   It would
be amusing after you have made your selection to
get the newspapers to start ballots of the twenty
their readers would choose!   It will be difficult
to get Dr. Hyde to sit again; he caught cold
and got a little cross at the last sitting. . . . Why
not write to ' Mr. Dooley ' of New York asking
him to sit when he next comes to Ireland ? "

Mr. Yeats took a studio in Stephen's Green
and enjoyed everything—" the light so suitable
for painting," and even the novel sensation of
envious eyes :—" My success is, I find, not very
good news to every one here in Dublin.   There
is a grotesque little person, Mrs. Blank, who is
very indignant, grieved that I should have taken
in so completely that poor young man your

nephew." Then he writes in great spirits: "I have just painted a portrait which is, I think, a masterpiece, and, besides, not at all unlike my sitter." And again: "Lily says that when she dreams of living fish it always means money. One morning I dreamed I was fishing at Coole and suddenly hooked a fish so big that it nearly pulled me into the lake. I had a really hard struggle, but got the better of it, when the dream vanished. When I got into town Hugh Lane met me with the Viceroy's consent to sit. I am now more superstitious than ever." That studio was not always a place of peace, though Mr. Yeats wrote, "Your nephew has an extraordinary knowledge of pictures and though, perhaps, we don't see eye to eye as the expression is, his errors are always corrigible and at the same time I learn a good deal from him. I thoroughly respect his opinion though I don't always share it."

I asked the artist's daughters lately about those days, but they could not remember much except that their father had not liked being interrupted in the heat of argument by having his clothes brushed from neck to ankle by Hugh, and had resented his putting roses in the bowls. And they remembered that Hugh had once rushed into that studio laughing and muddy and out of breath, someone had lent him a free-wheel bicycle, he had never used the free-wheel before, and in the short journey from Harcourt Street to Stephen's Green he had got in the way of the traffic; a tram had been stopped and the conductor had shouted: "I'll call the police to you, young man!" He carried that gaiety about with him, what their father has called "lightmindedness"—what Emerson calls the "incomparable advantage of animal spirits." They remember him in a crowd at the gate of the Civic Exhibition that was about to be opened. When the Viceregal carriage with the Aberdeens drove up and there was no greeting —there being no great haste to do honour to a Viceroy in any open-air crowd—Hugh had called out, "We must give them a cheer. They work hard!" and with the words he was out in the road, his hat off, the sun shining on him, and the cheer he asked for and led was given.

Yet the old artist and the young patron kept respect for each other, and Mr. J. B. Yeats wrote to me the other day:—

"It is good to have known him; that slight figure always wincing and shrinking to every chance and change and yet with such steadfast eyes. How well I remember his large dark eyes! —under heavy lids—and how tranquil they remained no matter what the trouble. He feared nothing; he did not even fear ridicule; he felt it, yet did not fear it, and for that reason he was never without an invincible hope that in some unexpected way he would throw the laugh back on his opponents. In those happy days luck was still with him; invariably he laughed last. I think he belonged to the genus 'Dandy.' Not because he was a vain or selfish man; because he was an artist in social life. He had the intrepidity of a man of action; and being always cool and collected never lost his sense of the ridiculous.

"The secret of his charm for me was that he read his fellow creatures better than I did. Anger, prejudice, or some cursed dogmatism of theory would blind my eyes, but he saw clearly. While I hated, his eyes would be laughter-lit, and laughter clears the air. I think he positively enjoyed his enemies, finding them more complex and therefore more interesting than his tried friends. He did not love his enemies in the Christian sense, nor was he specially magnanimous —it was a sort of natural aloofness, so that he could laugh at what vexed me. I think I may call it high breeding. . . .

" I think the mark of a superior mind is a certain lightmindedness, and this never abandoned him whether he talked of his friends or his foes. Whether victorious or defeated he remained light-hearted. Of course he did want to have things his own way, even in painting, but this being my business, I' resisted, and then he would give in and laugh at himself. . . .

" He was an artist in social life. When I lived in Dublin existence was feverish. There was the craziness of greed and of selfishness, the political craziness, and of course the perpetual war between the good artists and the bad artists. All this was so much amusement to him, and to me when I was in his company.

" I think he was one of the best bred men I ever saw, his courtesy was without a flaw, and don't you think that a really courteous man is always for the moment a perfect democrat ? . . . The really courteous man will take as much care of your dignity as of his own, and belongs to the time when all men were soldiers.

" The special quality in Hugh Lane's courtesy

was, I think, deference, and to be treated with deference by a man who looked as if he was the darling of society, so well dressed and elegant, and with a musical voice—I tell you that among the people of Dublin, who are not in the habit of giving or taking much deference, this was an experience as delightful as it was rare. Of course there were times when he was out of humour, discontented and despotic, yet afterwards he would be sorry and come round and make amends by laughing at himself, with that laugh which was so infectious.

" I have described him as an artist whose medium was action, and had he taken to politics he would have been after the type of Disraeli and not at all like Gladstone. Had it been poetry he would have turned to action like Lord Byron or D'Annunzio. I think it is characteristic of men of strong will that they must find an object, and he being a practical man and a patriotic Irishman, his object was the modern gallery in Dublin,—that was the star which he followed. Artists must be sensitive, but if there be no strength of will their sensitiveness betrays them into imbecility ; again, there are artists who lose their sensitiveness and because of their strong wills become the painters of philistine pictures. Hugh Lane was so sensitive it was to me a constant wonder how he could retain his strength of purpose.''

I don't think the portraits Mr. Yeats had come over to paint—those of Synge, Sir Horace Plunkett, Professor Dowden, William Fay—were so good as some others of his in the Gallery and elsewhere ;

he has the artist's caprice of choosing his own subject, he does not work well in bonds. Hugh called in Orpen later, and gave to the Gallery his paintings of William O'Brien, Michael Davitt, Lord McDonnell, John Shawe Taylor, Dr. Mahaffy, Nathaniel Hone. A fine collection altogether of notable men of the end and the beginning of a century. And as Hugh Lane's first work for Ireland, it is a page of her history.

CHAPTER V

SOMETIME in 1901 W. B. Yeats had written to me from London: "At the Irish Literary Society last Friday I made, and got accepted, a proposition to form a Parliamentary Committee to collect information and then to interview M.P.'s, inform public opinion, etc. I hope yet to see a row in Parliament as to why the Scottish Academy has £1500 a year from Government, and the Hibernian Academy £500. . . . We may be able to get up something like a vigorous agitation for the redress of intellectual grievances."

I had heard from his father also of this Government penuriousness, and we may be sure it was often talked of in that Stephen's Green studio. For many, to whom art was dear, were writing to the papers protesting in angry words against the threatened death by starvation of the Royal Hibernian Academy.

Hugh Lane, as was natural, was one of those who joined in the protest. But wherever Hugh came in, action had a way of coming with him, the deed was in the shadow of the word. If our Academy was threatened with death, he would show that it was yet living. He proposed that, all scanty as were its means, it should forthwith, in the manner of the wealthy Royal Academy of London, hold a Loan Exhibition of Old Masters. There was, of course, no money in its purse to pay for packing and carriage and insurance, perhaps not even for postage stamps. He had made some of his thousands by that time, he would take that burden upon himself, would take all risks. He took the work also on his own shoulders; his enthusiasm kindled the imagination of others. The President of the Academy, Sir Thomas Drew, lent him his own office. He wrote to owners of pictures in country houses, and many of these were already of his acquaintance, begging especially for pictures of his favourite eighteenth century. The owners were generous. Their promises of loans were published from day to day, and each county wore airs of consequence when it found that some one or more of its big houses had sent paintings bearing a great name. Of course there were prophets who grumbled that foreigners hearing of the display would come and carry off the greatest treasures, as they were used to carry off thoroughbreds from Ballinasloe Fair. And, of course, there were suspicious souls who believed him to be working for his own hand. Yeats, going on with his memories of him the other day, said: "When he came to Dublin to gather together that first collection of pictures, a Dublin painter, who afterwards became, and still is, his most devoted and unselfish and able supporter, spoke to me of the project with rage, saying, 'He knows that there are many good pictures in Irish country houses, he wants to find out where they are that he may buy them at a low price and trade with them in England.' For all I knew it might have been so ; I had not got over my first impression. But in a few weeks I met the new Lane and his sincerity. For months after that, the criticisms I met everywhere in Dublin were an almost hourly exasperation. They went on, indeed, for years. There was one patriotic man of whom I had a good opinion, for he and I had worked together in my early twenties to get collections of Irish books into the Irish country Societies, but after the foundation of the Municipal Gallery he met me with the usual opinion—Lane was somehow or other making a fortune for himself at the expense of Ireland. And when I said ' He is about to give it something about £70,000 worth of pictures,' he said ' But nobody would do a thing like that.' If I had said seventy pounds or seven hundred he might have believed me, but never had he met in his not selfish life any man whose gifts ran into thousands."

On New Year's Day, 1903, Hugh wrote to his friend, Mr. Caroline, from the Winter Exhibition of Old Masters in Dublin, "A Happy New Year to you and many thanks for your welcome letter. I am afraid there is no ' business ' in this show, it is simply ' *la gloire*.' I am trying to wake up these sleepy Irish painters to do great things, to get them a new R.A. building and a decent money grant. I also want to bring good pictures into the country rather than out of it. So that if you have anything good send it over. I gave up ' dealing ' some time ago, and hope sooner or later to get some appointment which will be more congenial work. Have I missed much at Christie's ?

And have you picked up any Franz Hals lately ?"

But this exhibition was to him not an end, it was rather a beginning. He had given ready ungrudging aid to the Academicians in making their case known. But his "seven - leagued thoughts" had already outrun even his desire for a new building for them on a new site (and this may yet be fulfilled in an unlooked-for way, for the Hibernian Academy was burned down in the fires that followed the 1916 Rising). His nursery dream of a wonderful gallery of pictures had now become "a clear pattern in the soul" to be worked out through the dozen years before him that were to be his sum of life. He would make the chief city of his own country a treasury and storehouse of art.

As to myself, then as now, being no politician, my desire was less to seek Home Rule, self-government, than to make ready for it. I had tried to give a helping hand to any work that might put out of fashion those outlandish labels, jocose or sentimental, that had been affixed to us in the course of Queen Victoria's reign ; any work that might bring back distinction and dignity to Ireland.* I was not content to rest on ancient heroic histories, splendid as are some of those I have helped to make known. So when Hugh

---

* Yeats wrote to me in 1904 from Indianapolis, when giving some lectures on the Theatre and the intellectual movement: "You would have been pleased if you had heard the compliments that have been paid to-day, for they commended me for doing just what you have wanted me to do. The Irish in this land often explain to me that I have done what no other Irishman has done for the dignity of Ireland here."

E

came, free, with money in his hand, filled with
the enthusiastic hope of his gallery, my heart
leaped to meet him; it is no wonder I was filled
with joy and pride. I had used my energy to
turn other millwheels before coming to that last
work of the Abbey Theatre; he had kept his for
the one. From that time we were fellow-workers,
comrades, not always agreeing as to means, but
at one as to the end. He set his seal to that
fellowship when he left to me the task that has
proved such a difficult one of having his " Codicil
of Forgiveness " carried out; his work as far as
this will do it, made complete.

When I was told towards the end of 1903 by
an official of the Department of Agriculture in
Dublin (which is also the Department in charge
of Art) that a collection of pictures by Irish artists
was to be sent to the St. Louis Exhibition, I said
" You will have to get Hugh Lane to do that for
you." I had said it as a mere statement of fact,
with no intention to offend; but I noticed a little
frown of annoyance, and understood him to
mutter in official language, that they were well
able to do it themselves.

So I could not but feel a little mischievous
delight when I read in a letter dated January 23,
1904, " Hugh Lane goes to St. Louis to organise
a Loan Collection of Irish pictures and miniatures.
He has only a month to get it all up in." Then
I heard from Hugh himself that though those who
had " tried to work the picture section for St.
Louis had failed and withdrew, they are now
furious at my doing it. But I am going on. I

never lose a chance." It seemed but a chance of difficult and thankless work, but the end proved that he was right in not missing it.

It is certain also (I have seen some of his " begging " letters), that he did not miss any chance of getting fine pictures together to go to America. He had, I think, even packed them in little more than a month. He was tired but well pleased. Then of a sudden the whole plan was turned topsy-turvy. He received a letter from the Board of Agriculture saying they had but just found that the Insurance rates for St. Louis were very high because of forest fires that had destroyed other cities ; were indeed too high for them to take the risk. They, therefore, requested him to return the borrowed pictures to the painters.

I was in London at that time, and Hugh came to me like one distraught. He was very angry. " They ought at least to have looked into the cost before they asked me to find the pictures." He did not grumble at his own lost weeks, but he felt bitterly the ungraciousness to the painters he had persuaded. Lavery, he told me for an instance, had through his urgency given up a week of his Berlin Exhibition to bring his pictures home before the appointed day of shipping. He sent me to see Sir Horace Plunkett, the head of the defaulting Board, to make clear to him that this unceremonious rebuff to artists was a matter less simple than the returning of surplus kegs of butter to a creamery. When Sir Horace understood the matter he grieved that a discourtesy so foreign to his nature should have been offered in his name, but he could imagine no remedy. When all hope had perished I went back to Hugh, downcast and disheartened. But already an idea had come to him that would, he believed, turn the defeat to a victory. There had lately been the Spanish Exhibition at the Guildhall. He would have an Irish Exhibition there. He was off again to Dublin and I had a telegram—"Theory I am working on is that though not immediately remunerative, Guildhall much greater triumph for Irish Art." He was back in London next morning. Sir Horace approved, and now that there was something to be done he did not spare himself but gave wholehearted help. But we were not yet over the Hill Difficulty. The Director of the Guildhall Gallery, tired after the work that had made the Spanish Exhibition such a triumphant success, hesitated to take upon himself this new fatigue. But he also, when he had once consented, put his heart into the work. And the painters, who had not without uneasiness agreed to let their pictures go across ocean and continent, were well content to have them shown so near their own door. Hugh was free then to do the work he loved. His days were spent not only in getting hold of the best work of Irish painters, but in convincing some, who had never claimed our nationality, that it was theirs by right of inheritance if not by birth.

Lavery had always been Irish, though with less intensity than has come to him in succeeding years; Mark Fisher was now claimed. Charles Shannon could only tell of a grandfather from across St. George's Channel, but that was enough; his pictures made the centre of the chief wall beautiful, and Hugh kept bringing them in till the Director (though all the while admiring and afterwards himself a purchaser) cried out upon their number. Once he even called out, "That picture must come down," but the artist proved his birthright and kept its place by the readiness of his answer, "That would break the glass!" On the very day of the opening, Hugh, not yet satisfied with the arrangements, got up early and rehung them according to his night vision.

For that opening (in the spring of 1904) there was a gathering of invited guests. I better remember than the speeches made, that the Curator of the Dublin Museum, who had been brought over to give, as it were, his benediction to the exhibition, said, as he escorted me in the procession, "I hope never to see a picture hung in Dublin until the artist has been dead a hundred years!" And there lingers also the memory of a bouquet of beautiful flowers given to me as to a few others to help the decorative effect, and that when in the evening I held it up with some pride to show Hugh, he said rather gloomily, "It was I who paid for it." But he was well content after all. Seventy thousand people came to look at the pictures during the eight weeks they hung there. Ireland had already, for a little time, been joined in men's minds with literature and drama as well as with the old political story, and now we found ourselves questioned with a new interest about our painters. Hugh did not let this interest flicker out. He looked on this success of the Guildhall Exhibition as another step towards the fulfilment of his purpose, now very definite, of creating a modern picture gallery in Ireland.

He had written in the Preface to the Guildhall Exhibition, " There is not in Ireland one single accessible collection of masterpieces of modern or contemporary art. . . . A Gallery of Modern Art in Dublin would create a standard of taste, and a feeling for the relative importance of painters. This would encourage the purchase of pictures, for people will not purchase where they do not know. Such a gallery would be necessary to the student if we are to have a distinct school of painting in Ireland, for it is one's contemporaries that teach one the most. They are busy with the same problems of expression as oneself, for almost every artist expresses the soul of his own age."

As to his idea of what a modern gallery should be, he was happily able to make that manifest in Harcourt Street. But he thus put it into words, when in an interview in America in 1914 his advice as to such a gallery was asked : " It should serve as a feeder and a sifter, a sort of artistic reduction furnace where a man's art work is held for the judgment of his fellows during his life, and if worthy passed after his death to that of coming generations, as such pictures are transferred from the Luxembourg to the Louvre, which is only for such works as have stood the test of time.

" It is impossible to make a collection of living men's work with any certainty of its representing properly and permanently the art of the period ; for instance, a certain tendency or movement in Art might have a useful effect in developing Art in a certain direction, while the works in the initial stages might not be worth keeping, though the final outcome might be good.

" In choosing work for modern collections you should give the artist the benefit of the doubt. Young men and women of talent will by public recognition develop much more rapidly than they would do if they were unknown and unappreciated ; and a gallery like this can afford to take some risks, for the outlay would not be great. The younger artists would accept nominal prices for their work as is the case abroad, and if one in ten increased in value, that would pay for the cost of the work taken out.

" As to the Director of such a gallery I think he should not be an artist, but a man of broad art culture and taste, and he should not be hampered by a Board of Trustees, for such Boards never agree on any artistic subject. It would be best to give him full power and a five years' appointment, so that he could be replaced if he was not broad-minded enough or efficient. I think a painter unsuitable as a Director, for a strong painter is usually a very narrow critic, he sees things from his own personal standpoint. Hals may have thought Rubens wrong in painting his shadows red, and conversely Rubens may have held that Hals was also untrue with his greenish and dark-grey tones."

I find a note of a talk with Lord Mayo, who " became more hopeful, indeed, enthusiastic, when I told him of Hugh's proposal to not only keep his promise of giving all his pictures if a building is provided, but to give £10,000 if the other £15,000 can be given to make the new building. His idea is to keep certain rooms in the building intact, rooms he would himself arrange with masterpieces and the work of artists who are, as far as he can judge, sure to keep their fame, other rooms to be for loan collections and experimental work."

But for all his desire to "give young artists the benefit of the doubt," he was often stern in his choice. In a letter of mine to Yeats, where I object to a certain play being sent to America with our players, I plead his example: "I don't think we could justify it to our conscience -- Sturge Moore's words were enough, 'the old stage traditional motive of drunkenness treated as broad farce.' . . . Now that there seems such good hope of getting the gallery for Hugh's collection I feel so proud that the collection is so fine, on such a high level—and I know he had to offend artists sometimes by not thinking their work good enough to buy. I should like the memory of our theatre to be at least almost as free from compromise. One should try and take the whole question before ' the long-remembering harpers ' and their eternal audience."

At the end of the year he wrote a letter to the Irish papers in which he said that the success of the Winter Exhibition showed that with good opportunities we in Ireland might produce a school of painting equal to any in the world. That towards the end of the eighteenth century there had been a small demand for miniature painting, and that such men then appeared as Reilly,

Horace Hone, Robertson, Hamilton, Chinnery, and Comerford, and deserved a place among the best miniature painters of the day. Then political misfortune (he might have said unrest and famine) put out Art for a while, till 1823, when the present Academy was built and new painters arose—Williams, Cuming, Hugh Hamilton, Nathaniel Hone, Hickey, and Sir Martin Shea. "Had these men in their youth had opportunities of studying in an efficient school, or had they even been surrounded by collections of fine pictures of past generations, their weakness in anatomy, and other academic defects would not have existed, and they would certainly have ranked with such men as Raeburn, Hoppner, Reynolds, and Lawrence." He proposes "the foundation of a gallery of modern pictures for the purposes of study." He tells of the effect of Art galleries in England. "Already the schools of Birmingham, Manchester, and Liverpool are world-famed. Glasgow also has come to the front. If Englishmen and Scotsmen can thus profit, how much more could we? There is no single accessible collection in the whole of Ireland that can give the necessary stimulus to beginners."

A piece of advice he both gave and practised was, "First make your collection of pictures, and the gallery will come to hold them." He had already begged of many artists to give him some of their work for Dublin, and as one artist at least has said of him, "He was the best beggar that ever stood at my door." Sir John Lavery was then Vice-President of the International Society of Painters, and he gave Hugh good help, sending

him to other artists with his introduction.
Whistler, in answer to a letter from him, promised
a picture. Sargent made a promise also. Lavery
himself gave his first gift to any public gallery,
as did Charles Shannon. A week after the Guildhall Exhibition closed Hugh was able to announce
that he had promises besides these of a bronze
by Rodin, of paintings by Blanche, Legros, Ricketts,
Orpen, and John. And of sums of money towards
building a gallery.

The Hibernian Academy offered its rooms for
the exhibition of the pictures already collected,
and a committee was formed. He was pleased
with Lord Mayo's answer to him when asked to
join it : " I will join your provisional committee
to form a collection of modern paintings for
Dublin—not because I think we shall ever get
the money to build a modern gallery to house
them in, but because you work hard and do
something which many Irishmen do not—they
talk." 1903 had surely been a well-spent year.

He tried to idle for a while. He says, in a
letter to Lord Gough, then H.M. Minister at
Dresden, " The reason that I have so much leisure
(when not engaged in public work) is that I have
given up for nearly three years selling pictures,
as I had made a sufficient amount to bring me in
a small income, and my great ambition has always
been some day to direct a gallery." And this is
the amusement he desires in that unoccupied
time (which did not last long, for he was soon
selling pictures again): " On my way from
Holland I stopped for a couple of hours at

Darmstadt, having read in my guide book that there were ' a few ' pictures of interest at the Royal Palace.   I was surprised to find that the collection, though in a shocking state of neglect, contained a great many fine pictures.   They are, however, for the most part very wrongly attributed to the painters whose name ornaments the labels.   The best pictures are in the worst lights, and much in need of cleaning and backlining.   The collection up to the present has evidently been considered of no importance.   They are about to be transferred to a fine new gallery, and they should have been attended to and a new catalogue should be made, but the great German and Dutch connoisseurs, Drs. Bode, Bredius, and De Groot, are too busy now to afford the time for such an undertaking.   There is nothing in the world I should enjoy so much as the doing of this work, of course gratis."   He is going back to Dublin to arrange the next winter exhibition and some other work.   " But after that I could go to Darmstadt for a month."

CHAPTER VI

OUTSIDE the portraits, which needed a living
artist to bring them into the world, Hugh had
for some years kept himself unmoved by, perhaps,
disdainful of, any modern work. I remember he
seemed puzzled, almost pitying, when I asked
him to bid at a sale for a little picture by Simeon
Solomon that I coveted, one that a few years
later he would surely have bought for the gallery,
for it was beautiful, and I did not reach its price.
He had not yet made that rule he practised later
and to the end of life, of " making money by
selling old masters that he might spend it on
living ones." I think it was the Hone Exhibition
that began his awakening, but even after the
Guildhall he continued unacquainted with any
new foreign school. Sir William Orpen said the
other day, " When he went to Paris with me in
1905 he knew nothing at all about modern French
painters. I was with him at Durand Ruel's, and
he would say to me, behind his back, ' What is
that ? A Manet ?—he had never seen Manet
before—and ' What is that other ? Is it one I
should ask for to bring to Dublin ? '—it was when

he was getting some on loan for the exhibition there. But in a very short time he had made that great collection you are fighting for. He trusted his own taste. That ' Seashore ' of Degas's he bought was a discovery."

This new interest in the French school had come with the suddenness of any Gentile conversion, and we may fix its date by finding that of an announcement made by the executors of Mr. Staats Forbes, who had lately died, that his great modern collection was to be sold. And this was to be no common sale, for in accordance with the testator's wish it was to be given for a lower price than in the open market, should it be purchased to find a place in some public gallery.

Hugh saw the opportunity for Dublin, and as was his custom he lost no moment. While others had hardly begun to think of the matter he had gone to the executors and had gained their consent to exhibit a chosen number of the pictures in Dublin. A price was put upon them that was, as one of the executors (Mr. Livesay) was afterwards able to point out, compared with later prices, a low one. There were in this collection many fine pictures of the Barbizon school; it was, indeed, best known by these.

It was to make the French side of the exhibition more complete that Hugh had made that visit to Durand Ruel of which Sir William Orpen spoke. Horace Cole tells me he was in Paris at that time, thinking its air favourable to an endeavour to keep awake, according to a bet he had made, for a hundred hours, and had met Hugh, in travelling clothes, just come from Monte Carlo, declaring he was without a penny, having brought away "nothing but this ruby pin." He had forgotten the name of his hotel, and they wandered until they found it, a shabby little one near the Gare St. Lazare. They went up many stairs to Hugh's attic, and there lying on the floor was his travelling bag, not locked, and in it, rolling about loose, were many pearls. Horace had taken him to make acquaintance with Mr. Tyler, the expert, who when he had talked with Hugh for a while had said, "I didn't think there was a man in the world who knew more about pictures than I do, but that man does." Horace had also spent some of these sleep-combating hours with him at Durand Ruel's, where, he says, Hugh, still proclaiming poverty, bought a Manet—Eva Gonzales?—for £10,000. I think, however, he did but borrow the Manet masterpieces then, and some others of the Impressionist school. His hopes were high; he thought that the whole collection might remain in Ireland, might be kept for the gallery that was as yet no solid building, but a vision.

A hundred and sixty pictures from the Staats Forbes collection were shown in the exhibition opened in the Royal Hibernian Academy in 1905. With these were hung the pictures already given by artists for the new gallery, should it happily come into being, and Hugh could tell of other promises to be redeemed. He showed there also forty or fifty pictures, his own possession. The greater number of these are now in the Dublin Gallery, given or bequeathed by him.

But there were still some who imagined in all his

work some secret purpose of his own enrichment.
Yeats says, " a rumour ran through the town that
if the Staats Forbes pictures were sold to Ireland
he was to receive a large secret commission. One
of the patriotic weekly papers had a paragraph
giving authority to this rumour without putting
it into words, by skilful innuendo. I went to the
office of the paper, which had till then been a
supporter of our movement, and had the most
substantial row of my lifetime, and acquired an
animosity that will last till my death. Yet what
could these people think and what could they
make of a man who, in the words of Charles
Ricketts, had ' joined to the profession of a
picture dealer the magnanimity of the Medici ? ' "

I have come upon a letter from Yeats, written to
me at that time, in which he gives a fuller account
of this quarrel : " At first the editor denied that
there was any insinuation that Lane is making
money out of the Forbes collection, but finally he
owned up and said he wrote it because three
Academicians had told him that Lane had made
large sums out of the Guildhall, and would make
large sums out of the present collection if it was
bought. You can imagine the scene that followed.
I said, ' My dear ——, you have published just
enough of a slander to give wings to it, while
keeping yourself out of the Law Courts.' He
promised some sort of retraction next week, but
I can imagine the grudging spirit it will be made in.
As I was coming away, I said, ' It is a custom of
gentlemanly life to presume that a man's motives
are good until they are proved the contrary.'
He answered without a smile, and in obvious

earnestness, ' I don't agree with that principle at all. If any Irish newspaper were at this moment to act on the assumption, or to say, that Lord Dunraven's motives were good, the country would be wrecked in six months."

I do not know who these three Academicians were, or if many gave credence to their statement that Hugh was making money out of his public work. I was given a letter but a few weeks ago that should if an assurance is needed be a sufficient one. The late Lord Gough, a man as thoughtful as he was generous, and always ready to help any Irish cause he could approve, wrote at that time, with a promise of ninety guineas towards the purchase of a picture from the Staats Forbes Exhibition, a private note to Hugh Lane in which he offers to pay for the paper and postage used on its business. Hugh wrote refusing the offer. " I would rather pay everything till the project has proved itself," and goes on to say, " My task would be a light one and a *very* pleasant one were there a few more such helpful kind people to do with ! . . . It is a fact that during the three years that I have worked for this cause, *no one* has as yet even asked ' who ' was paying the costs. I have circularised the United Kingdom on several occasions—got up deputations to corporations, a commission in the House of Commons last summer—and each exhibition has left me out of pocket very considerably, the last one at the Guildhall to the extent of over £1000."

But if he had been struck on the one cheek he was now to be buffeted on the other, and to suffer through those suspicions that are a malady of the mind of politicians on one and the other side. And he had not yet made up his mind on which side were the people of most importance to his work. So Yeats writes again, " I went to see Hugh Lane to-day and asked him if I should reply to a stupid little paragraph about him. I am not to do so, however, as he finds association with us Nationalists too injurious with the monied people. Many of his rich friends are saying that they will not help him now, that he is a part of the Movement. It's only the Gaelic League over again, etc., etc., and they had thought it something quite different. I am not even to speak of my father's lecture. All this amuses me very much. My father says that the Unionist classes are secretly angry with themselves, and that this is the one sort of anger a man never gets out of."

And a few days later: " The last event is that Sir Thomas Drew has written to Lord Drogheda, who had, as you remember, promised £100, remonstrating with him for belonging to a committee which included such rebellious persons as Edward Martyn and myself. Lord Drogheda is very valuable, as he is nearly the only entirely ' safe ' person Lane has. Even Mayo seems to be suspected of red republicanism. Lord Drogheda won't let his wife go on the committee as a result, but whether he has himself resigned I don't know. Edward Martyn is to be asked to resign and to state his reason in a letter to the *Freeman*, offering a subscription. I have offered to resign at any time Lane likes." Then I wrote, " Hugh came in to say Mahaffy was indignant at his

F

proposal to give his pictures, says such a gift would be ' ostentatious ! ' ' "

Yet if some withdrew their countenance there were many working in one way or another on his side. J. B. Yeats had written that if this collection should become the possession of Ireland it would " do more for the education of the people than a Catholic University." "Masefield is over, and writes for the *Manchester Guardian*." "Shorter is getting photographs of Lane's pictures made, and will help in every way he can." " Lane is in great delight with your article in *Claidheamh Soluis ;* he thinks it a most beautiful article."

I have looked back to see what had so much pleased him and think it may have been this sentence : " Ireland has no gift for compromise, and suffers often from the lack of it. But now and then she gains when some faculty is enabled to express itself with logical force through a single mind. Parnell did it in our day in politics, and it must surely be done in things of the spirit ; Sinn Fein—'we ourselves'—is well enough for the day's bread, but is not Mise Fein—'I myself' —the last word in Art ? "

And when I at last came to Dublin and drove straight from the train to the Gallery, I found it crowded. I was bewildered by a hurly-burly of committees, of groups collecting money to buy one at least of the pictures on the walls, and amused to watch Hugh's suavity amongst them all, for I knew he had to act as peacemaker now and again after hot discussions. Yeats had arranged a committee among Dublin Art Students, I myself among writers, Jane Barlow, Emily Lawless,

Martin Ross, Professor S. H. Butcher, "A. E."
and Douglas Hyde; Countess Markievicz, gay
and pretty, then one of the Castle folk, a Woman's
Picture League. From time to time a picture or
two was bought by some individual or some group
to add to the collection already given. President
Roosevelt was one of those who sent a cheque,
saying that he "believed this gallery would be
an important step towards giving Dublin the
position it by right should have." But as well as
Hugh some of his fellow workers may have had
need of patience. Dermot O'Brien, now President
of the Hibernian Academy, said the other day as
we talked of that excited time: "He didn't mind
what trouble he took—or gave—for the sake of
that Gallery. When we were buying pictures for
it from the Staats Forbes collection, there were
subscriptions for some particular one, and then
after it was bought perhaps he would think
another would be better, and I, as treasurer,
would have to explain to people—to my own
O'Brien clan among them—why, when they had
given their money for one picture yesterday, their
name would appear to-day upon another."

Mr. Bernard Shaw gave the bust of himself
by Rodin, and I find a letter from him to Hugh
about the pedestal. "Are you sure that green
marble is the right thing? . . . I am myself
convinced that what is wanted is a block of white
marble, not too smoothly finished but of the
same colour as the bust. However, you have a
good eye in these matters; and I confess to an
unpatriotic loathing for green marble, which will
be the ruin of Ireland."

He suggests trying experiments by painting a wooden pedestal, and adds, " These experiments, if you think it worth while to try them, will add a little to the expense ; but it is a poor heart that never rejoices, and I will go another five pounds to make the job sure."

Yeats had written towards the end of November, enthusiastic about the exhibition, but saying, " The wretched Academicians never go near him and are openly obstructive. They have lent the Academy to a Paper-Hangers' Exhibition for one week in January, so Lane will have to close after a month. The paper-hangers being Nationalists with some public zeal are very sorry, and are ready to do anything, but they have sent out all the announcements, etc. The Academicians are stony."

But Hugh would not suffer his work to be thus thrust aside. He gained leave from the executors to keep for yet another while certain of the Staats Forbes pictures, and no sooner were these turned out of the Academy than they were hung, together with the pictures which had been already given to " form the nucleus of a Gallery of Modern Art in Dublin," in the Kildare Street National Museum, " with the sanction of the Department of Agriculture and Technical Instruction and by permission of Colonel Plunkett, C.B.," my friend of the Guildhall ; we can hardly think with his approval, for he must now see in a place of honour in his own sanctuary pictures whose creators so far from having been dead a hundred years were yet living. I see in a letter to Hugh : " I went round the pictures on Saturday, Colonel P. was showing two showy-looking ladies the plate, and whenever they looked at a picture he turned them off it and on to the plate again."

Lord Dudley had all this time been a powerful friend. There was a story that Hugh, wanting to see him on some weighty matter at the very beginning of his scheme, was told on the telephone by the Private Secretary that it was impossible, " the Viceroy is leaving to-night for the Continent," and that Hugh had said in answer, " To what country is he going ? I will meet him there." Whether this be true or well invented, it is certain that he was met with a gallant eagerness akin to his own. So when the Prince and Princess of Wales, the present King and Queen, were at the Viceregal Lodge on their first visit to Ireland, they came to the museum where the pictures were hung, and the Prince buying two by Constable and two by Corot, the Princess another Constable, " A Seaport," they presented them, a generous act of faith and hope, to the yet unaccomplished gallery.

But where is the place so exalted that ill will cannot use it as a vantage point ! One of these pictures, a landscape by Corot, had been owned by Mr. Forbes for many years before his death, he had kept it in the room where his best Corots hung. (I take these facts from Hugh Lane's own note to the Municipal Gallery catalogue.) It is believed to have been the first picture Corot ever exhibited ; there is a letter now pasted to its back from Arnold and Tripp of Paris, the great experts in Corot's work, saying they believe it was painted while he was a boy working with his first master,

Michalon. It had often been exhibited. J. F. Millet looking at this picture once said to Mr. Forbes: "If I lived my life over again I would paint with this precision until I had mastered every detail in landscape painting." Sir John Millais had brought several friends to see it at a London exhibition, saying, "You see that even Corot began as a Pre-Raphaelite."

But (this is from the same note): "There appeared in an illustrated journal a photograph of a picture by a, till then, little known Hungarian artist, G. Mezzoly—a ' View of the Balaton Lake,' now in the gallery at Buda Pesth. On the left side of the canvas is a group of trees that resemble closely this small picture. The Mezzoly, which is a very large canvas, when reduced by reproduction to a few inches, gives a false impression of a similarity of execution; it was painted in 1877, so that when our picture was submitted to Paris experts in 1888 it would have had to have been painted during the previous eleven years. Our picture is painted on a panel, which, in itself, is enough to dispose of the idea that it is a fake. The Dublin Arts Committee had the picture submitted to some of the best-known experts in London, who are agreed that it is a very good painting, evidently by a young man; that it was, in their opinion, by Corot, and that it was unmistakably fifty years old at least. Some experts were sent from Hungary, who, on seeing the picture, decided that it was older than 1877 (the date on the Buda Pesth picture) and that it was not an earlier study by Mezzoly, as they had thought might have proved to be the case.

" This established the fact that our picture was
the original painting. It is said that Mezzoly
studied in Paris under Corot, and it is possible
that he made a study of this group of trees, or
that he possessed himself of a drawing for it.
The attack was never one of Art criticism, but
purely a campaign of extraordinary malice against
the project of a Gallery of Modern Art."

I am afraid that this accusation is true. It
gave an opportunity for excusing apathy, for
making a virtue of obstruction, for accusing Hugh
Lane of having brought over a collection of
forgeries to be sold at a vast price to Dublin.
What was first an acrid whisper grew to an outcry in the newspapers. His friends were anxious.
Orpen writes, " If you do not take an action
against *Truth* or the *Star* every one must come
to the conclusion you are in the wrong and know
it—you cannot let people say you are a swindler
in print and let it pass." " Any stick will do to
beat a dog," and Hugh was the dog who had
disturbed a sleepy peace, at a time when, as one
of the chief officials of the Board of Agriculture
and Art is reported to have said, " The time has
not come for encouraging art in Ireland," and
when the critic of one of the chief Dublin papers
spoke with a sneer of the whole collection as
" Botticelli and that." I was pleased when
I came across an Eastern proverb, " No one
throws stones at an empty tree, the tree stoned
is the one that bears the golden fruit."

My memory of all this annoyance had rather
died away, but I asked Mrs. Duncan, the curator
of the Modern Gallery, about it in Dublin the other

day and she said Colonel Plunkett was the chief
enemy, collecting any opinions he could against
it.   He had once asked her to get them into the
papers, not knowing her loyalty to Hugh.   But
other friends were loyal also, Sir Walter Armstrong
had threatened to resign, so angry was he at the
malicious attack.   Dermot O'Brien had said, " The
mean people hate him because of his splendid
generosity, it makes them uneasy."   And to me
Mr. O'Brien said, " That Corot attack was quite
unjustified.   I have never had the least doubt the
picture was authentic, it was one of Corot's
earliest exhibited paintings.   Lord Mayo had
bought it for the Gallery and then the Prince of
Wales liked it so much he yielded it to him, and
then when the attacks were made the committee
took it over to present themselves, they didn't
wish the attack to be associated with the Prince's
name.   It may have been through jealousy—
the Curator had a grudge against Lane—or he
thought the picture gained more attention than
the other things in the Museum.   Anyhow, when
the Prince and Princess paid their visit he was
taking them past the room where the pictures
hung, not intending them to go in there at all,
but Lord Mayo came out and took the Prince
by the arm and actually brought him in."

Yeats had spoken of this trouble in that
dictated talk : " When the pictures were being
exhibited in the Kildare Street Museum its curator
was so carried away by the popular spite that he
hung over it a photograph of the imitation he had
got from Buda Pesth for the purpose.   Sir Horace
Plunkett, and not the curator, was responsible

for the exhibition, so he felt himself free, without any statement showing there were two sides to the story, to exhibit daily what looked like irrefutable proof that the picture was really a painting of some lake in Hungary where Corot had never been. He gave the weight of official authority to an attack which was intentionally designed to ruin Lane's Dublin movement. It was then that John Shawe-Taylor went with a screwdriver, and in the presence of a bewildered policeman unscrewed and carried off the photograph, which the curator had, it seems, taken particular care to make, as he thought, irremovable. The family decision once more!"

And I remember that Hugh, always prompt in action, took John to lunch at the Viceregal Lodge, where he asked and received pardon from the Lord Lieutenant for his violent methods before the official complaint had time to reach the Castle.

Though Hugh used to declare that he had been converted to Nationalism by discovering that the Viceregal windows, which badly needed cleaning, could not be cleaned without long-pondered leave from London, it was certain from the time he began his work that he must incline to the side towards which the imaginative forces in Ireland had already tilted the beam. His nature, always unsatisfied, needed the vision of some Delectable Mountain on the horizon, and so long as he could see it as a home where art and beauty would exist, "would not have to be born," it mattered little whether it were called Beulah or Home Rule. I, with the theatre as my work, had kept free from any such entanglements as official society might have wound about me, but he accepted and used it for awhile, and made his success there one of his tools. I did not need much persuasion when, later, he took me to tea at the Chief Secretary's Lodge, for our host was George Wyndham and the pleasant talk was a pleasant interlude, and when a guest in the house whispered that she had been promised five pounds for a charity if she could keep us both to dinner, I felt a moment of sharp temptation. But I was working with Nationalists, and would not disturb them by what they would have thought a step into Bypath Meadow. But there was no such objection to the Castle visiting the Abbey, and all that gracious group pledged themselves to come on, I think, the next evening but one to see the plays and make acquaintance with the players. But, instead, there came a hurried note of change of plan. A change, indeed, for it was the sudden recall of the Chief Secretary, who had done so great a thing for Ireland through his Land Act, and was on the way to do yet more through his sympathy. It is fitting that we have in the Gallery a bronze bust of him given by its maker, that was Rodin.

But as to Hugh, there was a friendship that helped to bring him closer to Nationalists. Coole was not the only one of the family houses into which the new dawn had shone. There is in the Gallery a portrait of John Shawe-Taylor—he who had taken down that photograph put up in hostility to Hugh. Under his name in the catalogue these words of William O'Brien's are given: " It is one of the most bizarre of history's little ironies that a retired army captain, unknown outside his

County Club, the day before he wrote a certain newspaper letter of September, 1902 (calling for a Land Conference), should have succeeded where the genius of Gladstone failed."

I find written on one Christmas Day to W. B. Y. : "John Shawe-Taylor came over yesterday evening, rode over in the dark and stayed a long time. He looked tired; I think the excitement of working very hard for a while and then having to wait and do nothing for a while is trying to him. He says his Conference is all right. He is getting up meetings in Galway and Limerick.

" He has dreams which I am afraid will not be realised in his time, but which account for his enthusiasm. He sees a time coming when all who believe in invisible things will unite against unbelief. He thinks Protestants and Catholics will see then, as he sees clearly now, that differences of dogma are nothing, that their belief is practically the same. ' Our doctrine is that by Faith the Saviour enters into us, and lives His life through our body ; the Catholic believes that through the Sacraments the Saviour enters into him, and lives His life through his body.' I had never heard theology stated in this way before. Certainly John having that belief, need not be worried by little obstacles.

" But he wants some better National ideas. He had been telling the Castle people they ought every year to reward those who had done something for the country ; give Lord Dunraven a Marquisate, etc. I said that would be a very bad service to his own class, it would leave the Nationalists a monopoly of disinterestedness."

Yeats has written in his " Cutting of an Agate," of that unexpected letter that called the Land Conference together : " The calculation of his genius was justified.   He had—as men of his type have often—given an expression to the hidden popular desires, and the expression of the hidden is the daring of the mind.   It was as though some power deeper than our daily thought had spoken, and men recognised that common instinct, that common sense, which is genius.   Men like him live near this power because of something simple and impersonal within them, which is, as I believe, imaged in the fire of their minds as in the shape of their bodies and their faces."

And Yeats in talking to me of these two, said : " Hugh said to me once, ' Everybody loves John, he has personality, but I am only an eye and a brain.'   Yet his talent was just as much rooted in character as John Shawe-Taylor's.   To begin with there was the same audacity.   You will remember how when John was returning from America the boat reached Queenstown in a storm and he was the only man who left it in a tender, he had leaped into it before the ships were swept apart.   And I remember his arriving at Coole once, and telling how he had overslept himself in the train from Dublin and leaped out of the train when it had moved out of his station at Athenry.   The station-master had come running along the line to find if he was alive or dead. He was quite safe, for the action came from a power of calculation too rapid for the intellect to follow, like Hugh's in deciding on the authenticity of a picture.   I, too, have occasionally had

intuitions that surprised me afterwards by their
wisdom, but had I been one of your nephews I
would have acted upon them. The 'eye and brain,'
however, was this far true, that John had little to
say for himself, and that Hugh had a great deal.
I have heard him criticise everybody and everything, but not pictures. At any rate, I have heard
the uncertainty of others much more lucid and
explanatory on that subject than his certainty.
I remember his meeting at your rooms a certain
popular authority on painting. Hugh had just
given you that picture of the blind Homer playing
the fiddle, which hangs in the drawing-room at
Coole, and said 'It is a Poussin.' 'No,' said the
art critic, 'that is impossible,' and became full of
eloquent generalities. But Lane stuck to it.
'That yellow tree is Poussin.' He had nothing
else to say. I felt he could not have explained
himself in the least, I do not think that he could
even have named pictures by Poussin in which
he had seen a like handling, but he was quite
certain. The popular authority became angrier
and more eloquent. He had never heard of Lane
before and disliked convictions that could not
explain themselves. I think he was not really
certain of himself, for as we left together he said,
'I could have put that young man down, but I
had to remember that he is Lady Gregory's
nephew.'

"The astrologer in me was amused, for his
horoscope shows Mars in opposition to the Planet
Neptune, which gives—so far as we can be certain
about a newly-discovered planet—inexplicable
convictions one cannot reason over.

"But no man could have met Hugh in his later years without remembering ever after his intense restless nervous energy. Life was all bars against which he beat himself, and unlike John he had a single purpose that filled his life. He began like one of Balzac's heroes, like Rastignac, let us say, apparently all personal ambition, and would, I daresay, have shown himself as brutal as Rastignac, and like a Balzac hero put aside his personal ambition and become the providence of others. The meeting at the Red Lion, at any rate, was pure Balzac, though he did but shear the wolves.

"His own petulance and irascibility made many of his difficulties. He was constantly trying to hurry people, the Dublin Corporation particularly, by threats he did not carry out, until at last his threats lost all meaning, and Dublin lost the pictures.

"Shelley, a little before he was drowned, dreamt that some unseen being took him to the Mediterranean side and said, 'Are you satisfied?' and he answered, 'I am satisfied.' But Hugh was not, and subconscious revision, as I think, produced perpetual exasperation."

In spite of the unlikeness there came to be a very close comradeship between these two, my sisters' sons. The energy they both used for Ireland's good took hold of people's minds. Perhaps that is why Mrs. Asquith, meeting Yeats for the first time and doubtless finding him full of some enterprise, had told me she thought she liked him best "of all your nephews!" Yet Mrs. Asquith did a kindly thing for Hugh. The Prime Minister was going to Ireland for some meeting, and Hugh was very anxious he should look in at the Modern Gallery, take off his hat to it, as it were, as Lord Aberdeen had done more conspicuously to the old Parliament House. He had begged the officials to arrange this as part of the day's programme, but they said it would not be possible, there was no moment that could be spared. I, happening to meet Mrs. Asquith at a play, told her of this wish and this difficulty, and she said, "Write and remind me just before the visit, and I will see what can be done." The day after the visit I saw in the papers that the Prime Minister in going through Dublin, from speech to speech, had stopped to visit the Municipal Gallery.

I wrote in a note to my play, *The Image*, a play dealing with those who hold "a heart secret": "The Directors of our theatre are beginning to get some applause even in Dublin for its success; but only they know how far it still is from the idea with which they set out. And so it is with my sisters' sons, to whom I have dedicated this play. One brought together the Conference that did so much towards the peaceable and friendly changing of landownership. The other has made Dublin the Orient of all—artists or learners or critics—who value the great modern school of French painting. Yet I fancy it was a dream beyond possible realisation that gave each of them that hard patience needed by those who build, and the courage needed by the 'Disturber' who does not often escape some knocks and buffetings. But if the dreamer had never tried to tell the dream that had come across him, even though to 'betray his secret to the multitude ' must shatter his own perfect vision, the world would grow clogged and dull with the weight of flesh and of clay. And so we must say ' God love you ' to the image-makers, for do we not live by the shining of those scattered fragments of their dream ? "

The pictures saved from the Forbes Collection by gift or subscription (besides those of the Lane Collection), were :—Corot : Evening Landscape, Rome from the Pincio, Marseilles, The Fisherman, Woman Meditating, Early Landscape, On the Terrace Steps, The Punt, Landscape and Figures (charcoal), The Sempstress (pencil). Monticelli : Forest Scene, The Banquet. Troyon : Cutting Brushwood, Study of a Cow (drawing). Fantin Latour : Portrait of the Artist, Venus and Cupid, Blush Roses. Conder : The Gondolier, The Grey Fan (water colour and silk). Stott of Oldham : An October Morning. Constable : Brighton, Weymouth Bay, Study of Clouds, Elder Tree, A Seaport, Mill on the Stour, Near Arundel. Orpen : Reflections, China and Japan. Steer : A Summer Afternoon. Mauve : A Shower. Artz : Boats Ashore. Degas : A Peasant Woman. Harpignies : Village and Roadway. Millet : The Gleaners (drawing). The Bather (three sketches). Daumier : In the Omnibus (drawing). Legros : Evening Landscape. Jongkind : Delft (sketch). Segantini : Shepherd Asleep (drawing).

Hugh had hoped someone might from time to time give a picture in memory of one who had been dear in friendship or near in blood. And this

in Ireland would be a happy thing to do, rather
than to place a monument before the eyes of a
congregation of one or the other creed, as though
—and this, thank God, is not customary—
Protestant could not hold Catholic, or Catholic
Protestant, in honour and affectionate regard.
The Gallery knows no such divisions, but is wide
and liberal for all. A tranquil landscape by
Stott of Oldham was thus given by me and my
son to the memory of an old friend who had been
kind to us, and whose grave is on the headland
of Duras, by the sea. And lately, to Hugh's own
memory, and as a symbol of ultimate reconcilement, a friend who had stood by him through all
his work for the Gallery has given and put up
there portraits of John Redmond and Edward
Carson, those stout fighters for South and North.

CHAPTER VII

THE WATTS EXHIBITION

In 1906 there was yet another exhibition, when the Watts' pictures, which had already been shown in England, were brought to Dublin. The weight of preparation was not on Hugh's shoulders this time, he had been abroad, and the money for the guarantee was asked for by Lady Dudley. But when he came back and was told the exhibition must be made pay its way or the guarantors would lose their money, he put his hand to the work. He asked again for afternoon tea parties, and his friends were ready to help ; but this time the guests, or it may be some who wrote to the papers telling of their discontent, complained of the hardship of having to pay the usual shilling for admittance at the door. I am not sure if Hugh was used as Court of Appeal or was brought before one, but for all his suavity he was stern. He would not let off the guests from paying their fee, and he would not allow the hostesses to pay it on their behalf. It was a custom, he said, that had worked well in other places, and there was no reason it should be changed for Dublin. The guests were pacified ; concerts were sometimes given ; I am sure that at my own party there was no grumbling, for our Abbey players came and gave of their best. There were lectures also given in the great room. I find a note of mine to Yeats: "Hugh Lane hopes you will turn up for your lecture as your sisters told him sometimes you don't. He says you wouldn't answer him about a name for it, so he has had to invent one himself." And Yeats wrote to me: "My father has just come in and read me his lecture, he lectures at the Hibernian Academy on Thursday. Alas, he thought he had an hour's lecture written, and when he read it to me it took about a quarter of an hour."

"A. E." in his lecture gave cause for scandal, saying that "Ethical pictures, if anything, were immoral in their influence as everything must be which forsakes the law of its own being."

One of the pictures exhibited there was to find in Dublin its lasting home. When in 1903 Mr. Watts had been asked by Hugh for the promise of a picture for the new Gallery—should it come into being—he had promised "to give the matter his careful consideration," adding that in making his gifts to London he had always considered they were as much given to the Scotch and Irish people. This had already been his answer when asked to give a picture to the Scottish National Gallery.

Mrs. Watts had written to me in 1904 from Limnerslease: "You will forgive me for writing, for I hope it may give you pleasure to hear what pleasure you have given to us by your wonderfully beautiful rendering of Cuchulain. It has been quite *the book* to us of this last year, and I have often wanted to tell you what we feel about it, and how many beautiful evenings you gave us when we read it together. I see you have brought out a new book which I mean to get, but nothing can ever displace that wonderful Cuchulain.

" I suppose you know personally the poet who wrote ' Earth Breath ' and other beautiful things ? Mr. Russell ? I read them often and often. If you see him do tell him that chiefly for his poem's sake I got my husband to send his picture called ' The Slumber of the Ages ' to be exhibited at the Dublin Academy. It would be a pleasure to my husband to see you again. He is well and works very hard still at painting and sculpture."

When I was next in England I went to spend a day at Limnerslease, my son, who had just begun to work at painting, coming with me. Watts talked of the Cuchulain stories and said that if he had more time before him he would choose for the subject of his art some of these heroic people. And then he or Mrs. Watts said that on account of this newly awakened interest he intended to give one of his pictures to Ireland.

It was but a few weeks after this visit that the great painter died. I think his kindly intention had not been written in his Will, for I had a note from Yeats, " Hugh Lane tells me that Watts has left a number of his pictures to British galleries, not, it seems, specifying what galleries. He is very anxious that you should take the first opportunity of putting in a claim for Ireland. I promised to tell you, but write for fear of being delayed.'" I do not think Mrs. Watts had needed reminding ; and the beautiful " Faith, Hope and Charity " was sent by her to the Gallery in glad and willing fulfilment of his desire.

It was in the month when that exhibition was

opened, January, 1906, that Hugh was given by a few friends his portrait by Sargent "in recognition of his unselfish and untiring efforts to establish a Gallery of Modern Art for Ireland."

He was very much pleased, he was a great admirer of Sargent's work. He had been used to say, "If I ever marry it will be that my wife's portrait may be painted by Sargent." And as the money subscribed was but a little, and a painting seemed out of reach, he had asked that at least a drawing might be made. This was his story to me of how, when he was taken to the

THE HUGH LANE PRESENTATION. H. P. WEEPS TEARS OF ASTONISHMENT.

Sketch in a letter to Hugh from A. E.

studio, the painting was accomplished in its place. "Sargent has a fancy for ears that stick out, and mine stick out. And he has a fancy for red ears, he has coloured a model's ears sometimes, and mine are red. So he took his brush instead of a pencil and began working in colour, and went on, and after a while when a sitter came who had an appointment he was put off, and he went on with me. Then he told me to come again the next day, and after another long sitting it was finished." But when later I met Mr. Sargent and spoke to him of the beauty and value of the portrait he said, "I could not help doing it, I was so attracted by the great nobility of his face." Through whatever cause it came into being, I thank God and the artist that it exists. It hung on the staircase at Lindsey House until Hugh's death, and is now, as a part of his bequest, in the Dublin Municipal Gallery.

CHAPTER VIII

THE NATIONAL MUSEUM

IN his letter to Mr. Caroline in 1903, Hugh had said he would like to find some official work in place of dealing. And we know that even when at the Marlborough Gallery he had hoped to be some day Director of a National Collection. So when in 1907 he was asked to apply to be made curator of the Dublin National Museum, it was natural that the idea pleased him. Not only this, but his imagination took fire. He determined to make it one of the great Museums of the world. He at once began buying precious gifts for it. He would take no pay, that should (as afterwards at the National Gallery) go to its enrichment. He would come and live in Dublin or near it, he would buy a house. He was told by those in authority to wait quietly, that the place was certain to be given to him, for there was no other candidate with anything like his knowledge. I wrote to him: " I never thought you would take the Museum, and am overjoyed to know you think of it, it would make a great difference having you there, for all Ireland as well as to me personally. I have written to T. W. Russell and to Stephen Gwynn and to John Redmond threatening to turn Sinn Feiner if they don't all support you ! They will be perfect idiots if they don't, they will not find any one to do the work as well as you."

Redmond could not, as leader of the Nationalists, help towards any official appointment, and Stephen Gwynn wrote: " Russell himself, I may tell you in confidence, suggested Lane to me as the best man he could think of, if he would apply. I had gone to him to say we would raise Cain if he continued Colonel Plunkett in the post. . . . "

So I was spending the summer tranquilly at Coole when one day I had a troubled letter from Hugh who was in London, saying there were rumours that the appointment was to be given to another, asking if I could find out from the authorities what was being done. The letter came by a late post, and I sent it over to John Shawe-Taylor, five miles away, saying I didn't think any writing or telegraphing of questions would be of use, and asking if he could go at once to Dublin to see the President of the Board of Agriculture. The answer was a disappointment, he was not able to go. I had a wakeful night, and in those " tiger-clawed " hours I resolved to go myself to Dublin, and so I got up early and caught the morning train. When I arrived in Dublin I drove to the President's office and to his hotel, and at last to his private house in I forget what suburb. He spoke kindly, but his news was unkind. The appointment had already been made. It had been given to one who, if he had no great knowledge, was, in the opinion of the Castle officials, "a safe man." I drove back through Dublin and again crossed Ireland, a railway journey with as its end a nine-mile drive on an outside car hired at Athenry ; and I got home close on midnight. I had sent a telegram home, as well as one to Hugh in London, telling the dreary news. Yeats was staying with us, and had raged when it was received. It was, in his mind, one of the worst of crimes, that neglect to use the best man, the man of genius, in place of the timid obedient official. That use of the best had been practised in the great days of the Renaissance. He had grown calmer before my arrival, because when walking in the woods, the sight of a squirrel had given him a thought for some verses, the first he had ever written on any public event :—

> "Being out of heart at Government
> I found a broken root to fling .
> Where the proud wayward squirrel went
> Taking delight that he could spring ;
> And he, with that low whinnying sound
> That is like laughter, sprang again
> And so to the other tree with a bound.
> Nor timid will nor the tame brain
> Nor heavy knitting of the brow
> Bred that fierce tooth and cleanly limb
> Nor threw him up to laugh on the bough—
> No Government appointed him."

Hugh, having a certain reverence for writers, was pleased, though a little puzzled, by the lines, that do but put in form of fantasy what another poet has called " the difference between men of office and men of genius, between computed and uncomputed rank."

This, now printed with Yeats' poems, was written out by him at the time on a blank leaf of one of his books that he had given me, and looking at it just now I find written above it, " On the appointment of Count Plunkett to the

Curatorship of Dublin Museum, by Mr. T. W.
Russell and Mr. Birrell, Hugh Lane being a
candidate."

It had seemed strange to me that it was Mr.
Birrell who had thus acted, he who had so often
helped even hazardous work at the Abbey Theatre
and elsewhere. He was away from Dublin when
we " defied the Lord Lieutenant " in the *Blanco
Posnet* business; but I was told that on his
return he had spoken of the attempt to banish
the play in language beside which that of Blanco
was "as moonlight unto sunlight, and as water
unto wine." But it happened the other day,
just before I left London, I was talking with him
on many matters, and among them on this book
I had undertaken to write. And at the mention
of Hugh Lane's name he said, " How scandalously
he was treated about that Museum." I answered
that I had believed him as " a Castle official " to
have been responsible. " So far from that," he
said, " I was never told of the appointment until
it was made, and when I heard of it both I and my
Under-Secretary raged at it in the office for half
an hour." I ought to have acquitted him in my
thoughts, for it had been a time when, as Yeats
wrote, "against Lane all the incompetents com-
bined."

Although so gracious in matters he looked on
as of a lower importance than Art, Hugh would lose
his natural affability when that matter was in
question, and speak his rapid decisive words even
in the presence of dignities. He had but just
been put upon the Senate of the New University
when Yeats wrote to me: " He has succeeded,

after an encounter with old Z., in getting the Board to agree, provisionally at any rate, to give £300 instead of £100 to a Professor of Art. Old Z. said that the professor 'should confine himself to beautiful old Irish Art,' and Lane retorted that 'we have got all we can from that art, considering we have covered match-boxes and table-legs and everything we could lay hands on with it.' Old Z. said he had no doubt Mr. Lane wanted a professor of Impressionist painting, a school which he would venture to say would soon cease to be heard of. Lane thinks the encounter rather shocked the Board."

Yeats says also that Hugh " had said in a moment of irritation to one of the officials of the Museum, ' If I am ever head of this Museum I will make you work,' and that official became a very active agitator. While it was another official, who would have been his superior, dreading a strong-willed subordinate, had justified his opposition with the sentence, ' The time has not come to encourage the arts in Ireland.' At least this is the account given generally in Dublin at the time. Though I imagine that what weighed most with the Government was that the time had very definitely come to appoint a Catholic. To them it was an entirely theological question."

I had sent Hugh a telegram, and I wrote him next day an account of my journey and the failure of my errand, and I said, " Mrs. Russell (who was very nice, indeed they both were) told me you were coming over, and I am thinking with amusement to-day of your interview with them, so far as I can be amused with anything, for I am

passionately indignant at the whole system of
Irish officialism which is driving one after another
the best out of the country. Standish Hayes
O'Grady, the greatest Irish scholar who is also
an Irishman, was treated just the same way about
the Royal Irish Academy, a man with no Irish to
speak of being appointed, and nobody cared. I,
for one, will fight on till I die, and in a way, over the
Playboy fight I have been treated worse than any
of you."

And as fate would have it, he who had been
pitched upon as a " safe man " was arrested as a
rebel by Government after the Rising in 1916,
carried off from his Museum and sent to England
in banishment, his son shot in prison ; and that
tragedy has pushed aside any carping words.

Had Hugh been given that work and made
Dublin his home, perhaps one of those deserted
Georgian houses he so much admired might have
been made as beautiful and as rich in its influence
as the house by the Thames. For one feels he
had but to imagine it and there would appear
one of those grand buildings, full of music and
fine people and beauty, that our country people
see built up in a moment by the enchanted hands
of the Sidhe. Yet that rejection may, after all,
have been for Ireland's profit ; would Joseph have
had the means so to enrich his brethren if he had
remained in hunger-stricken Canaan ?

As to " The *Playboy* fight," when an attempt
was made through a week in January, 1907, to put
down Synge's play by violence, I have written
in the story of " Our Irish Theatre " of Hugh's
part in it: " A caricature of the time shows him

in evening dress, with unruffled shirt cuffs, leading out disturbers of the peace. For Hugh Lane would never have worked the miracle of creating that wonderful gallery at sight of which Dublin is still rubbing its eyes, if he had not known that in matters of Art the many count less than the few. I am not sure that in the building of our nation he may not have laid the most lasting stone. No fear of a charge of nepotism will scare me from ' the noble pleasure of praising ' ; and so I claim a place for his name above the thirty, among the chief, of our mighty men."

CHAPTER IX

On the 24th March, 1905, the Municipal Council of the City of Dublin decided to allow a yearly grant of £500 for the maintenance of a Gallery " in which the valuable pictures offered to the City by Mr. Lane and others might be safely housed." At a later meeting, in June, the Council authorised " the hire and maintenance of temporary premises in which these Works of Art can be preserved and exhibited, pending the erection of a permanent building in a suitable locality." A fine old house in Harcourt Street, once, I think, the town house of the Earls of Clonmel, was hired for a term of years, and Hugh set to work with great enjoyment to improve and embellish it. I remember coveting two beautiful small carved frames in an antiquity shop, I thought they would look well in a room I was arranging at Coole. But while I was making up my mind they vanished, had been sold, and the next time I saw them they were over the doors of one of the Gallery rooms. And while the house was yet being put in the disorder that comes in the van of order, grates and chimney-pieces being torn out to be replaced by Georgian brass and marble, the large upper room

was used for a while as a studio for Mancini.   Hugh
enormously admired his work.   Even when he
was arranging the Irish room at the Franco-
British Exhibition, many pictures by Mancini kept
tumbling out of the hurriedly-opened cases, as
though he also was to be swept into our nationality.

He had hurried back from Spain, or Italy, to
collect and arrange pictures for that exhibition.
He had but one day to spend in Paris ; it was a
Saints' day and Durand Ruel's was shut.   But
he carried off three of Lavery's paintings, one a
loan from Rodin, the others from the Luxembourg.
In gratitude he gave the Luxembourg one of Hone's
paintings, and Paris welcomed it ; the Tate Gallery
had refused such an offered gift.   He was all but
late with his Irish Room, but the workmen, I
know not by what persuasion, or maybe it was
but that of example, worked through the night,
and on the opening day, as he was able to boast in
triumph, the only one of the Art collections ready
was the Irish.

It may have been at this time it happened
that coming back from Monte Carlo with his
pocket full of diamonds he ran short of money,
so that he had to pawn some of them in Paris
before he could take his ticket home.   For there
are some entries in his pocket diaries written at
Monte Carlo : " Won £540.   Bought diamond and
pearl necklet, £280."   Then, " Lost in evening all
capital, £400.   Bought three pearl strings and
olivine ring for £233," and then the purchase of
a rose diamond necklace is put down ; all this
written as conscientiously as the " Bun and pear

3½d." and " two penny gingerbreads " of his careful needy days.

Having established Mancini and his easel in that large room of the Dublin Gallery he set him to paint his sister Ruth Shine's portrait, and then mine. I sat in a high chair in an old black dress,in front of a brown curtain lent by Miss Purser. Mancini set up a frame in front of me. He pinned many threads to this, crossing one another; their number increased from day to day, becoming a close network. The canvas on which he painted was crossed little by little with a like network. This—as he would explain in almost incomprehensible French, though sometimes turning to little less comprehensible Italian—was not his own method, but had been the method of some great master. Having put up a new thread or two he would go to the very end of the long room, look at me through my net, then begin a hurried walk which turned to a quick trot, his brush aimed at some feature, eye or eyebrow, the last steps would be a rush, then I needed courage to sit still. But the hand holding the brush always swerved at the last moment to the canvas, and there in its appropriate place, between its threads, the paint would be laid on and the retreat would begin. I was well repaid for my patience or courage, for at the end his portrait of a woman growing old, and a dusty black dress, and a faded brown curtain would have lighted up a prison cell. Synge, not often enthusiastic, spoke of it as " the greatest portrait since Rembrandt." Mancini himself liked it, though he was not quite satisfied, as towards the end he begged me to come to London

and sit for another portrait that would immeasure-
ably excel this one. It is one of my lasting regrets
that I allowed opportunity, that "winged nymph,"
to escape me then. The portrait was photographed
and Yeats, writing from London, tells me: "I had
a long lesson in the mathematical part of astrology
from Ralph Shirley yesterday, I think I must ask
you to meet him, he was struck with your horoscope.
'Those Jupiter and Scorpio people,' he said,
'have such a grand way with them.' I showed
him the Mancini photograph to prove it."

Yeats himself was not quite so fortunate, he
says:

"At some time or other Lane asked me if I
would sit to Mancini for a pastel. The pastel,
which I still have, was an evening's work. Mancini
put his usual grill of threads where the picture
was to be and another grill of threads correspond-
ing exactly with it in front of me. He did not
know anything about me, we had no language
in common, and he worked for an hour without
interest or inspiration. Then I remembered a
story of Lane's. Mancini, Italian peasant as
he was, believed that he would catch any illness
or deformity of those whom he met. He was not
thinking of microbes, but of some mysterious
process like that of the Evil Eye. He had just
been painting someone who had lost a leg, and
whose cork leg he believed was having a numbing
effect on his own. He worried Lane with his
terror—' My leg is losing all power of sensation,'
he would say at intervals. The thought of this
story made me burst into laughter, and Mancini
began to draw with great excitement and rapidity.

H

In a few minutes he had produced a most vivid likeness, not indeed of me, but of some dark-skinned Italian café king, in whom I see a curious resemblance to myself."

Meditating, I sometimes wonder how that visit now appears in Mancini's memory, should a thought ever drift back to it from Naples or from Rome. Even to me there seemed to be a little touch of tragedy under the laughter that rippled about him in Dublin. I think an immense loneliness as of a prison must have encompassed him sometimes, when evening closed in, and there was drizzling mist around him, and he hurried to his lodging under a sky without stars, through streets without chatter or gaiety, and open spaces without the music that would have been a speech he could comprehend. There were but few—perhaps because of the difficulty of language—to show him hospitality.

Hugh said the old gentlemen of his club had already been startled by the entrance of Augustus John, who on his way from a visit to us at Coole had called upon him there, in blue jersey and gold ear-rings, and that he must give them time to recover before he brought another artist among them. But when at last he brought in Mancini, half hoping that the elderly round-shouldered little man might fit better into its composition, Mancini, always doing what was least expected, put his hand on his heart, went up to each chair in succession and bowed low to its occupant. That civility was yet more disconcerting to the members than John's disdainful air of a strayed apostle come from converting, or being converted by, a camp of gypsies. So when Hugh was not with him at the hotel his dinner would be a silent one, and finding his best interpreters in chalk or charcoal, he would go to his room, and, failing another model, draw his own portrait from the looking-glass. There is one of these self-portraits in the Gallery, I was given two or three, and they show, I am bound to confess, no mark of melancholy, whether the laugh may have been at himself or at the town. One day, I forget with what companion, he broke away as if to search for some distraction in the city's shops, returning puffed with pride in the possession of a fine gold watch and a heavy gaudy chain. Hugh reproved him for his extravagance, and above all for his taste, declaring that no one would believe he was a real artist if he flaunted so ostentatious an ornament. It was a very dejected man who painted me the next day. And Hugh also was dejected as he murmured, " and the bill has been sent to me ! " For Hugh was keeping back his money till all the work was done, lest he should squander it, he said, or it may be with some misgiving that with a full purse and the packet boat at hand he might make one day his escape. It was in their bargain that all materials should be provided, and Mancini made at times an over-liberal use of paint, white especially, slapping it on as a mason slaps mortar on the stone. So rumour was, perhaps, well informed in saying that Hugh, returning after dusk to the Gallery, would scrape some of the most extravagant lumps and masses from the canvas, putting them back upon the palette for the unsuspecting artist's use next day.

Sometimes Mancini would write him a letter, not very legible but very much in earnest, demanding sums of money in advance. Even in tranquil moods his writing was difficult. Hugh had once received one of his letters torn in pieces; he had torn it in impatience, probably at not being able to read it himself and intending to write another, but had then, repenting, put the bits in an envelope for Hugh himself to mend and find the sense of. I liked to see them together, Hugh, but just out of his twenties, responsible for so irresponsible a grey-haired genius. They had their little quarrels but forgave one another quickly, one because of his great admiration for the other's work, the other because of that appreciation. As for myself, even when my portrait appeared but a thing of dabs and blotches I forgave the long waiting and the chilly hours in that evening dress, because I had within sight at the end of the room the "Maker of Figures," that portrait by Mancini of his father given to the Gallery by Mr. Sargent, and one of the pictures in which I take most delight.

When Hugh had been making a motor journey with friends, Lady Phillips and her party, he had persuaded them to go to Rome to be painted by Mancini. He himself had been painted by him there, the large portrait in the Gallery, having, I think, rather too much confusion of background, yet friends notice that his custom of sitting on the edge of his chair shows something of his character, as if he was but poised for a moment. He gave a fine picture by him to the Leeds Gallery, another portrait of the artist's father. Besides the portraits he had ordered and the pictures he had bought direct from him he once recognised his work in a shop window, when in an English country town. The friend who was with him doubted it, and bet him £5 it was no Mancini. They went in, and Hugh having won the £5 offered it for the picture (it is one now in the Gallery). The shop-keeper accepted it, saying, "My word, it is a funny looking thing!" and told him, to his mischievous delight, that it had been taken away "with other rubbish" from the house of a rival admirer of Mancini. It was by no witchcraft, however, he divined the artist that time. He had recognised on the canvas the marks of Mancini's threads.

Mr. J. B. Yeats, writing to me last July and again mentioning Hugh, says, "I don't think humour derives its satisfaction from a sense of superiority so much as from a sense of difference—a sense of difference with as practical result a sense *not* of superiority (your true humourist will deprecate the idea) but of *giving protection* (it must be one of the attributes of God the Father). When the helpless Mancini was in Dublin Hugh Lane went about with him everywhere and conducted him everywhere, spending every evening with him, and obviously enjoyed every moment of his time ; was that because he wanted to gratify his sense of superiority, or was it from some mysterious enjoyment in the sense of giving a constant protection, and a laughing protection, because Mancini by his queer ways and crazy nature was a constant shock ? I think a shock, a sudden surprise, always makes us laugh unless one is frightened or angry—and it was not easy either to frighten or enrage your nephew.

" I first heard of Mancini in this way. One morning in Dublin I met Lane and he stopped me to say that he had just had a letter from him to say he had arrived in London and asking when was he to come to Dublin to paint Lane's ' illustrious sister.' It seems that when your nephew sat to Mancini for his portrait in Rome he did mention his sister with the remark that she was a much better subject for a portrait. On this Mancini meditated and finally came to London. Evidently Hugh Lane was both perplexed and amused, for of course he knew that Mancini would be no ordinary handful. I again met him and asked about Mancini ; it was all right, he had written to Mrs. —— I forget the name of a lady who was a friend of Sargent and artists generally. She had taken him into her house, and that he might not be lonely hired another Italian of whom she made a footman, and they were such friends that they went about together all day with their arms round each other's necks. Again I met H. L. He was in great perplexity. Mrs. —— had written to say that the friends had quarrelled, and that this mattered greatly, because they both took up and threw at each other ornaments and bric-à-brac in her rooms, which were valuable."

There is another portrait of me in the Gallery. It was at a little dinner, in Burlington Street, in an ante-room after a lecture that had been given by Yeats, that someone praising Epstein's work, Hugh said with sudden agreement that he would like me to sit to him for a bust for the Gallery. I had pleasant hours enough in those sittings, and my thoughts went to placing a replica of it for my grandchildren to remember me by. But one day some writer came in, asking questions about the work of our Theatre, and I was over ready to answer and grew eager in talk and forget the calmness that befits sculpture, that is for eternity, and I did not notice how time passed or watch the artist's hand. And then suddenly I found that, pleased with some gesture, he had cut through the clay throat, tilting head and chin in an eternal eagerness. Hugh grumbled at it, and it was thought too revolutionary for the company of the serene marbles that preside at Coole. It is very clever and I do not quite dislike it ; yet when set beside Mancini's radiant transfiguration the thought has crossed my mind that as if for balance and by some star less magnificent than Jupiter, Epstein had been beckoned in as Devil's Advocate.

CHAPTER X

WHEN Hugh was asked, as sometimes happened, for advice as to the right way to found a Gallery, he was used to say, "Get your pictures together first and then think of your building"; and in his own practice he ever conformed to this rule. So now that the splendid collection made by him was lodged in the house in Harcourt Street, the time seemed to have come to give it an enduring home. I say "lodged," for although the rooms where we still go to look at the pictures have great beauty and charm, an intimacy of which something will be lost in a new building when it comes, the windows are those of a dwelling-house, many of the pictures can only be seen in their full beauty at certain hours of the day, there is not space or light for any who would copy them, and besides and beyond this, as it stands with houses joining it on each side, it cannot be guarded from even probable accident. Mr. MacColl had advised us to be content with "a simple carcass—a shell, well lighted, and rain and fire proof," but this house has not one of these qualities. I am anxious in every one of the troublesome days of the present year, for some of the Harcourt Street houses are used for their business by the Sinn Fein committees, and while soldiers make their sudden raids and searches, rumour keeps one in mind of that Easter time when O'Connell Street was shattered into ruins. So both for lighting and for safety's sake an open space on which to build a Gallery was needed.

Hugh Lane had written in the Preface to the Catalogue of the Municipal Gallery in December, 1907 : —

" I now hand over my collection of pictures and drawings of the British School (seventy) and Rodin's masterpiece, ' L'age d'Arain.' I also present the group of portraits of contemporary Irish men and women. . . . I have also deposited here my collection of pictures by Continental artists and intend to present the most of them, provided that the promised permanent building is erected on a suitable site within the next few years. This collection includes a selection of the Forbes and Durand Ruel pictures bought by me after the Royal Hibernian Academy Winter Exhibition, and some important examples of Manet, Renoir, Mancini, etc., which I have purchased to make this Gallery widely representative of the greatest masters of the nineteenth century."

The pictures in this conditional gift were :—

Les Parapluies, Renoir ; Le Concert aux Tuileries, Edouard Manet ; Portrait of Mademoiselle Éva Gonzalès, Edouard Manet ; Printemps, vue de Louvecienne, C. Pissarro ; Vétheuil, Sunshine and Snow, Claude Monet ; The Mantelpiece, E. Vuillard ; La Rivage, entrée de Tourgeville, E. Boudin ; La Plage, Degas ; Jour d'été, B. Morisot ; Duc D'Orleans, Ingres ; In the Law

Courts, Forain; Portrait of Marquis del Grillo, Mancini; En Voyage, Mancini; Aurelia, Mancini; La Douane, Mancini; The Mountebank, John Davis Brown; Portrait Study of a Woman, R. Madrazo; Portrait of Honoré Daumier, Charles H. Daubigny; Forest at Fontainebleau, Ant., Louis Barye; Avignon, Ancient Palace of the Popes, J. B. Corot; Landscape, A Summer Morning, J. B. Corot; The Slave, Eugene Fromentin; The Snowstorm, G. Courbet; The Pool, G. Courbet; In the Forest, G. Courbet; The Offspring of Love, N. Diaz; Portrait of a Naval Officer, Jean Leon Gérôme; Still Life, F. H. F. Fantin Latour; Still Life, Francois Bonvin; Moonlight, Theodore Rousseau; The Toilet, Puvis de Chavannes; Decollation de S. Jean Baptiste, Puvis de Chavannes; The Hayfield, A. Monticelli; Don Quixote and Sancho Panza, Honore Daumier; Feeding the Bird, James Maris; The Present, Alfred Stevens; An Italian Peasant Woman, J. B. Corot; Skating in Holland, J. B. Yongkind;, The Artist, G. Courbet.

The condition being, as I have already said, that a suitable Gallery should be provided. But after the Harcourt Street house had been taken there were difficulties even in keeping it open. The Corporation had been obliged to apply to Parliament for power to carry out that vote of £500 a year made in 1905, and this power was not granted by " a too-occupied Parliament " until 1911; the Gallery through these years was maintained by friends of Art, and by Hugh himself. While there was no money even for lights or fires

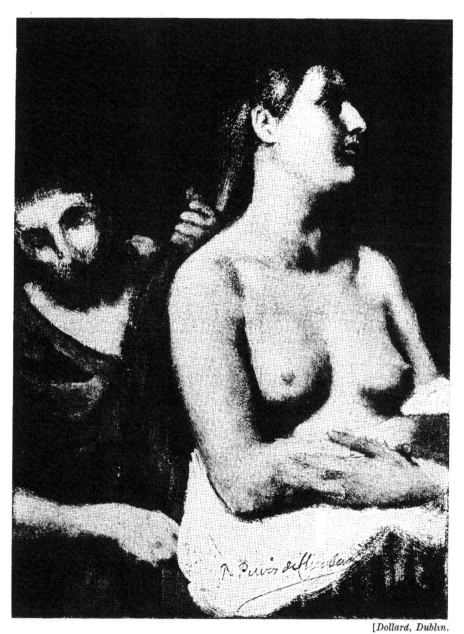

THE TOILET.

By Puvis de Chavannés.

or doorkeeper's wage, there was of course none for making a new building. Hugh worked on in patience, but even in 1909 Yeats had written to me from Dublin: "I met Lane last night; he is once more threatening the Corporation with the withdrawal of his pictures and he is taking a house in London 'with a nursery' as he puts it. He says also that he has told his landlord that 'a bachelor wants room to expand in.'" And a little later I wrote from London: "Great pressure is being put on Hugh Lane to give his pictures to the Tate Gallery here, where the value of his gift would be understood and appreciated."

In the autumn of 1912 he was growing impatient. He wrote to me in September from North Devon: "The hunting is slowly bringing me back to life, though I don't expect to put on flesh till the Gallery question is settled one way or the other in January." And he wrote to the Lord Mayor reminding him that his promise had been only "for the next few years" and that already five of these had passed, and asking him to take immediate steps toward the fulfilment of the condition. The Lord Mayor was entirely in sympathy with him. He invited the Citizens' Committee to call a public meeting at the Mansion House. The Committee wrote from there that "it ought to be known to the people of Dublin that the pictures lent by Sir Hugh Lane at present housed in Harcourt Street are in immediate danger of being lost to the city unless a suitable building be provided for their custody and exhibition."

The meeting was held in November; the Lord

Mayor gave an assurance of sympathy on behalf of himself and his colleagues in the Corporation. "But," he said, "we can only levy a halfpenny tax which will not be sufficient, and so we have to appeal to the citizens for contributions to keep such a treasure in Ireland and in Dublin." It was told also at the meeting that these pictures had been valued some time ago at £60,000, but that after the sale in Paris of the Henri Rouart collection, Sir Walter Armstrong, a very high authority, had written : " Great as was the market value of the collection a fortnight ago, its value has been greatly increased by this sale, great enhancements of price were shown by every master included in these whose works are at present hanging in Dublin." Among the letters read was one from Mr. Robert Ross, saying, " Some of the pictures at Dublin are already regarded as marking an epoch in European Art, and they are the envy of every modern Art Gallery Director with whom I am acquainted." Mr. Birrell had written of the collection as having " already obtained world-wide celebrity," and Mr. George Bernard Shaw, having asked me in a telegram, "Is the Lord Mayor Right Hon., or what ? " wrote to him: " Sir Hugh Lane has placed in the hands of the Corporation of Dublin an instrument of culture the value of which is far beyond anything that can be expressed in figures by the City accountant. . . . A good Gallery is the best of investments, because people will give you pictures to hang in it which you would not get otherwise except by buying them in competition with American millionaires." John Redmond gave the meeting his blessing, and

Professor George Baker of Harvard "wondered the people of Dublin could sleep at night knowing that collection to be in a building that is not fireproof."

There was great enthusiasm at the meeting and no doubt as to what was the desire of the citizens; and the Municipal Council holding a special meeting in January, 1913, agreed to give £22,000 for the building of a Municipal Art Gallery provided that a site was given by the Citizens' Committee, as well as a sum of £3000 towards the building. A Committee began to collect money for this, and of the various possible sites which had long been spoken of one had now to be chosen.

I have been looking at some notes written and sent to me about this matter of a site. The first mentioned is on St. Stephen's Green, the large oblong square in the very centre of Dublin made by Lord Ardilaun at much cost into a garden with green turf and flower beds, and shrubberies, and ponds where wild fowl swim and are the delight of children. I have been looking at a letter written about this site at the time: "It has the advantage that the cost of acquiring it would be nil; the excellence of the situation and the beauty of its surroundings. But it is hopeless, as Lord Ardilaun when he acquired the Green for presentation to the citizens of Dublin had to do so under an Act of Parliament under which certain powers are reserved to him. He is strongly opposed to the scheme, and consequently his opposition will be fatal to the passing of an Act which would be essential."

It was on this place that Hugh Lane had set his heart. He wrote, 21st August, 1912 : "Lutyens has promised me to architect the new Gallery (Dublin) and *garden* in exchange for an Old Master, so that now we only want the £25,000 and Stephen's Green." He found it hard to believe that the Gallery he had already asked Lutyens to design would not find its welcome where it would be " like the Luxembourg in its garden on the only good site in Dublin." If this was given he would add £10,000 to what he had already promised, for he was sure it would be for the enjoyment of the people on whose behalf Lord Ardilaun had turned the Green into a pleasure ground. So he was very sad when he wrote to me in 1912 that it had been refused. He had still some hope, and said : "I will let Lutyens go on with his design for St. Stephen's Green and hope for a miracle to carry it through." And he asked me to find out if there was yet any hope for it. But Lord Ardilaun believed that the building would " totally destroy the proportions and beauty of the most attractive part of the Park. It is only twenty-two acres in extent, and the loss of space would be serious." Hugh, on the other hand, was convinced that " properly designed the gardens would look very much larger than they do now, and the building make very little impression on it."

But although Lutyens' fine design had been made—" a beautiful low building with a pillared portico on the garden front for a rest and shelter "— it had to be put aside. Another place proposed was Merrion Square, but the Mansion House

Committee were against a new Gallery being
" added to the already large number of free public
institutions grouped together in a residential
quarter at a distance from the business centre of
the city." Lutyens gave his opinion that it
would for architectural reasons have to be placed
in the very centre of the Square, and as for Hugh,
" he wanted it built on a thoroughfare." When
someone said later of his Bridge site that only
workmen would be passing there and they would
not care for the pictures, he said, " I shall be
satisfied if they only go in to warm themselves."
But he was not asked to make a decision, for the
cost was found to be heavy and mortgages made
the business complicated, and the idea was for
the time given up.

There were other proposals. There were the
old Turkish Baths in Clare Street. But that site,
like one of Upper Ormond Quay, and one in
Dawson Street, would have cost close on £50,000.
Another was proposed directly opposite the
buildings of the National University, then being
built. But Yeats wrote : " Hugh will not
hear of this, he says he has seen the designs
and nothing would induce him to put a beautiful
building opposite such an ugly one." An addition
to the Mansion House was thought of ; an addition " which could be used as a ballroom or for
banquets," Sir E. Lutyens reports, " and the
reception of public guests. . . ." But, besides
other reasons against it, Hugh said, " The Mansion
House site does not give us any scope for a fine
building which is even more necessary to Dublin
than pictures. It is more than a hundred years

since a good piece of architecture has been raised in Ireland."

Dec. 15. It is near Christmas time and the letters and papers given to the keeping of poor dead Martin Wood have not yet come to me. I have still to work without them. That vexed me when I began to work this Monday morning, for my story had come to the year of the proposal and rejection of the Bridge site for the Gallery, a project that was so loved and so hated that it led to much rancour and bitterness in Dublin, and even to-day the branches of the bitter root then planted are bearing their sour fruit in London where Hugh's coveted pictures, taken out of Ireland in that unhappy quarrel, are being held from us by some who would put an unforgiving name upon one whose nature turned always to forgiveness. But, thinking of the ungraciousness showed him by his own countrymen at the time, I begin to be glad that so much of the record is missing, and that I must of necessity shorten the history to a few necessary pages.

And before I go on with those pages I would like to write here a passage from a letter that came to me only a few days ago, sent to me by Yeats who had searched for it in vain till he came into a settled house at Oxford. It was written to him by that good friend now gone, the Right Hon. W. F. Bailey, on January 17, 1917, and told of some words that Hugh had said to him one of those last days in Dublin in the Spring of 1915: " He came to see me, bringing with him a pair of Chinese statuettes as a present. We talked about his French pictures and I remarked that it was a tragedy that such a proffered gift should not have been accepted by Dublin. He replied that this was largely due to misunderstanding, that there were mistakes and misapprehensions on both sides, and that if the matter came up again he thought things would take a different turn. 'Then,' I said, 'there is still a hope that we may get the pictures?' 'Certainly,' he replied, 'with some give and take an agreement will be come to on the question of a site for the Gallery and Dublin will get the pictures.' He added that too much had been made of this site question."

I am putting this near the beginning of my chapter because I do not wish to blame unduly those who went against him or to hold him altogether free from blame. I know that many of those who were not with him believe now as he did at the last, that the "mistakes and misapprehensions" were not all on the one side. To-day also I am thinking of one who believed in him all through, and supported him against his own companions and fellow-workers for a long time, although at the last he gave his voice against him through honest belief that in so doing he was upholding Ireland's rights, and who but a few dark mornings ago, having been roused from his bed by soldiers in the night-time, was put on board a warship and taken to a prison in England— Thomas Kelly, an alderman of Dublin. Hugh always held him in affection and respect. It was but a little while before he left Dublin for that last voyage that they, meeting in the street, talked over this matter of a building, and at Hugh's urgency the other said : " Why don't you give us a little more time, why are you in such a hurry ? " And the answer, "Because I have not long to live," had lingered in his ears but some thirty days when that fatal news from Queenstown turned it to an immutable memory. This might well have served for " the Binding " at my chapter's end, but, as I say, I would like the thought of Hugh's placable words to be carried through its harsh record.

It was soon after the Mansion House meeting that the great idea that was to prove so great a disaster came into being. It was that, no plot of earth having been found on which to place the Gallery, it should be built upon a bridge, poised, as it were, between air and water, in the manner of the Uffizi Gallery at Florence. So daring an idea was, I think, Hugh's own. He wrote to me, to America, on February 15, 1913 : " The Committee and the Press, and the principal Corporation Officials have agreed to pulling down the hideous metal bridge (covered with advertisements) and to build a Gallery on a stone-faced bridge. It will be a most beautiful and sensational ornament to Dublin and will in no way spoil the existing view and will bring more life to the centre of the old city." Lutyens approved of it as " an idea so full of imagination and possibility that it is almost impossible to resist," and made his design forthwith. The City Architect, having seen the design, considered it would be " a very great ornament to the city." Yeats wrote me of it :

SIR E. LUTYENS' ORIGINAL SKETCH FOR THE BRIDGE GALLERY DESIGN.

"I hear it is most beautiful, it seems to be conquering everybody," and later in the same letter, "I have just seen the Lutyens' design—beautiful. Two buildings joined by a row of columns, it is meant to show the sunset through columns, there are to be statues on the top."

The practical advantages were that this site could be obtained by a grant from the Corporation, without an Act of Parliament or Law difficulties. It was near the centre of the city, would take the place of the ugly metal foot-bridge, and as the Corporation intended sooner or later to pull this down and build a more worthy one the cost would not be for the Gallery alone, it would still act as a foot-bridge. The Gallery would be detached, and especially safe from fire. But there is no doubt it was the beauty of the design that awoke and kindled enthusiasm. As to Hugh, he already saw (even beyond this) a new Parliament House with a river front, the rebuilding of all that was poor and ugly, all Dublin put in harmony with what it already possessed of beauty.

Sir E. Lutyens made an estimate of £45,000 for the Bridge Gallery. Of this the Corporation would have to find £22,000, and they agreed to this in accepting the design. The site was to be paid for, as already agreed, by private gifts. Hugh was hopeful, and before January was out Yeats wrote: "He has just bought a Degas for £4500 to go to the Gallery if the money for building it is found." But money came in very slowly. For, good givers as most of us in Ireland are, we are not used to give for anything that is not to help charity or politics or religion. We are but slowly learning the value " to the life of the soul " of " the great unselfish interests—science, love of knowledge, love of beauty in all its forms." The Dublin citizens had already accepted taxation for the building of a Gallery, and dwellers in the country, it may be, looked on such a building as a luxury for a well-to-do Dublin.   And the few rich men in Ireland were also slow to help.   Yeats, hearing that one of them had refused to add to what he had given at the first " unless it could be proved the people wished for pictures," wrote a vehement poem, " To a Wealthy Man "—

> " You gave but will not give again
> Until enough of Paudeen's pence
> By Biddy's halfpennies have lain
> To be ' some sort of evidence '
> Before you'll put your guineas down
> That things it were a pride to give
> Are what the blind and ignorant town
> Imagines best to make it thrive.
> What cared Duke Ercole, that bid
> His mummers to the market-place,
> What th' onion-sellers thought or did
> So that his Plautus set the pace
> For the Italian comedies ?
> And Guidobaldo, when he made
> That grammar school of courtesies,
> Where wit and beauty learned their trade
> Upon Urbino's windy hill,
> Had sent no runners to and fro
> That he might learn the shepherds' will.
> And when they drove out Cosimo,
> Indifferent how the rancour ran,
> He gave the hours they had set free
> To Michelozzo's latest plan
> For the San Marco Library,
> Whence turbulent Italy should draw
> Delight in Art whose end is peace,
> In logic and in natural law
> By sucking at the dugs of Greece.

Your open hand but shows our loss,
For he knew better how to live.
Let Paudeens play at pitch and toss,
Look up in the sun's eye and give
What the exultant heart calls good
That some new day may breed the best
Because you gave, not what they would
But the right twigs for an eagle's nest ! "

Early in 1913 I was in America with the Abbey
Company. Yeats wrote to me there telling me
the Gallery matter was still urgent. He went
on : " I dined with Gwynn last night at the
House of Commons, Hazleton, member for North
Galway, and several of the other Irish members
came up. One was lamenting that a Home Rule
Bill did not give a House of Lords. He was
interesting on the subject; he said, 'The towns
are hateful and it will be their influence if the
gentry go away. An honest man can be a dreamer
in the country, but a town dreamer is a loafer and
a drunkard.' Later on Devlin came up. They
were all excited about the Gallery, complained
they had not been told of its peril until the last
moment."

I had written to Hugh before leaving home in
December : "Is it to the beginning or end of
January that your offer holds ? If to the end I
would have a month to try for help in America,
if all else should fail."

And the letters that followed me there told me
of the increasing danger ; that nothing could be
done without more money towards the building,
that the time had all but run out when Hugh
would take his loan collection away from Dublin.

But the Citizens' Committee still needed some thousands to make up the necessary sum for a site and for their promised contribution.

I again begged him to stretch his patience a little farther and he did so by degrees, at last as far as to my birthday, the fifteenth of March. I knew that Americans were generous, and especially towards Ireland, and would in all likelihood help us. But I was bound to the business of the Theatre, going here and there with the Company, and it was difficult to make our need known. But when we came to Chicago I spoke of it to those kindly lads who came to see me from the newspaper offices—one of them a nephew of my old friend Chenery, the Editor of *The Times*—and they were good in finding a place for what I said. And I told some of the friends of our Theatre of this anxiety about the Gallery, and spoke of it at a matinée we gave to help the Citizens' Fund. Before the end of January had come I wrote to Yeats from Chicago :—

" I have used up a good deal of time and energy trying to do something to save the pictures, and after endless efforts at last, last night, got a few men together to start a subscription list. I am afraid it is rather late for much to come of it, but even a small sum from abroad might set a good example. We made about £200 by the matinée. I will cable news of it."

And next day I added to the letter : " Oh, my dear Willie, 'the help of God is nearer than the door '—and hardly had I put up my letter when the telephone rang and said there were gentlemen downstairs waiting for me, and there I found nine or ten business-like people, Judge Cavanagh, Judge McGowan, Mr. McCormack (just going to receive three million dollars at his bank), Mr. Ira Morris, Mr. Dillon (my old enemy), and others. They listened to my few minutes' statement, all said they would try and help, some had to go, some stayed to lunch given by Mr. Morris, and before lunch was over the cable was written guaranteeing £1000, and more will certainly follow, though I am sorry to be leaving to-night, but of course my hopes are up. I am so relieved. I had worked so hard and seemed to have done nothing, but at last when those blessed men came in and the spark was struck every one knew the facts. The atmosphere was ready. . . . I had cabled to know how much is still wanted for the Fund and had heard ' Four thousand,' which is nothing ! ''

And then from Philadelphia : '' The Gallery still first in my mind. Hugh cables that the decisive meeting is to-morrow. I am still trying for a little more American money, but not sure of much, and this morning we had a consultation, Company and I, and decided to cable guarantee for £1000 inclusive of £180 already sent. I guaranteed against personal payment and they will work it out by Matinées, New York, Boston, Dublin, London, Oxford, etc. I am sure you will approve. It was very nice of them. . . .

''Our last triumph, or chief one, in New York was the conversion of Bourke Cochrane. I brought him one night to the plays in the last week and he came two other nights—says all the genius of Ireland is in us—wants to make a public announcement of his opinion—and is to give us a reception and make a speech before we sail.   He was less amiable about the Gallery—which I had hoped he would have helped—says it would do Dublin good if all the pictures were sold at Christie's and they found what they had lost.   It was at a lunch at Mrs. Guinness's and she sided with him, and I should have had a hard time but that Peter Dunne (Mr. Dooley), to whom I will never forget it, was not only kind but full of tact, and at last proposed to Cochrane that he should see John Quinn to-day, and they arranged to lunch with him and he is to come and tell me by and by what happened, but I am not very hopeful."

Then when we came to Montreal we, the Players and I, were asked by Mr. J. C. Walsh, President of the St. Patrick's Society, to luncheon at an Irish Club or gathering.   And before the lunch was over another cable had been sent to the Lord Mayor guaranteeing another thousand pounds.

And I wrote from Boston in March, before we sailed for home : " We give a Matinée in New York 22nd to clear off part of Gallery guarantee. Mrs. Bourke Cochrane is to sell tickets and will give tea on the stage after, and B. C. will then make his speech—he has given £50 for the Gallery. They asked me to dine on Sunday, so I set out from Philadelphia on Friday night, travelled all night, arrived here morning, did business at the Plymouth Theatre and had interviewers for a couple of hours, went back to New York Saturday evening and back here Monday, rather tired, but well content.   For, after all my vain efforts for the Gallery, they had asked a young man, Mr. C., to dinner to meet me who at the first mention of it promised £1000 ! So I had a cable from the Lord Mayor of Dublin : ' You have worked wonders for us, I do not know what we should have done without your powerful advocacy. Ireland could not afford to lose these pictures—that they shall not be lost to Dublin is the one point as to which I am concerned.' ''

For the then Lord Mayor, Mr. Sherlock, was a staunch friend to Hugh, as well as the present Lord Mayor, Mr. Laurence O'Neill ; Miss Harrison, in or out of the Corporation, was always a devoted and tireless worker ; Alderman Foley also, and, above all, Alderman Tom Kelly. But of those whose minds suspicion had clouded there is no need to give the names.

I was still anxious and I had written to Hugh on my way home on board the *Cymric*, April 26 : '' The day I left Boston I thought I must have some beautiful thing to remember, and I went to Mrs. Gardner's ' palazzo ' and sat with her, just moving from room to room to look at the pictures. She told me to tell you how little help she had had, and how much ingratitude and annoyance. And at first the Boston people didn't care for the pictures, used to ask to see her own rooms, but now they are growing more intelligent. So Dublin has comrades in ungraciousness.''

Yeats had written while I was still away :—

'' I saw Lane last night. I think all is right for the Gallery largely through your success in America, I believe. I wrote at .his dictation a long wire to Dublin stating the conditions on

which he will hand over the pictures.   He insists
on the river site—the Gallery to be put on a bridge
over the river close to Grattan Bridge.   I, knowing
we had not enough for this site, tried to get him
to accept a site opposite the new University, but
he is unshakable on the Bridge site.   He wants
to put up a beautiful building in fine surroundings.
He says the most beautiful buildings would be
lost in front of the ugly architecture—he has seen
designs of the New University.   He goes to Dublin
at end of week and will, I think, make over pictures
on the Corporation finally accepting Lutyens'
and the River site and will be content till the
money has been raised.   The estimate for making
the Bridge Foundation is £12,000, but he thinks
it will cost more."

Hugh wrote: "It may be some satisfaction
to you to know that if the pictures are saved
to Dublin it is entirely owing to you and the
generosity of your American friends."

Want of money was no longer the stumbling
block.   But already another difficulty had arisen.

CHAPTER XI

THE REMOVAL OF THE FRENCH PICTURES

THERE had always been some who had looked coldly or with scorn on the scheme of a bridge building, while some others, though allured by it, feared so dazzling an idea could never be brought into solid being. One of the letters sent to me says, after putting the case for it, " but against this is put the likelihood of serious engineering difficulties; the damp situation and danger from effluvia ascending from the river, which is most injurious to the paint in pictures, attacking the lead in the paint." Lutyens, however, in his report in favour of the bridge says of this danger, " It is a question of fact that could be easily proved," and asks to have the matter submitted to certain simple chemical tests. But there were also ill-wishers who saw an opportunity to blast the whole project. First in whisperings and then in the newspapers accusations were made of the sort to which " this man contributes his Malice, another his Wit, all men what they please, and most upon Hearsay." Yeats has written an account of what took place in this vehement note to his book " Responsibilities " : " During the thirty years or so during which I have been reading Irish newspapers, three public controversies have stirred my indignation. The first was the Parnell controversy. There were reasons to justify a man's joining either party, but there were none to justify, on one side or on the other, lying accusations forgetful of past service, a frenzy of detraction. And another was the dispute over *The Playboy*. There were reasons for opposing as for supporting that violent laughing thing, but none for the lies, for the unscrupulous rhetoric spread against it in Ireland, and from Ireland to America. The third prepared for the Corporation's refusal of a building for Sir Hugh Lane's famous collection of pictures.

"One could respect the argument that Dublin, with much poverty and many slums, could not afford the £22,000 the building was to cost the city, but not the minds that used it. One frenzied man compared the pictures to Troy horse which 'destroyed a city,' and innumerable correspondents described Sir Hugh Lane and those who had subscribed many thousands to give Dublin paintings by Corot, Manet, Monet, Degas, and Renoir as 'self seekers,' 'self advertisers,' 'picture dealers,' 'log-rolling cranks and faddists'; and one clerical paper told 'picture-dealer Lane' to take himself and his pictures out of that. A member of the Corporation described a half-hour in the temporary Gallery in Harcourt Street as the most dismal of his life. . . . Someone asked, instead of these eccentric pictures, to be given pictures 'like those beautiful productions displayed in the windows of our city picture shops.' Another thought that we would all be more patriotic if we devoted our energy to fighting the

Insurance Act. Another would not hang them in his kitchen, while yet another described the vogue of French impressionist painting as having gone to such a length among 'log-rolling enthusiasts' that they even admired 'works that were rejected from the Salon forty years ago by the finest critics in the world.'

" The first serious opposition began in *The Irish Catholic,* the chief Dublin clerical paper ; and Mr. William Murphy, Mr. Healy's financial supporter in his attack upon Parnell, a man of great influence, brought to its support a few days later his newspapers *The Evening Herald* and *The Irish Independent,* the most popular of Irish daily papers. He replied to my poem, ' To a Wealthy Man ' (I was thinking of a very different wealthy man), from what he described as 'Paudeen's point of View,' and Paudeen's point of view it was. The enthusiasm for ' Sir Hugh Lane's Corots '—one paper spelled the name repeatedly ' Crot '—being but an exotic fashion ' waited some satirist like Gilbert,' who killed the æsthetic craze, and as for the rest, ' there were no greater humbugs in the world than art critics and so-called experts.' As the first avowed reason for opposition, the necessities of the poor got but a few lines, not so many certainly as the objection of various persons to supply Sir Hugh Lane with ' a monument at the City's expense ' ; and as the Gallery was supported by Mr. James Larkin, the chief Labour leader, and important slum workers, I assume that the purpose of the opposition was not exclusively charitable.

" These controversies—political, literary, and

artistic—have showed that neither religion nor politics can of itself create minds with enough receptivity to become wise, or just and generous enough to make a nation. Other cities have been as stupid—Samuel Butler laughs at shocked Montreal for hiding the 'Discobolus' in a cellar—but Dublin is the capital of a nation, and an ancient race has no place else to look for an education. Goethe, in 'Wilhelm Meister,' describes a saintly and naturally gracious woman, who getting into a quarrel over some trumpery detail of religious observance grows—she and all her little religious community—angry and vindictive. In Ireland I am constantly reminded of that fable, of the futility of all discipline that is not of the whole being. Religious Ireland—and the pious Protestants of my childhood were signal examples —thinks of divine things as a round of duties separated from life, and not as an element that may be discovered in all circumstances and emotions; while political Ireland sees the good citizen, but as a man who holds to certain opinions and not as a man of good will. Against all this we have but a few educated men and the remnants of an old traditional culture among the poor. Both were stronger forty years ago, before the rise of our new middle class, which showed as its first public event during the nine years of the Parnellite split, how base at moments of excitement are minds without culture."

When I talked with Yeats of writing this book he was insistent that all the truth about him he called that " bitter-tongued man " should be put down. I reminded him of Plutarch's counsel to beware how we speak ill of the dead, "and so make immortal enemies." And I said, "I have here a letter written to me at the time by one of Hugh's best friends and supporters, who says, 'I don't wonder at your being upset and mortified —as indeed we all are—at the action of the Dublin Corporation in regard to the princely gift of your nephew. The sad part of it all is that I really don't believe the Corporation would have acted as they did but for the unaccountable part which Mr. Murphy played in the transaction, and the intensity of his opposition throughout. Those who know him assure me that he was not actuated by personal or unworthy motives, but honestly believed he was speaking in the interests of Dublin.'" "Yes," said Yeats, "I am ready to admit that, but what I object to are the methods he used, and the unworthy attacks. And you see even in that letter the writer says, 'I confess I find it hard to believe.' But whatever he thought, no man has a right to use such methods."

The other day, in Dublin, I went to see Sir —— to tell him how the matter of the pictures stands ; of the breaking off of the discussion in the Cabinet, and of the word spoken by one of the Trustees to Sir John Lavery.

Someone who was listening said then, "I think Sir Hugh Lane's face was the most beautiful I have ever seen." We talked a little of his treatment in Dublin and I said I rejoiced that it had been outdone in ungraciousness in London, and to this they, like Mr. Birrell, agreed. Another said how fine the Bridge design had been, and our host said, "But for Murphy there would never have

been that trouble." The first who had spoken
said, " Yet I believe his opinion was sincere, that
is an excuse." But he said, " No, that is no
excuse, it is no excuse for him that he formed an
opinion on a matter on which he was entirely
ignorant, and that was the value of the pictures.
He knew nothing about it at all." And then he
said how splendidly the National Gallery had been
enriched by Hugh's gifts and his bequests.

The opposition went on growing through the
spring and summer. In March Yeats wrote : '' I
am afraid there will be a great deal of opposition,
some of it genuine, to this particular site. The
Arts Club is in a most quarrelsome state ; everybody wants a different site and hates everybody
else as a result." And I wrote later, after my
return from America : " I am not very happy
about the Gallery, there are constant letters in
the papers about it and hardly any one seems
really enthusiastic for the Bridge site. And I am
not really sure myself it would be good. I had
forgotten the Liffey was so small till I drove across
Dublin the morning I came. Lutyens seemed to
be fairly well pleased with the Mansion House as
an alternative, and I said something about this
when writing to Hugh, but he answered that
Dublin wants a good building even more than the
pictures, and the Mansion House wouldn't give
scope. But I don't think the Lord Mayor will
hold out about it, there are so many against it.
And I am in terror of Hugh losing his temper and
spoiling all he has done."

And again : " Things look bad. I have written
to Hugh about Merrion Square site, but expect a

violent refusal. I am more anxious about his reputation than the pictures, and hope the Corporation will put themselves altogether in the wrong by going on with opposition to Lutyens." And to Hugh I wrote: "The papers make one indignant about the Gallery, and it is hard to have patience with the carping group, and still one has to be oneself and not disappoint those who believe in you. I am very anxious about Monday's meeting. I suppose as Lutyens seems fairly content with the Mansion House site you will agree to that if necessary. My own feeling is that whatever you wish ought to be done in recognition of what you are doing for Dublin, but I suppose there may have to be a compromise, you of course holding on to Lutyens. As I drove past the Parnell statue yesterday I remembered that opportunity was not given to an Irish sculptor, but to St. Gaudens. As Yeats says in a letter I am giving in my Theatre history, 'I will not feed my country's stomach at the expense of its brains.'"

And again: "'Looking from things visible to things invisible,' that is what has given us power, you, and John, and I myself to do anything at all —we have to think of the invisible witnesses."

But Hugh wrote in return: "A building will take about two years to build, and from the late (and in fact the constant) experience I have had of the Corporation's ways, I feel that the *only* thing that would enable me to go through with the project would be the thought of a beautiful building to recompense one. . . . You never seem to mind much how bad the scenery or costumes (or wigs!) of your plays are, but I feel

K

that the importance of a proper setting is *quite* as important as the pictures. . . . I am trying a 'Hypnotic' treatment for nerves, twenty guineas first week, and two guineas for every half-hour after that, but it has done me no good so far."

His patience was hardly tried. He wrote to me again, putting his case :—

"August 15, 1913. If the pictures are removed at the end of six weeks (from the first of August), the only thing that I will have to regret is that I did not keep my earlier threats of removing them and thereby saving every one a lot of trouble and annoyance.

"A committee was formed with the consent of the Corporation to choose a site. They chose the river site. The Corporation on the 19th March passed the river site. Lutyens then came over and made his design and becomes daily more enthusiastic on it, and does not want to consider any other.

"The opposition to the project is entirely got up by the anti-galleryites, who would have done just the same thing over the St. Stephen's Green or Merrion Square sites.

"I refuse the Merrion Square site. I have told them that if I am offered the Mansion House site I will give them my Barbizon pictures and all the recently acquired British pictures. It will be a second-rate building (at the back of the Mansion House) and therefore a second-rate collection is quite good enough for it.

"I am worse than useless personally. If you will ask a doctor what an advanced state of neurasthenia means, you will understand that one's fighting days are over.

"I was going to open up the question of St. Stephen's Green again, when I received your enclosure from Lady Ardilaun, this seemed to close that site. If it can be got instead of the Bridge site within the time I shall of course be satisfied."

I sometimes asked for sympathy as well as gave it. Writing from London, I said: "I feel your troubles are nothing beside mine! The Manets don't turn and rend you, and the hall porter anyhow is grateful for a means of living— at least I hope so. Anyhow, I am at the end of my strength and must go. I may have to come back for a few days later, and, of course, would come here or go to Dublin, or go anywhere that would help the Gallery, which seems to me the one bright and restful result of all our labours in Ireland. Of course if we turned the Abbey into a music hall and you turned the Gallery into a picture palace all would go easily, but we are 'image-makers,' and must carry out our dreams. But we need much patience sometimes!"

He writes: "I am very sorry to hear that you are ill. Goodness knows you have worked. Your wonderful combination of gifts has carried through what you have set out to do. I, with my one talent of 'taste,' should never have attempted to work in Ireland."

Yeats was writing to me in increasing indignation. "I think the dislike to the Gallery can only come from fear of culture, which was described by a man—who is, I believe, on the staff of the New

University—as ' the enemy of faith and morals,' at least I am told that was his description. All the Irish orthodoxies—political and religious— are at this moment in fear of a dissolvent."

He wrote again from London in July : " I made a good speech on Monday. Lane was anxious about some vote coming on in Dublin that day, but I know nothing, of course, of what has happened. I spoke with him quite as much as the possible subscribers in my mind. I described Ireland, if the present intellectual movement failed, as ' a little huxtering nation groping for halfpence in a greasy till,' but did not add, except in thought, ' by the light of a holy candle.' "

And in August: " I have just seen a paragraph in the *Morning Post* in which the Lord Mayor states that he believes the Gallery project is at an end, as the Corporation will not accept an English architect. It is lamentable, but I would sooner it failed because of this than anything else. If it had been Lane's insistence on a bridge site it would have put him in a bad light. I think if the bad news is true, and if nothing can be done —if it is quite certain the thing is over—we must insist on the principle of a great connoisseur being free to choose where he will. I do not want to say anything now because, of course, I would sooner have the pictures in a barn than not at all, but if it is finished we must make as good a statement as we can for the sake of the future. Ireland, like a hysterical woman, is principle mad and is ready to give up reality for a phantom like the dog in the fable."

For the sharpest opposition was now directed

against the employment of Sir E. Lutyens, for no reason save that of alien birth, just as one of the causes that years ago brought to naught Newman's planned Catholic University, was the objection to his having chosen one or two professors who were English. And that reason was but half valid in our case, for Lutyens had an Irish mother. More than any rebuff to himself, Hugh felt this ungracious rejection of his friend.

Those vehement words of Yeats in his speech had made the foundation of a fine poem. He gave it to the Irish papers, although he wrote : "It is not so appropriate now, as the Corporation are appealing to a hysterical patriotism to escape, I suppose, from a position Murphy has made difficult. I had not thought I could feel so bitterly over any public event."

> "What need you, being come to sense,
> But fumble in a greasy till
> And add the halfpence to the pence,
> And prayer to shivering prayer, until
> You have dried the marrow from the bone ;
> For men were born to pray and save,
> Romantic Ireland's dead and gone,
> It's with O'Leary in the grave.

> "Yet they were of a different kind,
> The names that stilled your childish play,
> They have gone about the world like wind,
> But little time had they to pray
> For whom the hangman's rope was spun,
> And what, God help us, could they save ;
> Romantic Ireland's dead and gone,
> It's with O'Leary in the grave.

> "Was it for this the wild geese spread
> The grey wing upon every tide ;
> For this that all that blood was shed,
> For this Edward Fitzgerald died,

And Robert Emmet and Wolfe Tone,
All that delirium of the brave ;
Romantic Ireland's dead and gone,
It's with O'Leary in the grave.

" Yet could we turn the years again,
And call those exiles as they were,
In all their loneliness and pain,
You'd cry ' some women's yellow hair
Has maddened every mother's son ; '
They weighed so lightly what they gave—
But let them be, they're dead and gone,
They're with O'Leary in the grave."

For all this time, although there was enough
money in hand, or all but enough, the building
of a Gallery seemed as far as ever away. ·Meetings
of the Corporation were held, but brought it no
nearer. It was said, and I am afraid it was true,
that the opponents put in agendas for the sole
purpose of making a decision impossible. At last
at one of these meetings several of the members,
to block the business and make· a decision impossible, stayed outside the door. They got their
way, and at another meeting the Bridge site was
abandoned, and the City architect was directed
to make estimates for another. And then Hugh,
who was waiting for news in England, was invited
to come and talk things over.

He came, indeed, but passionately indignant,
less I think at the defeat than at the unworthy
methods by which it had been brought about, he
came to take down the French pictures, his
conditional gift, from the walls on which he had
hung them in Harcourt Street.

I think, and others say, that had he been in
Dublin all would have yet gone well. Even

Alderman Tom Kelly, who though he had worked for him "in season and out of season," went against him at the last upon this question of Irish birth, said afterwards, "If he had stayed here with us all would have been right." And I believe that he who had so often in his public work kept great civility and good nature and had showed himself a "Master of Temper" under outrageous personal accusations, would have won over with more frequent companionship that fractious part of the Corporation. But incivility in written words is harsher than in the spoken word, and his patience would no longer stand against "the Ebbs and Flows of Popular Councils and the Winds that move those Waters," and that were sending his plans that seemed so near accomplishment to wreck.

He had asked me to go to Dublin when the meeting of the Corporation that was to decide the matter was coming on, and I did so, but finding what was its temper I could do little but attend it as an onlooker. A friend of his, Miss Swan, told me the other day that she had been staying at the Reeves' country house with him at the time of the decision. He was anxious and told them he had left it in my hands. "And if she cannot get it nobody can." Then my telegram came saying I had failed. I asked if he was very much cast down and she said, "Yes, but I think he had still hope."

I wrote to him a few days later: "I haven't written since the meeting. For one thing I made a dash for home, and drove on a car from Athenry, and rain came on, and between that and the exasperating days in Dublin I was quite knocked up with cold and headache. . . . I am glad in a way I was at that meeting. It took away some bitterness, the aldermen were so far from any understanding of what was offered and what the gift would mean to the country. It is not their fault, it is the fault of the system that puts our precious things into the hands of a democracy. I am pretty sure English corporations are much on the same level. One said the ' Beheading of John the Baptist ' was ' a travesty ' ; another that Irish artists could paint pictures like that if they liked ; some one quoted what I had said about the appreciation of those pictures in America, and Alderman Quaid said, ' She's his aunt, a family affair—a family affair," and another said Lutyens' design was an exact replica of a picture of a bridge he had seen somewhere. But it is not for them we went to work, but for the young generation, and with the desire of giving dignity to the name of Ireland for the sake of all those we have cared for who have belonged to this unlucky country. I am afraid it will become a laughing stock now for a while, we shall all suffer for the stupidity of a few."

And in other letters I wrote : " One has only to go ploughing on, ploughing on, knowing that some day or other our work will be recognised, though not probably in my lifetime." And then again : " Your letter is rather a heartbreak. You could hardly say anything about Dublin that I could not cap ! And if you have had ingratitude, have I not had a threatening letter with a picture of a coffin from a countryman while in Chicago ?

. . . But one must go straight on, that is all I have learned from life so far. ' Even a fool, if he continue in his folly, shall be counted wise.' If you knew how I hate ' Playboy ' that I go out fighting for! And all for the sake of this unfortunate country that doesn't think it possible for any one to walk in a straight line."

He wrote on September 27 : " I have been very busy hanging pictures here (in Belfast). . . . I am always anxious to get out of Ireland. My early romantic notion of it was got in my childhood in Galway, and I am now so completely disillusioned that I don't want to be reminded of those early happy days. As soon as the London N.G. has hung my pictures I will be off to Cape Town. The Lord Mayor is taking me to a review of the Ulster Volunteers this afternoon ! "

Again, " I am too ill to do anything more for this horrible country where one can only collect advice ! "

And I answered: " It is a real heartbreak. I am very sad, and ashamed of our country—or one should say Dublin. The ungraciousness of it all ! I am glad you are going to the Cape. . . .

" I hope with all my heart you will sell the collection at Christie's—it will be the best object lesson. ' He came unto His own and His own received Him not.' I keep thinking of that, and of all you have gone through. One looks beyond present surroundings to the ' cloud of witnesses,' but it is hard to keep patience sometimes. . . . It is like a death, one keeps thinking ' is it possible that hope is dead and gone ? ' I am trying not to cry !

"You are one of the 'Image-makers,' and you have done more for the future than any one else. Our Theatre will pass away before your pictures."

I find quoted in a letter to Yeats much later—during the war—a passage with something the same thought: "I have just to-day got Rolland's 'Au dessus de la Mêlée.' It begins: 'A great people assailed by war has not only its frontiers to defend; it has also its reason. It must be saved from the hallucinations, the injustice, the follies flung up by the flail. To every one his office: to the armies to guard the country's soil; to men who think, to defend its thought. If they put it in the service of the passions of their people it may be they will be of use, but they run the risk of betraying the mind (esprit) which is not the least part of the heritage of this people.' Does not that apply to all our long struggles in Ireland?"

I think "the young generation" understands these matters now, and that at least Synge's name and Hugh's are held in honour. *New Ireland* has told that Pearse some time before his death had said he was sorry he had ever opposed *The Playboy;* and I wrote last summer: "On Wednesday I was sitting in the Abbey Theatre watching the rehearsal of *The Saint* when the author, a Sinn Fein M.P., came in and sat beside me. I asked if he had been writing much, and he said, 'Only when I am in prison.' He said he had been chained to De Valera as they were taken to the gaol. I told him my sympathies went a long way with his friends, 'but,' I said, 'such is the

irony of Fate, I am praying for the health of Sir
Edward Carson, because he is taking up the matter
of the return of Hugh Lane's pictures to Ireland.'
' Then,' he said, ' we must all pray for his health ;
for I found when I was living in Paris the thing
that seemed to interest the French in Ireland more
than any other thing was the possession of those
pictures by Dublin. They would say, Is it
really true that Dublin holds that great collection ? "

He said also (and this is what Hugh himself
might have said), " Is it not a great burden this
feeling that drags us back to Ireland. I was so
happy in Paris and in Brittany, but that force
brought me back to a troublesome life. It is so
with De Valera also, who hates politics and wants
to begin building, and feels the long separation from
his wife." I said all of us workers knew the Hill
Difficulty and the Slough of Despond. Did not
Hugh also leave the open doors of pleasant houses
for a fight that was all the harder because it was
with his own countrymen ?

But it is no wonder that Hugh suffered sharp
trouble of mind under the defeat and the discourtesy. Had not I myself in a moment's
bitterness given my opinion that the best thing
would be to sell the pictures by auction and
let those ungracious enemies know by this the
value of what had been lost.

He was ill, he was about to go into the
surgeon's hands, and on October 11, 1913—less
than a month after that disastrous Corporation
meeting, and in a resentment that was natural—
made his new will. In it, having left a few

thousand pounds and some keepsakes to family and friends, he says: "I bequeath my Sargent portrait, the modern pictures now being shown in Belfast, and any modern pictures of merit (John drawings, etc.) that I possess, to the Dublin Gallery of Modern Art, other than the group of pictures lent by me to the London National Gallery, which I bequeath to found a collection of Modern Continental Art.

"I bequeath the remainder of my property to the National Gallery of Ireland (instead of to the Modern Art Gallery which I considered so important for the founding of an Irish school of painting) to be invested, and the income to be spent on buying pictures of deceased painters of established merit. I hope this alteration from the Modern Gallery to the National Gallery will be remembered by the Dublin Municipality and others as an example of its want of public spirit in the year 1913, and of the folly of such bodies assuming to decide on questions of Art instead of relying on expert opinion."

Even now I sometimes hear idle clamour against him among some who have seldom spent but on themselves. "He ought to have made his brothers and sisters rather than the Galleries rich." I wonder if there were, in like manner, carping voices when Cæsar's will was read. For it often happens that what a man has taught and lived seems to be broken from in that last settlement of life's affairs; William Morris's disciples have spoken sorrowfully of this. And I am proud that Hugh has carried on his life work over the borders of death.

And yet, as one of his friends has written, "while he endowed his country with all his great treasures of art he also remembered to leave trinkets to children he was fond of, and fifty pounds to an old friend to buy a horse. This will help to explain why his death which was a European loss was also a bitter personal grief to many an obscure simple man."

I went back to my tree-planting at Coole; and Yeats went on through that September making those noble and indignant "Poems written in dejection" that will always help to keep Hugh's work and name in mind. The first has for title, "To a Shade," the shade of Parnell—

> "If you have visited the town, thin Shade,
> Whether to look upon your monument
> (I wonder if the builder has been paid)
> Or happier thoughted when the day is spent
> To drink of that salt breath out of the sea
> When grey gulls fly about instead of men,
> And the gaunt houses put on majesty :
> Let these content you, and begone again :
> For they are at their old tricks yet.

> "A man
> Of your own passionate serving kind, who had brought
> In his full hands what, had they only known,
> Had given their children's children loftier thought,
> Sweeter emotion, working in their veins
> Like gentle blood, has been driven from the place,
> And insult heaped upon him for his pains,
> And for his open-handedness, disgrace :
> An old foul mouth that once cried out on you
> Herding the pack.

> "Unquiet wanderer
> Draw the Glasnevin coverlet anew
> About your head till the dust stops your ear,

The time for you to taste of that salt breath
And listen at the corners has not come,
You had enough of sorrow before death—
Away, away ! You are safer in the tomb."

This he has called " Paudeen "—

" Indignant at the fumbling wits, the obscure spite
Of our old Paudeen in his shop, I stumbled blind
Among the stones and thorn trees, under morning light,
Until a curlew cried and in the luminous wind
A curlew answered, and I was startled by the thought
That on the lonely height where all are in God's eye,
There cannot be, confusion of our sound forgot,
A single soul that lacks a sweet crystalline cry."

And this is to Hugh, to " A Friend whose Work
has come to Nothing "—

" Now all the truth is out,
Be secret and take defeat
From any brazen throat,
For how can you compete,
Being honour bred, with one
Who were it proved he lies
Were neither shamed in his own
Nor in his neighbour's eyes ;
Bred to a harder thing
Than Triumph, turn away
And like a laughing string
Whereon mad fingers play
Amid a place of stone,
Be secret and exult,
Because of all things known
That is most difficult."

It was with all this in mind I spent a while
in the Gallery the other day, looking at the pictures
given in remembrance of Hugh, and those given
by him. One of the caretakers recognised me.
He spoke of Hugh, how he had loved that Gallery.
" He worked harder than any of us. He would

be moving pictures and hanging and shifting them
till far into the night ; he never would ask any one
to do what he would not do himself. He never
spared himself, and if he went out for lunch or
his dinner, he wouldn't take as long at it as you'd
be drinking a cup of tea.

"I know he was sorry to take the French
pictures away. For every other day he would
have a smile for us, but on that day when he was
taking them down his face was all sadness.

"It's a great pity they didn't let him build
in Stephen's Green ; there's room enough, and,
above all, where he wanted it, where the rockery
is that is of no use to any one.

"He was very happy the day Mr. Asquith
and his family and Mr. Birrell came here. They
stopped forty minutes. I could hear his laugh
on that day.

"It is wonderful what insight Sir Hugh had,
there would be a heap of pictures sent here for
him to look at that I, knowing nothing about it,
would have jumped at. But with one look he
would say they were to be taken away.

"With flowers, too, he was wonderful. He
would put them in so quick, and they would look
just as if they were growing in the bowl. But
when I would take them out to put in fresh water
I never could make them look like that.

"There was something going on upstairs—I
forget what it was—and some speeches made,
and he called to us to come up ; that was kind of
him, he thought it might amuse us.

"Often upstairs, and in this room, he would
put a paper into my hand and would bid me to

sit down and read it, that I would be tired with so much standing. He was very gentle. Too gentle nearly for a man.

" We have a hundred people coming here every day, more than three thousand in the year, that is more than goes to the National Gallery.

" We had a great many students that had joined the army during the war, they would come from morning till night, and many of them would say the pictures in English Galleries were rubbish beside these. And a gentleman that came several times said that the Louvre in Paris is better, but he wouldn't say there's any other Gallery that is. I am sure Sir Hugh was fonder of this than of·the National Gallery to the end."

And a friend tells me that as she stood looking at the Sargent portrait one day she listened to like praises. " You had a loss not to have known him, for there never was any man that ever I knew like him. He never thought of himself; it was always for others he was thinking and working. And he was so good to the poor, he was so good to me, and when he'd see poor people especially looking at the pictures, he'd leave whatever he was doing, and he'd go round the Gallery and tell them all about the pictures and explain things to them.

" And there was no pride in him. There's people who wouldn't like to be seen carrying a small parcel, but Sir Hugh was that good he wouldn't care what he carried. Many's the time I've seen him carrying up from the Club or some place a picture, and he'd come in and he'd say, ' Another little gift for the Gallery.'

"I'm always thinking of him, he loved this place ; ah, it's a pity you didn't know him. And when he'd be talking to you he'd always look straight at you, but his eyes were very sad, sadder than what they are there. I could say no words good enough for Sir Hugh if I was talking the whole day."

CHAPTER XII

In 1909 Hugh Lane " brought together the collection of modern paintings in the Johannesburg Municipal Gallery." We in Ireland best remember this by a sentence written to Mr. Thomas Bodkin, when he gave up buying for it : " I find that one cannot buy for two Galleries (the same sort of thing), as I want all the bargains for Dublin."

I find in a note of mine written at that time : " I lunched with the Lionel Phillips at Beit House. Mrs. Phillips is quite ready to start the Johannesburg Gallery with Hugh's help. He has already persuaded her to buy three of Steer's pictures as a beginning. 'I didn't want to, but he told me to, and I hadn't any money, but I found a little sum I had forgotten and bought them.' She is going to get money from other millionaires, £50,000 if she can. She says very sensibly, ' When there is a man like Mr. Lane to be had, one should use him.' "

When I was in London in October, 1919, Mrs. Norman Grosvenor came to see me, and knowing that Hugh had written her name in a catalogue he had sent her as " the godmother of the Johannesburg Gallery," we talked about it. Lady Phillips had first thought of building a Gallery to be filled with loans from English museums, of ancient craftsmanship as well as pictures. But she found there would have been legal difficulties in getting such loans. So then her thoughts turned towards a collection of pictures by old masters. Mr. Beit had promised her to spend £10,000 in gifts for such a Gallery if it could be provided, but he remembered that his brother had given a fine collection of casts to South Africa, and they had been left in packing cases for want of such a home. I asked Mrs. Grosvenor how she had gained the name of " godmother," and she said she had been staying with Lady Phillips in Hampshire, " and she talked of pictures and said she would like to found a Johannesburg Gallery if she knew how to go about it. I told her I knew the man who could best help her in that—Hugh Lanc—and she asked me to telegraph him an invitation. He came in the afternoon, and at once he told her it would be a mistake to try and fill such a Gallery as she wished for with pictures by old masters ; there are but a few of the best to be had, and the price of these is enormous. He pressed for a modern Gallery for the work of living men. She said she didn't like modern paintings, that they did not interest her. But before nightfall she had promised him to come next day to London, to see on its first day's opening an exhibition of Steer's pictures."

I had heard also that she pleaded that she was not ready to buy pictures at once, that the Gallery had yet to be founded, and must take money and time, and that then Hugh had said (as one feels certain he did say), " Sell this fine house and its surroundings, and use the money to make a great Gallery." But that was not possible had she wished it, for they belonged to her husband, and he had returned to South Africa.

Next morning, Mrs. Grosvenor said, they all set out for London and went straight to the Goupil Gallery, where the pictures were being shown. Lady Phillips did not at first appreciate them, she, as Hugh himself had been a few years before, was out of sympathy with modern art. But whether from growing admiration of the paintings or from Hugh's urgency, or the fear that he would, if disappointed, lose his interest in the matter, and she would be left without his help, she made a sudden resolve. She would sell her blue diamond (for that, as I am told was the " little sum she had forgotten ") and buy the first pictures for the dream-gallery.

" He left Goupil's before us," said Mrs. Grosvenor, " and I passed him at the end of the street and stopped the cab to ask him to come back with me to lunch. He refused, and I said, ' You must be tired.' ' Tired ! ' he said, ' I am running all over with perspiration ! ' "

It was announced in the evening papers that Mr. Steer's great landscape " Corfe Castle," with his " Limekiln " and " A Chelsea Window " had been bought for South Africa.

That was a battle won with more - than the sweat of his brow, and I take pride in his all-conquering intensity. Though sometimes that insistent parochial voice in me murmurs ,Sars- field's last words at Landen, " Would that this had been for Ireland ! " as I ponder on what such a blue diamond might have wrought in our own city by the Liffey.

Then later Hugh, in the autumn of 1910, had gone out to Johannesburg to give what help he could to Lady Phillips in her efforts that were akin to his own. There were troubles there also, not unlike those of Dublin, about the choice of an architect. The committee wanted some one belonging to South Africa. Yet, when none of the designs satisfied those most concerned, they decided that a beautiful building would be of such value to the country that whatever man could best bring it into being should be chosen. And so they took Hugh's advice to call in Lutyens. He was in Rome when the telegram came, and hesitated for a moment, but then accepted—" What fun it will be ! "—and Johannesburg is proud now of his beautiful building.

Their country gained more than this by their brave humility in looking outside their own borders for a skill and knowledge greater than was to be found within them. For largely through that action South Africa of to-day has her own architect to take pride in, and the noble design for the great Cape Town University has been made by one of her own sons, who, still young, might even now be struggling towards the mastery he has attained to were it not for the influence, the help and friendship of those two " outlanders " brought to Johannesburg, Hugh Lane and Edwin Lutyens.

Hugh would call out sometimes impatiently that all had been done so easily in South Africa, as he fretted at the long Dublin delays. I had written this at some troublesome moment to Mr.

Bailey, and he answered, " Your letter and enclosure filled me with concern. There is so much in Hugh Lane's objection that no one has been able to do much to *force* the Gallery on here. The political situation is partly responsible, as people's minds are diverted to so many things. South Africa is now in the position of ' building up.' We are in the fluid and formative state, and to one so full of his subject as Hugh Lane, that does not explain the difficulties sufficiently. If one had a Government that would help us as in South Africa, it would be all right, but there we are ! "

" Full of his subject ! " That, indeed, he was. I thought of him just now as I read in a review by Mr. Birrell : " It has been shrewdly said that when the Almighty wants anything really done, He creates a man or woman foolish enough to believe that if the thing were done all would be well with the world." And as to that Divine foolishness, was it not in Johannesburg that it was said by one of his own near kin, " I can't think what any one can see in Hugh—he is such a fool ! "

Soon after my talk with Mrs. Grosvenor, I went to see Sir Edwin Lutyens at his office. He was soon to go out to India, where he is making the Delhi Memorial, and business calls by knock at door, or ring of telephone, hardly ceased. But for Hugh's sake he sat and talked with me for a while. I asked how Hugh had lived out there, if he had felt astray in that strange atmosphere. But he said, " No, he brought his own atmosphere." In the mornings he enjoyed his leisure

at the Phillips' hospitable house, lying under
mosquito curtains—a luxury of the imagination,
for no mosquitoes came—" smoking cigarettes and
reading news cuttings." For in no rummaging
behind shop-counters could even his eyes discern
any old masterpiece in Johannesburg. And he
had pictures to hang, he talked and persuaded,
he was angry with his friend for his proneness to
treat lightly the serious committees, for making
a play-game of attending them, not treating them
as solemn assemblies. " I never could look on
them as serious things." Hugh's own laughing
time was not when business had to be got through,
the laughter and the gaiety came on the way
home, on shipboard. The architect, for all his
bubbling jests, had made a noble temple for the
" Corfe Castle," the " Limekiln," and " A Chelsea
Window." That was Lutyens' firstborn picture
gallery, beautiful in the design he showed me.

They sparred and quarrelled and made friends
again, there at Johannesburg and later in London,
and had their merry plans, Hugh telling him he
must design for him one day a room with twelve
panels, in which should be placed twelve portraits of that never-to-be wife of the future, by
twelve separate artists. Mancini would surely
have been one, and Sargent, and Orpen who
had painted his sister's head so finely, and Steer,
and Kelly, and Charles Shannon, and Augustus
John. And then perhaps that shadowy wife
would have come by degrees to the water-shed of
life, and its descent, each new generation of
painters adding grey to the brown and white to
the bleaching head.

And amidst these soaring ideas Lutyens had been taken to dine at that favourite little Chelsea restaurant, and when they had eaten the three scanty courses, and Hugh had asked him to admire the meagre dinner, " So wonderful for eighteen pence," he had cried out. " Yes, wonderful! Let's have it over again ! " And he used to declare that when he sent a telegram with prepaid answer, Hugh would come on foot bringing the answer, to save the sixpence for another time.

But now that Hugh is gone, he tells how kind he was and liberal and straight in business, a trafficker in pictures, but never making money out of his friends. And he speaks also of his love of Ireland, and says his heart was there, and he always meant to bring back the French pictures, and did but make use of London " as threat for Dublin."

And while Sir Edwin talked, he was fingering the drawing he had made for a tablet to be put up to his lost friend.

At Christie's I made the acquaintance of an old man, knowledgeable in pictures, who said he well remembered Hugh and his wonderful instinct, that discerning sight that is as mysterious to common men as is the power of the desert man of Arabia to see the constèllations at noonday. And he told me that Hugh had been wise, and had gained knowledge in South Africa, and of a time when he had given him good counsel.

There had been a sale in Holland, a collection had been broken up, and some of the pictures had come to London, and, " escaping Christie's," had been held for awhile. Berlin wanted them, saw them, bought them, but the money could not be paid until the Kaiser gave his consent, and I know not for what reason, this he could not be brought to do. Then Berlin tried to go back from the bargain, but the English owner refused. The bargain had been made, the pictures had been held, there was no breaking it; still the Kaiser hardened his heart, and at last, that his country might not be shamed, some rich German brought the money, £20,000. But then he asked that they might be sold again, he did not want to keep or to make a gift of them. " Then I said to myself, ' Hugh Lane is my man ! ' I sent for him and I said, ' Would not these be a great thing for some South African millionaire to buy ? He could hang them in his dining-room and point to them and say, boasting, " Those are the pictures the Kaiser could not afford to buy, but I bought them ! " ' But Hugh Lane said, ' No, you will not find an African millionaire to do that. He would not think it neighbourly.' And I saw that was quite true, for there is a comradeship of feeling between the rich men of South Africa and of Germany. He had a very wise head."

CHAPTER XIII

In November, 1912, Hugh had written to me from Dublin: "I have to return to London at latest next Monday, and I must use my remaining strength on finishing my South African work. It is a great satisfaction to me to have created an 'Old Master' Gallery for a Continent that wants one so badly."

And in May, 1913, he wrote: "We look forward to the 31st, your coming. . . . I am frantically busy on the Cape Town Gallery Exhibition which opens the day after to-morrow."

I had written some months before: "I am really glad that South African scheme is coming off, for when you were buying the pictures I asked you if there was any real prospect of it, and you said none, except that you usually found when you made up your mind a thing ought to be done, that somehow it was done in the end; and this is good augury for the Gallery in Dublin."

Mr. Solomon has thus written of this in a South African paper: "It was General Smuts who first inspired in him the desire to make a collection of Old Dutch masters for South

Africa, and together we conspired to get our South African magnates to start a National Art Collection Fund, which might purchase works over a period of years. When at the end of 1911 I went to stay with Sir Hugh in London, he had added to his own collection a completely representative collection of Dutch and Flemish seventeenth-century masters, which, by a great and unique act of generosity, Mr. Max Michaelis decided to present to the land where he had acquired his wealth, and so for ever link it with the great European centres of Art. South Africa thus became possessed of one of the choicest collections of its size and kind in the world. The debt this country owes Lane is incalculable. He pushed forward the boundaries of Art into the Southern Hemispheres, and by his genius brought a light into the life of our land which Eternity alone can extinguish."

I was at Lindsey House after the pictures for Cape Town had been acquired by Mr. Michaelis, and I was sad to think of one of them, the Rembrandt, going overseas. Of all his pictures it was the one I cared most for. Often when I came back late from the Court Theatre I would go into the drawing-room where it hung just to look at its radiant serenity, the "continual comfort" in that face. It has been known and was famous as "the Demidoff Rembrandt." The highest price ever given for a Dutch picture was said to have been once given for it. Hugh had paid for it £25,000. But Dr. Bredius of the Hague, the learned authority on Dutch Art, now gave it as his opinion that it might not be by Rembrandt, but by Bol. Sir Claude Phillips followed this opinion, and Mr. Michaelis could not make up his mind as to whether, with this doubt hanging over it, he would send the picture to the Cape. He wanted this collection to have the immunity of Cæsar's wife. Hugh entirely believed it was Rembrandt's handiwork, but he was willing to withdraw the picture and fill its place with other Dutch masterpieces. He did so, and the whole collection was the richer for these, and Cape Town and the donor were well served.

Mr. Alec Martin writes: " The collection of pictures which Mr. Michaelis presented to Cape Town, and now hanging there, contains more than one example of the first importance. It is, perhaps, worth noting that the attributions under which the pictures were bought have, in the great majority of cases, received the approval of Dr. Hoplede de Groot. I would like to single out the ' Portrait of a Lady ' (1644) by Franz Hals, the two ' Landscapes ' by Jacob van Ruisdael, the ' Fruit and Still Life ' by A. van Beyeren " (Mr. Martin had telegraphed to Hugh from Christie's that it was the finest van Beyeren he had ever seen, and he, telegraphing to him from Rome, gave his authority to buy it), " ' The Landscape ' by P. de Koningh, the ' Harrowby Metzu,' and the fine ' Portrait of John Oxensteirn.' The great merit of the collection, however, does not lie in its star pieces, but in its general level as a representative of Old Dutch Art, and in the characteristic subjects interpreted by the painters ; the latter is, Mr. Michaelis considers, an important point, in view of the fact that these pictures hang in a community largely Dutch, and supply examples Art in a country where the opportunity of seeing Old Dutch masters are otherwise of the rarest, and indeed almost non-existent."

I asked Mr. Charles Ricketts to write me his impression of the Rembrandt "A Lady with Gloves," as he calls it, for he had studied it closely at Lindsey House. And he writes : " This picture may be confidently classed with other works dated about 1632–1633, such as 'The Wife of Jan Pellicorne' in the Wallace collection, and 'The Woman Seated' in the Hof Museum, Vienna ; it belongs to that early golden manner of which 'The Anatomy Lesson' is the most popular example, with this difference, that in 'The Lady with Gloves' the sense of form is more searching and the workmanship more delicate and intimate than in the above-mentioned paintings. Later, with the advent of the early Saskia portraits, the handling becomes more romantic and Rembrandt's taste for about a decade somehow less secure ; we have to wait for the bejewelled 'Saskia' of the Berlin Gallery, better still for the 'Lady with a Fan' at Windsor, for portraits of women which surpass this one in the qualities of vision and for a more searching and exquisite quality in workmanship. 'The Wife of Jan Pellicorne' is inferior to 'The Lady with Gloves'; the portrait at Vienna, to which it bears the closest technical resemblance, is a colder work. In the Lane picture the golden light emphasises the construction of the face, the differing texture values of bone and flesh in the brow, cheeks, and nose—the painting of the lips is miraculous.

"Ferdinand Bol has imitated works of this period, but with him the light is artificial as if the figure were lit from within and the draughtsmanship always vague and vulgar. The distance between the master and the imitator could not be better illustrated than by this picture in which the cool reflected lights from the ruff emphasise the construction of the chin. Apart from qualities of draughtsmanship there are little 'mannerisms' in pigment and colour, in the treatment of the bracelet and cuffs, which leave a student of Rembrandt's painting in no doubt ; for its date it is a first-rate specimen of the master's work, more cool in colour and more reticent than is his wont during the thirties."

Mr. Michaelis had asked him to leave the matter of changing the Rembrandt for other pictures open for a while, and in agreeing Hugh wrote : " I wish that you would write to Dr. Bode and beg him to come over or give a written statement." He was ready any one should examine the pictures ; " as I have offered to sell the pictures subject to Dr. Bode's opinion as to their genuineness there was no risk in the matter whatever."

Dr. Bode did not come over, but it was not in Hugh's nature to accept the belittling of a picture he loved so much. It needed cleaning, and he packed it up and sent it straight to Berlin, that the cleaning might be done under the very eyes of the man counted as the master critic upon Rembrandt. He, having full opportunity, declared it to be undoubtedly Rembrandt's work. Hauser, of Berlin, who had cleaned most of the famous Rembrandts, declared the same

PORTRAIT OF A LADY WITH GLOVES.

By Rembrandt.

certainty. It is well that Hugh had made no delay in sending it abroad, for the picture was safely back in England before the breaking out of the war. Rescued from a second danger of exile it hung again in its old place of honour as long as Lindsey House was unsold, and now it has been brought to its lasting home in the National Gallery of Ireland. Though I grieved at the time in sympathy with Hugh's annoyance over the matter, I cannot but feel that no wilderness of Metzus and De Koninghs could make up in Dublin for that tranquil loveliness.

But all this matter troubled Hugh. I wrote from his house: "He ought to be lying up, the doctors ordered him three weeks in bed for the concussion and giddiness he suffers from, and when I begged him to take warning by John and take care of himself he said he had this picture business to do, arranging the collection for South Africa."

But he wrote after I had left: "Dr. Friedlander came at last—to-day. He says that he was against Michaelis exchanging the Rembrandt 'as it is in my opinion by the Master!' But he says now that he, Friedlander, sees how many good pictures I have to offer in exchange, he will advise him to do so. This will suit me quite well."

I had grieved because of his health and because there were some days that were broken and wasted while he waited for a decision to be made, and Dr. Friedlander, and others consulted on the matter, to come to the house; for of all things wearing to the patience surely the hardest when work is to be done is being forced to sit still waiting on the time or good will or energy of others. And such waiting filled perforce many days and hours of Hugh's short working life, while his own fiery spirit would gladly have burnt itself out could it thus have swept away obstacles.

He had once designed, leaf by leaf, a beautiful ornament, a rose formed of moonstones, as a gift for his sister. I begged of him to continue such designing, and even learn the jeweller's handicraft, that he might have that slight occupation for eye and hand found by women in knitting or embroidering, and that a wise doctor has ordered as a soothing medicine for the nerves. There is something in the act of making, the adding of stitch to stitch, row to row, leaf to leaf, that tends to quiet restless nature through its hour.

But at last all was settled as to the pictures, and he wrote to me: " We are in daily communication with Botha about a building for them, —they will probably give either the old Court House or Government House in Cape Town." And in a note I have seen he wrote: " I sold the Dutch collection at practically what it cost me, to fulfil my ambition of forming a picture gallery of old masters for South Africa."

Mr. Solomon has lately been in London looking for draughtsmen to go back with him to help him with the work he has in hand—the new University. I talked with him of the Cape Town Gallery, and he said: " It is well known through the world now, so many from all countries, landing during the war, came to see it. They are astonished to see so splendid a collection there. The Franz Hals portrait of ' A Woman ' is one of the finest to be seen, no one can make a real study of Hals without seeing it. And the De Koningh and about twelve are masterpieces.

" When I was in America I went into one of the largest architectural offices there, and when the Principal heard I had rebuilt the old Dutch house for that Gallery he said : ' Oh, we all know of that collection, it is one of the first.' The Dutch house where it is placed was built about the time when Rembrandt was painting."

I said I was glad we had got the Rembrandt in Dublin, but he said : " I am not glad, and I think Michaelis regrets it now. It is a wonderful thing. It was a great annoyance to Sir Hugh at the time that attack was made on it. He told me of a day when he and Michaelis sat in different rooms, with a lawyer taking messages from one to the other. But all was amicably settled in the end."

October 6. Mr. Solomon wrote to me from Cape Town on August 12, " I have had a rather trying time since I returned to the Cape owing to the breakdown of my colleague, which threw a great deal of additional work of the Office on my shoulders, and in the midst of it all I was laid low with a very severe attack of influenza from which I am only just beginning to recover enthusiasm after a long period of listlessness. . . . I am going to send you some snap-shots of my home and family shortly. . . ."

But before this letter reached me news had been flashed from South Africa of the sudden death of " a famous Architect " ; and it was with grief I learned that one Hugh had cared for and who had so lately helped to honour his memory with grateful words had passed away.

M

CHAPTER XIV

LONDON LIFE

I HAVE gone straight on telling the story of the Gallery in Dublin and of Hugh's help in beginning those South African ones. He used sometimes to say: "I am best at beginnings," but to that all we who know the Dublin story will be slow to agree, knowing how his courage, patience, and tenacity had stood many an assault before that disastrous September of 1915.

Yeats wrote in 1909 from London, where our plays were being given: "A full house last night and great enthusiasm. Sir Hugh Lane was there, very pleased with his honours, and Kelly the painter with him. . . . Lane thinks that his knighthood means that the Government is going to give his Gallery the £500 a year it wants." For he had just then been knighted "for his services to art."

I think the distinction was of real value to him, especially in foreign galleries, giving him a sort of official rank without having to explain what he had done, and this helped his work.

He was very much pleased later at being given the freedom of the City of Dublin. He bought an old silver vessel shaped as a ship wherein to keep the parchment. But this was yet on its way to him when he died.

As to his life in London, while life grew harder in Ireland it had become easier there. When he had made a little money he had moved from his lodging in the Harrow Road to one in Duke Street, and then to Jermyn Street, where he began to take a pride in his rooms, putting up pieces of brocade against which to hang his pictures and bringing in the pieces of old furniture he had already collected and stored in the houses of his friends. It was there he began inviting friends of an afternoon for tea and for the music he loved. Later again in 1907 he took the rooms adjoining Orpen's Studio in Bolton Gardens. It was in that studio "Hommage à Manet," now in the Manchester Gallery, was painted, in which he and certain critics are standing in contemplation of the great *Eva Gonzales.*

Though he lived alone he went in and out of the Orpens' house almost as a home, and Lady Orpen would tell him as he played with her children, that when all trades failed he could take a place as children's nurse. Then in 1909 he bought Lindsey House, 100 Cheyne Walk. He needed a house of his own with large rooms in which to lodge his pictures, for he liked to have them around him, and never put them in a shop or showroom away from his own abode. "If ever I want to marry," he said, "I shall now have a house to settle on my wife." And certainly that riverside dwelling would have made a noble show in marriage settlements. A part of old Lindsey Palace, it had its own high ancestry.

The date 1674 is cut over the porch; Charles the First's chief physician, Sir Theodore Mayerne, had lived there; there is a legend that the first opera ever given in England was performed there by Nell Gwynn and was attended by the King. Passing afterwards to the earls of Lindsey, it took its present name; the Chelsea Parish book tells of "ten shillings paid for ye Ringers when the King came to the Earl of Lindseys in 1674." Lady Plymouth, with her son Lord Windsor, had lived there in the eighteenth century, and Lord Conway; Francis, Marquis of Hertford, was born there; the Duchess of Rutland was its tenant in 1727. In 1750 it was sold to the son of the Duke of Ancaster; a year later to Count Zinzendorf, who thought to make it the headquarters of a colony of Moravians. The Brunels lived there early in the last century, but that was after the house had been divided. They were in number ninety-eight, while Hugh Lane's house contained the two numbers thrown together, ninety-nine and a hundred.

It was fortunate for Hugh that before he had been long in the Chelsea house his sister Ruth Shine, her husband having died, came to make it her home. She, like Hugh, had not let her life run to waste. She had set to work to learn gardening at Glasnevin, and had then taken charge in its early days of Lady Wolseley's garden at Glynde. She was young then as well as beautiful; Lady Haliburton told me Lord Wolseley had spoken of her as the most beautiful girl he had ever seen. One of Orpen's best portraits is of her; Mancini's was not of his best; other artists painted her and there is a drawing by John.

She married a country gentleman in the South of Ireland, and occupied herself ceaselessly with her home. She loved, and still loves, the beauties of the country better than those of the cities, and when Hugh talked of restoring some great mansion her dream was of a cottage within its shadow. She had less approval for his plans for filling Dublin with beauty than for, his gifts to charity, and these were large. " Money is nothing in itself," he used to say, " but only in what it can bring," and he liked to use a part of it in bringing comfort to the poor. His many guests recall her ready welcome, her cheerfulness and courtesy, even at the time when her own sorrow was new and the new life jarred with it. Hugh's heart could safely trust in her ; to the end and after the end his interests were her unceasing care.

An American guest of Hugh's at Lindsey House—and often some friend or acquaintance of his or of mine from across the Atlantic would be invited there—has written in a Michigan paper : " There was a pond in the small square garden at the back of the house, with a mulberry tree spreading over it, and after tea the visitors would be invited into the garden to enjoy the berries. Lindsey House was built in the reign of King James, so Sir Hugh Lane told me, and I believe he said that monarch planted the mulberry tree. If he did it is much to his credit as a planter of mulberry trees, for they were the largest and most wonderful berries I have ever tasted."

Hugh called in Lutyens to re-make the garden,

and he put a marble floor in place of tiles in the great hall, and put up old panelling upon the walls. The mantelpiece in the Green Room had come from some famous house and the massive fire-dogs in the drawing-room, with the Lion and Unicorn, were said to have been stolen from Windsor Castle. The octagon dining-table had been made by Chippendale himself for Queen Charlotte's summer-house at Kew; and to that table he called what company he would.

The Michigan writer goes on: "At Sir Hugh's house one met many people, they came to afternoon tea, all kinds of people from everywhere and nearly always interesting. The guests were not dotted about the room at random, as is invariably the case at a London 'At Home,' endeavouring to carry on a conversation across the room while desperately trying to balance a cup on the knees; here all were gathered around a large circular table which appeared to have an unlimited capacity for seating people, however many came. Sir Hugh was untiring in his attentions to his guests and had the faculty for making each guest appear at their best; reticent and inclined to be nervous at meeting new people, yet one of the most delightful hosts I have known; a man with a keen sense of quality, artistic to his finger-tips. No description of the man could be more apt than one made in a letter I received recently from a mutual friend and great admirer of Sir Hugh's who describes him as 'a vivid soul.'"

But one of those cousins who used to tease him in Pall Mall Place tells me that when he began giving those afternoon parties he suffered such misery from nervousness that he sometimes had even to take a little brandy. But the arrival of the first guest would act as a sedative and he would be at once quite at his ease and making others so.

Hugh had written to me of his friend Mr. Solomon: " You will meet here a young architect who knows more about London and more about English history than anyone I have ever met "; and that young architect has written of those afternoon gatherings and how, among the great people, " It was Sir Hugh's delight to search out some poor young artist who, on the verge of starvation, he had brought thither that he might be helped," and how " he would take one who couldn't afford a frame for a picture up to that room where he kept frames, and let him choose one for himself that had perhaps cost him £15 or £20; or would recommend another for a commission for a portrait. No effort was too much for him if in any way he was able to help a friend. Often when from sheer physical weakness he found it impossible to attend to his own affairs, he might be found going half-way across London to keep an appointment which he had made to look at some young painter's work. Lane possessed a gift beyond anyone I have ever known for bringing out the best in his friends. Chelsea is full of young artists who will mourn his loss."

There are very many others who could tell of his kindness, his liberality. All those he met he seems instantly to have divided in his mind in two groups: those who could help his work, or the work of his friends, and those to whom he could be helpful, and these not artists alone. I remember his saying of someone who had written to ask him for a loan of money: "I scarcely knew him, but I was going for a motor drive and I thought he looked sallow and took him with me that the fresh air might do him good."

Once when looking for a frame for my portrait painted by Gerald Kelly, I found that he had but lately given away several to set off the work of some yet unknown painter. Mr. McColl said to me: "The first thing that interested me in him was finding that he was making people do what I had been so long begging them to do, buy the work of living men." His plan in business was the "selling pictures by old painters to buy pictures by living painters," and that was a fine thing to do. I had written from New York that a certain critic was there "lamenting that no one in London will buy a picture without leave from Hugh Lane, and that —— is starving and —— growing fat and lazy thereby! I am very proud of this!"

Often like our wandering folk-poet Raftery, he had "made a wedding of what was no wedding" by his presence and his gaiety and his gifts. Sometimes a lovely picture given by him would make some little shabby sitting-room its shrine. It seemed as if he hardly walked through a friend's house without adding to it some beauty, through discovery or arrangement or through a gift.

I have liked to give memories of his winning courtesy from travellers belonging to two

PORTRAIT OF A GENTLEMAN.

By Strozzi.

Continents, and I can add yet other testimony from a third, that is Asia. I find in a letter I had written from Lindsey House in the Coronation summer : " I went yesterday to lunch with the G's and met a young man in some regiment just back from India. He said there were a great many beastly natives about and he wouldn't take any notice of them, had seen one he didn't know well at a party, and another that he knew very well at Ascot. ' I suppose you spoke to him,' said Lord G. ' Indeed I didn't, I hate natives, I think them beastly.' I said I supposed we were all natives of some country, but Lord G. hurriedly changed the conversation. Lady W., whom I found when I came home, said she had been in an omnibus the other day opposite a respectable old Indian in a turban reading his guide book, and a man who had sat down next him bounded up again and said audibly to a friend he ' wouldn't sit next a nigger.' Hugh said he met some young natives of India at a country house where he was staying the other day, and he was surprised when his host said as he was leaving that they were very grateful to him ; ' they say you are the finest gentleman they have met.' He had been but courteous and friendly to them as one generally is to fellow guests, and had asked them to come and see him. His host said they go back to India filled with rancour from the way they are treated over here. If we have another mutiny it will be from the doings of that young man and his like."

The other day I was sitting with Mrs. Childers. She had told me, looking so fragile as she lay there ill, about the gun-running and how she had steered the yacht into Kingstown Harbour. Then I told her what I was writing and she said : " I only saw Sir Hugh once, when I came to see you at Lindsey House, but I remember him very well. For it seemed strange to me that a man who was in the habit of meeting so many people and had affairs on his mind should come in as he did, and shake hands as he did, giving the impression that he expected to find a friend in each of us, just as a child does when brought in to meet strangers. I thought of what Emerson says, ' I carry the keys of my castle in my hand, ready to lay them at the feet of my friend wherever and whenever I shall find him.' "

He always took delight in the company of children. Mr. Dermod O'Brien, talking of his Dublin troubles, said, " He felt the way he was treated, and yet he had a sort of frivolity that helped him. He would come into our house vexed and jaded and out of heart. And then, perhaps, the children would come in and call to him, and he would romp with them and roll over on the floor for half an hour and then he would suddenly jump up and remember he had an appointment, and would try to smooth his frock coat." He was always doing them little kindnesses. I remember asking a poet's child which of his father's guests, and they were many, " gentle and simple," he liked best. He thought for a minute and said, " Do you know Mr. Lane ? He gave me half a crown." Once he had invited the Orpen children to tea at Lindsey House to play with Tinko, his little Pekinese. But before the day came Tinko had fallen ill and died, and Hugh spent his morning at a very busy time in searching for another Pekinese—he would not hear of a puppy of less distinction, " These children must not be disappointed, they must have the best." He found one at last, or I think Mr. Alec Martin found it for him, and he borrowed it for the day, being first obliged to insure it for £100. And he took risks in doing that, with lively children awaiting it, and unaccustomed cakes. And although, after all, the costly puppy had refused to play with them, Lady Orpen tells me they had enjoyed that party very much ; it had been hard to get them to leave. He had intended to get some Christmas crackers for them but had failed, perhaps because of the time given to the quest of the dog ; but in place of them he had given each child a little enamel bowl to put flowers in.

But almost every day brought its guests. I was saying to his cousin, Ida Cunningham, the other day how I had urged him, and have ever wished I had done so with more insistence, to go to Rodin for a bust ; I had written begging him to do this while he was still young and in his good looks. At that time we were arranging for one of John Shawe-Taylor after his death, and I said, " I won't be living when your time comes, and I do hope you will have it made while you are still young and handsome, for you will be so far-appreciated by that time that X, or rather his successor, will be entrusted with a memorial that will annoy your ghost." He could easily have arranged it, she said, for he had told her one day that he was busy unpacking in the cellars any bits of bronze he possessed because Rodin himself was coming to visit him that day.

I had sent a note on I forget what small matter, to Ellen Terry, and it happened it was not given to her for some days, on one late afternoon, and she hurried to Lindsey House in her sudden gracious way to explain, and bring the answer. Hugh was out, he had gone to Mr. Steer's studio, and I sent to tell him of our visitor and he hurried in, delighted to pay his homage to one he so much admired and had never met. He showed her the treasures of the house, and when she was leaving he took from a cabinet a crystal figure, a Chinese version of the Madonna and Child, made after the Christian missionaries had brought the story there, and asked her to accept it. It was pleasant to look on at the offering and the acceptance, a courtly unrehearsed scene. It was not the only time I saw him take down and give away some treasure to a guest. Yet he did not give idly, and I have seen Royalty so keen in admiration of some cup or vase that I thought it must surely go to his country, but it was put away in safety again. Yet Mr. Solomon tells me " he gave a fine Chinese figure to Herbert Baker, just because he admired it so much. He packed it up after he had left and sent it to him. He thought it would be in its right place."

Another visitor who came to see me there was Henry James. It happened that although *The Outcry* had already been written he and Hugh had never met till then. Their first meeting was on the staircase where I was going down with my guest as Hugh came in, and they had a long conversation there. Hugh told him how he had bought *The Outcry*, having been told he was its hero. Mr. James declared he had not founded his novel upon Hugh, but confessed he had heard much of him ; and I was pleased again to witness the meeting of two such courtesies. Another visit from Henry James was not so fortunate, for a young and pretty countrywoman of his asked him with mocking intent if he had ever been in America, and he was ruffled, and spoke of it after she had gone with some indignation, saying, " It was not ignorance, it was impertinence."

Of all his visitors the least welcome were people with whom he had but slight acquaintance, bringing small properties or doubtful pictures for him to set a price on. To one who questioned his opinion he spoke sharply, " You may set your judgment against me in anything else, but this knowledge of pictures is my gift." One guest he told me of as never coming without " an old knocker in his pocket, or some rubbish of the kind." " Tell me the secret of getting rich as you did," they all seemed to call out. That same persevering guest had one day come with a proposal that they should go into partnership, saying complacently, " We shall get on very well together. I have *flair* and can do the buying, I will leave the selling to you." Hugh did not often use strong language ; I don't know if he used it then, but that acquaintance ceased to come to his door.

One of my letters to my sister says : " On

Thursday the Crown Prince of Sweden came to
tea, a very nice, bright, unaffected young man.
Ruth and I and Lady C. were waiting to receive
him, when Lady W. and Mrs. T. came in to call,
and sat down with us in the drawing-room. I
wondered if Hugh would be annoyed as he had
not invited anyone ; however, he ran up having
left the Prince downstairs—they had been driving
together—and simply took them by the shoulders
and sent them away ! They didn't seem to
mind, and it was very sensible of him. I had
just received a request from a Swedish editor
asking leave to translate some of my plays and
Synge's into Swedish. I showed H.R.H. the letter
and he said it was a very good paper, very literary,
and he would send me some numbers if I liked.
He was a long time going over the house with
Hugh and meanwhile I took Lady C. into the
garden where Richard" (my grandson) "was
sailing his boat, and she made friends with him
and fed him with grapes.

"And next day Richard came to play in the
garden and then Steer appeared to do a sketch of
it as a background for a picture he was painting.
Nurse asked who he was, and seemed disappointed
and said, 'I thought he might be the Duke
of ——.' I said he was a greater man,
an artist, and she, more satisfied, said, 'Yes,
I heard something about Baby being *hand-
painted !*' "

He lived very simply in his stately surroundings.
For he who had been acquainted with poverty had
no mind to be cumbered with a large household,
nor did he hanker after a fat larder, though he

used to say he was no niggard in housekeeping because he had no idea what should be its cost. His Cunningham cousins tell me that the first meal at Lindsey House, where they came unexpectedly one evening, was little more than bread and bovril. He was not yet well settled and the new housekeeper was crying out because when he had gone to a sale promising to buy a bedstead, he had but brought home a pair of bronze vases. But just at that time of moving into the house he was tormented, agitated, walking up and down, because of a lawsuit that was going on, one that he lost. I think he had but three in his life, and this was more distressing than the rest, because it was with a friend, Robert Ross. As well as memory holds the tale, a picture had been left by him at Carfax's for sale and it had not been sold, and he took it away at their asking, selling it afterwards to some man who had first seen it at the Carfax rooms; and lawyers found their delight in prolonging the argument, and he, helpless, took an enduring hatred to their trade. He believed he was right and he was very angry with Ross at the time, but I knew this had passed away because he had pleased Ross by putting him in his own place as buyer of pictures for Johannesburg, and I remember his taking him to Bagshot to see the Duke of Connaught on some of its business. Indeed, I had forgotten the quarrel until the other day Alec Martin, telling me how good Hugh had been in friendships, said, " Just after that Ross case he was giving one of his big parties and said, ' I must ask Robert Ross.' I said, ' Some of the people coming here won't like that,' and he said, ' Then those people who don't like it may stay away.' "

Though I think he often read character well he had not the same discernment in the matter of living servitors as of Old Masters, and it was desirable that what is called " a treasure " should be found to guard that house so richly stored. But the search was not always rewarded, and I remember when arriving one early morning after the night journey from Ireland I was forced to go in search of a constable, and misled by a passer-by crossed Battersea Bridge on the errand, all ignorant that " the force " had its headquarters but a hundred yards or so from our gate, while Ruth (for neither of us would disturb Hugh's morning rest) held fast the key with which she had locked the " treasure " of thàt period with a confederate into his own pantry. But Hugh was placable in such things and did not even lose his gentleness when the sweeping of a room once led to a hole being knocked in a canvas that had cost him many thousands.

He kept something of the Evangelical religion of his childhood ; a certain austerity in morals and admiration of good works and of " the Good." General Booth had once come to his father's rectory for lunch, and had sat next Hugh and talked to him, and as he left had taken off his own badge and pinned it on the child's little coat. It had been lost, stolen by a servant they thought ; and Hugh among all his jewels lamented this loss to the end. But though a church-goer he was a little impatient of observances, and when a clerical relation staying with him at Lindsey

House said grace before dinner, he murmured to me, " I think I who provided it might have had some of the thanks."

Even after he had come to live in Lindsey House he would go to dine at some little restaurant —" such cheap dinners "—but I protested, saying that there was no economy in paying for food you could not eat. I was a little insistent upon this because I saw that any meal at home, however simple, in his quiet beautiful dining-room, would be better rest to him after the unrest of the day. And so in May, 1912, he wrote to me : " I hope you will be more comfortable this time, we have engaged another servant in honour of your coming and will be able to give you dinner in the house." And it was not long before the little dinner parties that host and guests enjoyed so happily were begun. For these were among his greatest pleasures. They were seldom arranged beforehand, he would ask one or two friends for the next day or that same day, though his sister would beg for a longer notice, and then another and another till the octagon limit was reached. Once or twice he went beyond it, and the guests on whom the lot fell were put at another table. But that enforced banishing proved so irksome to his courtesy that he often put a curb upon a hospitable impulse rather than repeat it.

Mr. Tonks writes : " To dine with him in Cheyne Walk, and at one's leisure look at the pictures on the wall, was undoubtedly one of the greatest pleasures of my life."

I told Miss Cunningham how a critic, Mr. X., had lamented his turning to Bridge in the evenings,

N

and she said, " Yes," she remembered well meeting him at Lindsey House, just, she thought, in that last year, at a small informal dinner. Her sister and some others had sat down to the game with Hugh, " and poor Mr. X. had only me to talk to, and then he tried to decipher a name on some picture that had been brought in, and would call to Hugh to look at each letter as he made it out. But Hugh would not turn from his cards, and besides if he had not already made out the name it is not likely he thought X. could do it."

The guests would sit after dinner around one or another picture; the latest treasure was usually put upon an easel for a while. One evening it was the portrait of the Duc d'Orleans by Ingres, that is now in his French collection. Mr. Francis Howard told me he had been with Hugh in Paris once when he had set his mind on buying an Ingres, and they went to many dealers' shops but there was not one to be found. But he did get one after all, that portrait. I remember someone saying on one of those evenings as we looked at the refined pallid face, " He looks as if it was time for him to marry a comedy actress and put vigour into that worn-out aristocratic race." I had written when he brought it home: " Hugh has just got an Ingres and means to keep it, it cost a thousand pounds. He thinks in thousands now."

Mr. Howard said, also, that after one of these long searches Hugh had promised and given him a costly dinner. " But," he had said, " I am doing this with pain."

The Titian portrait of the author of " The Courtier," Baldassare Castiglione, now in the

PORTRAIT OF BALDASSARE CASTIGLIONE.

By Titian.

Dublin National Gallery, had its turn upon the easel, and Mr. Charles Ricketts, having seen it there, allows me to use this note from his diary: "Lane's newly discovered Titian is of superb quality, it belongs to that stately and magisterial type of portrait which the painter initiated during the later thirties and early forties. I imagine it slightly later in date than the 'Francesco Maria Della Rovere' and the 'Eleanor Gonzaga' portraits, not so late as the 'Antonio Porcia,' and at a rough guess I think 1540 might be a probable date. The landscape vista is magnificent, the quality of the clothes very fine. The lettering is a seventeenth-century addition and may be based on traditional evidence as to who the sitter was."

I remember an evening at Lindsey House when Mr. Ricketts sat for a long time gazing at this picture. And I was not the only one to notice the strong resemblance between his absorbed face and that of Baldassare, he also absorbed in meditation upon some noble beauty.

Mr. Solomon wrote of one of the evenings: " Three years ago in the drawing-room at Lindsey House the talk had turned on Synge, the Irish playwright, who had died all too early; and one of us, I forget who, suggested that the volume with which he laid claim to be remembered by posterity was even slighter than that of Thomas Gray.

" I can recall the evening well; the quiet, rather sombre dignity of the long, oak-panelled room; the marble Venus in the bay window which overlooked the river where the light of the barges, the warehouses, and the tall chimneys, becoming campanili in the night, reminded one irresistibly of Whistler's 'Nocturnes'; and whilst the fire in the grate between two fire-dogs, which years before had been stolen from Windsor Castle, caught in its zone of light Rembrandt's 'Portrait of a.Young Lady' and Goya's 'Femme Espagnole,' Sir Hugh sat among his guests, nervously smoking his cigarette, perhaps a little melancholy at the turn the conversation had taken.

"By the dim light this pale, slender, dark-eyed knight, with his trim black beard, his slim hand, and his poised, nervous, illusive manner, presented an appearance similar to the figures in the paintings of that strange seer, El Greco.

"The guests were few; . . . George Moore, talking even more wonderfully than he writes; Henry Tonks the artist, who has distinction written in every line of his form; and Wilson Steer, quietly nodding a disinterestedness in all that was being said.

"Sir Hugh talked little, perhaps over-tired, as he often was in those days, but it was evident that his mind worked and he was serious. When the guests had gone and we were about to climb the stairs for bed he turned to me saying : ' How foolish to talk of Synge's small volume of work. Why, generations after I, who have created nothing, am dead and forgotten, Ireland will be watching his plays.' This was the pathetic thought of one who had tried to paint and had failed, but in his modesty forgot those other creations, his galleries in his native land and far-off Africa."

Mr. Solomon said also to me : " You remember

that Snyders, ' A Concert of Birds,' that hung over the sideboard, it is now in the Cape Town collection. One evening Yeats and Moore dined there, and as they were looking at it Yeats pointed to a parrot and said, ' That is Moore on his perch,' and it really had a look of him, and everyone laughed. But then Moore pointed out the raven and said, ' And that's Yeats, very much disgusted to see me on the perch ! ' "

Another friend tells me with amusement of an evening when she met John, and other artists. '· We dined at Lindsey House. Martin Wood was there and kept saying, ' This is a very remarkable gathering.' We went upstairs after -dinner to look at the Titian, ' Philip II.,' and I, venturing to speak to John for the first time, said, ' How can the wonderful brilliancy of that colour keep its freshness so long ? ' And John said, ' Ah-h-h ! ' ' "

If Hugh was not grudging of food in his own house, it did not interest him, his first look and his criticism would be for the flowers on the table. An American friend at Rome once said to me, " I can do without necessities but not without luxuries." (And I remember that as she spoke I noticed that, perhaps as an example, she had diamond rings in her ears and a hole in her veil.) That was in part Hugh's feeling. The flowers were a necessity, a part of the beauty of life ; they must not only be fresh but of the right colour for the harmony of the room. I hardly remember him more indignant than when coming suddenly home one day he found guests in the drawing-room and noticed that (through accident rather than neglect) the flowers had not been changed. " I have nothing but my taste," he said, and he felt this outrage to it like an insult, a blow in the face.

He was glad when he could tempt his friend Alec Martin to dinner and an evening's talk, or snatch him away from Christie's for a drive. He did this one Saturday when he motored me to Buckhurst, where I was to spend Sunday with the Robert Bensons. I was in the garden when they were leaving and came to say good-bye; my hands had been filled with roses by my host, and I thought it greedy to keep them among that abundance, and gave them to Mr. Martin, because he had told me his little ones were going to a flower service for children next day. But when I met Hugh again he was rather sad and said, " I should have liked those roses for myself." Fruit also was a luxury and so necessarily must be also good to see; the cakes also for his tea-table must be chosen with care, good to see and to taste. But the meat, fish, the ordinary courses for a dinner, though not outside his notice were outside his care, his housekeeper might look to those.

Even when there were no guests the evenings were not without excitement; he would come in with a story of his doings. " Hugh, who had been talking as if near the workhouse, confessed he had been to Christie's and bid up to £3000 for a 'Gainsborough, but was outbid. So he felt he owed himself £3000. Then he took Colonel Poë to Nicholson's, and the Colonel could not make up his mind to anything. There was a wonderful picture of an orchid there, unfinished. Nicholson said the Duke of Marlborough had asked him to come to Blenheim and paint it, and afterwards they talked of price, and Nicholson asked £600 which the Duke refused to give, though he said he had spent a fortnight painting it, shut up in a hothouse as there was snow on the ground. Hugh wanted Colonel Poë' to buy it, but he thought it too much for Still Life, and then Hugh said, ' Well, I offer you £500 for it, and you can wire that to the Duke and see if he wants it.' Just before we went to dinner the telegram arrived from Nicholson : ' Duke withdraws, you possess orchid.' So now he only owes himself £2500."

In his earlier days he had accepted and even been ruled by convention. I sometimes said to his mother when I went to see her in her Dublin house, " I would have brought you this or that, but was afraid of meeting Hugh while I was carrying the parcel ! " But all that had changed with his character, " like the turning of an oyster-shell from black to white." And as his surroundings had grown stately he had come to practise simplicity. One evening, giving the gossip of some fine dinner I had been at, I said for talking's sake, " One is given all delicious things in plenty except cucumber. That is handed round in one tiny plate for all the table. I never feel greedy except for cucumber." A little while after this Hugh came in one Saturday evening hurrying over the marble pavement of his hall looking as if he had just discovered a Giorgione. " I have brought you this ! You said you liked them and they were on a stall and so cheap." And he held up in triumph a cucumber ! He was very kind to me, taking me here and there though I would tell him that people didn't expect to see an old woman when they were expecting a young man. I told him one night at a Stafford House party that people would think from his attention to me that he was expecting a legacy.

Late one afternoon he rushed in his impetuous way into the little yellow room used by me as a sitting-room at Lindsey House, and said that I must go with him to the Shakespeare Ball at the Albert Hall that evening. I thought it was a jest, I whose balls could be counted on my fingers far more readily than the number of years since I had attended the last, I think at Buckingham Palace in the old Queen's time. But no one could stand against his vehemence, and in an ancient black brocade and carrying a bundle of black lace, I saw nothing better to do than to drive to the Lyceum Theatre where kind, clever Mrs. Martin Harvey was playing, and there she arranged with quick, skilful fingers my veils and diamonds until I could pass muster in a crowd. And that I might not loudly challenge immediate criticism of my dress I chose the name of Lady Woodville, because she is only once mentioned in Shakespeare. So with Ruth, who looked extremely well as Katherine of Aragon, we set out and I enjoyed looking from my box at the brilliant unexpected scene, and at Hugh, impressive in a ruff, making up for those young days starved of beauty, and enjoying the freedom given by a little unmortgaged wealth ; greeted from their box by beckoning royalties of the day as well as by his fellow masquers in Drake's and Raleigh's attire.

Another letter says, " Hugh called for me at

Rumpelmeyer's and took me on to the Grenfells' party. He had been to lunch with the Asquiths and there was royalty there, and the governess had said to the little Asquith girl, ' Look at the Crown Princess of Sweden ; see how she holds herself up and behaves better than anyone else,' and Hugh, hearing this, had immediately repeated it to the Princess, to the indignation of the governess though the amusement of the Princess. The Grenfells' party was very pleasant ; I met Lord Roberts and we talked a little of India where I had stayed in the same house with him, Sir Alfred Lyall's. . . . Then ' God Save the King ' was played and the Connaughts arrived, the Duke looking very lively and amiable. Hugh introduced me to the Duchess, who apologised for not having had time to come to the plays and hoped to see them in Canada and asked when they would be there ; and then someone came between us and I went to tea with Lady Tree, who introduced me to a young man as ' the great Lady Gregory,' and he seemed so excited I thought perhaps I really was great, but it was only because he had a friend who wants to get into the Abbey Company and thought I might see her, which I promised to do " (Miss Cathleen Nesbitt, who I am proud to say became a member of our Company for a while). " The Boy Scouts, two or three dozen of them, came running on to the lawn, and were reviewed by the Duke and Lord Roberts and Lord Grenfell —such a small army and such big men ! Lord Grenfell asked me if *Spreading the News* had been brought over, says it is his favourite play. Garden and lawn, and house beautiful, it was very

pleasant altogether, but we were going on to the
Martin Harvey's garden party, and only arrived
when the last guest was leaving. However, they
forgave us and I was glad that we came. . . . Yeats
came here and we all dined at the Good Intent,
and he and I and Hugh sat and talked in the drawing-room and had tea, until Hugh went off to two
parties or balls, one at the Grand Duke Michael's."

Then, " I lunched at the Shaws' yesterday,
G. B. S. in great good humour. Hugh came in
afterwards to fetch me and they got on very
well, he was amused at G. B. S. having said that
' Lane had been wise to take to picture dealing ;
he would not have been fit for any useful job,
whereas Lady Gregory, if she had been a washer-
woman would have been an excellent one ! ' " (But
Bernard Shaw, before many had understood what
Hugh was doing had written on coming back to
Dublin of a difference made there by those two
new facts, the Abbey Theatre, and the Gallery
in Harcourt Street ; and he has written in the
preface to his latest book that he " understood,
perhaps better than most people, the misfortune
of the death of Lane.") " Mrs. Shaw was talking
with satisfaction about the advance in the position
of women in the last few years, and of all the
things they did now that they would not have
thought of before. I was listening cautiously
when L. R., who was there, said in his slow Cork
accent, ' The young lady at the box office was
saying that yesterday, she said it was surprising
how many ladies now paid for the gentlemen
they bring with them, and if they borrow sixpence they say, ' I will pay you back again ! ' "

Once, a few years before Hugh's death, marriage had seemed near at hand; marriage with a young girl, gentle, charming, in whose presence he felt content and rest. He was pleased that I liked her and made easier the informal meetings at Lindsey House away from the balls and receptions where they used to see one another, for it was a period at which he went a great deal into Vanity Fair, wanting to know it through and through, getting its best in great houses among great hostesses, and meaning then to put it away as a memory. He was never bewitched by all this fine company, but used, and in a measure enjoyed, it for a while. I say in a measure, for I think it was with children and music and his pictures, and a few close friends and fellow-workers that he made his nearest approach to felicity.

That dream of marriage near fulfilment stilled his restless nature for a moment. I had left London thinking all was going on well. Then in a little time he wrote that " the early intimacy that had been so delightful " would never come to more than " a warm friendship." Meanwhile, the shadow of ill health, never far away, had deepened; a motor accident had increased it, and it was in a Nursing Home, recovering from the surgeon's hand, that the sweet vision died away.

I wrote from Coole: " I am a little sad at your news, for I hoped there was a happy future for you and her, and one's life becomes more and more engrossed by the happiness and the hopes of the young. . . . But, indeed, I had not been very content about it at the end, for I am sure you

ought to lie by for a while and let your strength
build itself up, and it was difficult to do that
while you had so much to think of.   I do hope now
you will lay aside business and have a real rest of
body and mind.   Money is such a little thing now
that you have no immediate use for it, in com-
parison with health, and poor John S. T.'s sudden
breakdown is a warning.   I have only had your
letter this afternoon so have not quite looked at
all sides of it. . . . I had been looking forward
to welcoming you both here, and planning to hide
our weak points from you."

I have sometimes said, "Marriage legitimises
selfishness," and I think that had Hugh married
it might have been to Ireland's loss.   Yet even
during that short dream of a possible married
life he said he would never endow a child of his
with riches enough to make him idle.   He had
worked, and any son of his should work.   The
chief endowment he would provide would be for
what he never lost sight of, a Gallery in Dublin of
great pictures, of great art, free to all.

When someone had once asked me, "Would
Hugh be happy in married life and would his
wife be ? " I had said, laughing, "Yes, if they
lived in separate houses."   Yet there was some
truth in those jesting words.   His vivid life, and
the excitement of his work, and air and sunlight,
restored his strength each day.   But there was
nostril trouble that made sleep broken and breath-
ing difficult.   I would find him in the morning
exhausted, white, taking his light breakfast in
bed, lying late, irritable and nervous.   Even to
me at those times he would say some sharp word,

so that it was not all in jest that I said to him once,
" You are like Jephthah in the early morning,
going out determined to slay the first person you
meet, even though it should be your dearest."
And often coming home in the evening white and
jaded, dark rings under his tired eyes, the little
frown of annoyance that I remember on his
mother's face when she was crossed, he would sit
down at the piano and play himself to a happier
mood ; or would stroke Tiger, the big Persian cat
that I had never quite liked since it had come
in at my window one morning with a torn bird
in its mouth. But Hugh loved it, and did not
wince when it walked among his costly China ornaments. He writes to his sister : " Tiger was found
mewing before one of the pictures in the hall this
morning, and a pigeon was seen on top of the
picture, its best tail feathers all over the floor !
It had come down the chimney of the yellow
room and strewn it with soot."

But he loved yet better little Tinko, the tiny
Pekinese given to him by his friend Alec Martin.
His face would light up at the sound of its tiny bark
or its bell. Mrs. Hinde told me that sometimes
when she asked him to stay to lunch he would say,
" and there's Tinko—is there enough for him ? "

Yet late at night, coming in from the plays
that were my business, I would find him sitting
up answering letter after letter, for he never would
consent to have a secretary, about many things,
but especially about the Gallery. His cousin
Ida says, " I think he must have hated that Dublin
gallery at times, as we did when he stayed with us,
because he was always writing hundreds of letters

about it, he was so much its slave." But then he would lay down his pen and turn round in his chair, unruffled, uncomplaining, kindly interested in all I had been doing, telling me of his own day's doings, till at last he would finish the letters in a hurry and carry them off to the pillar-box in Beaufort Street. I was glad it was no nearer at hand, and that he was forced to go out even for those few minutes into the empty road and the fresh night breeze from the river. He was always glad at that hour to linger and talk. I think he had come to dread, without confessing it to himself, the night and the awakening. I wrote to him at the time of the Louvre robbery: "I am so glad you are taking that much needed rest cure, though I always wonder how one's mind is kept quiet, for it is in the middle of the night, when one is supposed to be resting, it works most determinedly, and what I call 'tiger-clawed thoughts' rise up and seize one by the throat. . . . I hope you will have patience to get really strong. We think you will be accused of stealing the 'Monna Lisa' because no one will believe you are really taking a rest, they will think you have got someone to personate you here, while you were securing the Leonardo for Dublin!"

A little hunting now and then was a great help to him. He wrote to Ruth on the day after Christmas, 1913: "I had my first hunt to-day, the New Forest foxhounds. The meet was eight miles off, and no one else would go, so I went with a groom who knew the way. He was very tactful and looked the other way when I funked any rather big jump. There were a good many

spills owing to the bogs and big holes hidden by
heather, but I brought my priceless horse back
safely (the sire was a famous racer). We also
rode on Christmas Day and yesterday. I hope
to hunt on Monday and will perhaps return to
London that night." Yet he had written only a
month earlier : " I went to the Drag hunt on
Saturday—but never again. It was as fast as a
steeplechase, and more devious. I fell off twice,
once badly, right on to my head and broke
my hard riding hat to pieces, and nearly my
neck as well."

And a friend, Mrs. Reeves, writes : " Did
you ever realise his extraordinary courage ? With
so nervous a physique it was remarkable. I
noticed this concerning riding. He knew nothing
of horses but didn't mind a mount of any
kind."

The doctors thought that he might find his
needed tranquillity in the peace and quiet of the
country, and the search for a house was added to
his occupations or perhaps his amusements for a
while. He wrote me in 1914 when I was in
America: ". . . I have a motor now and have been
taking trips into the country looking for a ruined
palace to restore. It will be some time before I
can hope to recover from this neurasthenia, and
as I am ordered quiet, fresh air, early hours, I
must not live in London. I think that ' restoring '
some wonderful old house will give me something
to do. At times I feel that I shall never be well
or able to work, but this depression is the principal
result of the illness."

He enjoyed the search for the " wonderful

old house " though he never found one quite to
his mind.   Mr. Bodkin tells me how, tempted for
a moment by a beautiful old Elizabethan house
near Lewes, with yew trees and a moat, but falling
to decay and used but as a lodging for harvest
labourers, he planned not only its restoration but
its furnishing with old oak and old Elizabethan
plate, the walls to be hung with masterpieces by
Holbein, John Batty, Zuccano.   " He would show
England a perfect Elizabethan house in good
order."   Mr. Solomon tells me he went with him
sometimes and that " he wanted something built
by Wren.   He liked Kirby Hall best, it was a
mere ruin, but he would have liked to restore it
and fill it with beautiful things.   I told him it
would cost £100,000 and he said it would not be
so much, that I was giving South African prices.
But then he asked Lutyens, and he said £200,000.
He would not have lived there much, though he
said he would like the country, that London was
too near Christie's.   But he used to say of Johannesburg that it was too far from Christie's."   And
Mrs. Grosvenor writes :   " You will remember his
keenness to buy and restore Kirby, the beautiful
house belonging to Lord Winchelsea, which had
been allowed to fall into the most lamentable
state of decay.   He only asked to be allowed to
live in one corner of it, spending all his time,
money, and energy on rebuilding it with the
most faithful care and understanding, in order to
restore it at the end either to its original owner
or to the nation for exactly what it had cost him,
without making a farthing of profit on the transaction.   Had his offer been accepted, I feel sure

THE SAME PORTRAIT "IMPROVED."

MRS. EDWARD TAYLOR, AS PAINTED BY ROMNEY.

that it would have ended in his spending much of his own money on it without asking for any return."

He happily did not buy that splendid ruin or, with his grand ideas of rebuilding, the war would have brought yet greater disaster to his fortunes. Oliver Gogarty tells me that when he was himself looking for a house outside Dublin, Hugh had gone with him on some of these excursions—admiring Delville above all—he would see at once what could be made of such a house, but his ideas would outrun possibilities. They had passed by a terrace that looked out in full sunlight upon coast and sea, and he had cried, " Buy that whole terrace ! You could turn part of it into such a wonderful picture gallery ! "

But all this time money had to be made. A critic said of him, " His acuteness in discovering master-pieces is almost uncanny."   And it was oftenest at Christie's he discovered them, so that in time if he was seen to look closely at a picture its value would go up. It was there he bought for £1000 Watteau's " Contre Danse."   It was in a very dirty state and bidding had begun at £5. But later, when I first met Alec Martin at Lindsey House, Hugh, introducing him, said, " There is no chance now of bargains at Christie's. This man knows too much."

The Romney portrait of Mrs. Edward Taylor, now in the Dublin National Gallery, gave him great delight. The day before the sale he came to lunch at 1, Old Burlington Street, where I was staying, and he talked of a picture he was going to bid for at Christie's. It was put down in the

o

Catalogue as a Romney, but experts said it was
of the "school of Lawrence." It had the
Lawrence dress, a dark gown, dark hair, a great
muff; the critics who looked at it said it was
impossible that Romney could have painted
fashions that would not be in existence until a
quarter of a century later. But Hugh was
certain. He said, "I cannot be mistaken in those
Romney eyes." He bought it at the sale for
£756; his bidding had perhaps sent up the price.
He told us afterwards of the impatience with
which he carried it home. Mr. Solomon was
there, and tells me of the tremendous excitement
when he began to rub at the heavy black paint
of the hair and white began to appear. Then he
rubbed away the blue scarf that covered the
shoulders, and the black gown, and large muff,
and again white was seen and the outline of pale
arms. With this certainty he brought in his
cleaner, and when all the overpaint was very
carefully removed there appeared the lovely
portrait with its powdered hair, light blue plumed
hat, gauze handkerchief and bare hands.

Romney's receipt for the money paid him
for this picture was afterwards found by Mrs.
Taylor's representatives. They suppose that as she
grew older she thought a more sombre dress would
best befit her, or it may be that among her
neighbours Romney had gone out of fashion. It
was all for Ireland's good, for the original paint
had been protected by the late daubing. The
Medici Society published a print of this picture
later, and Hugh liked to bestow a copy of this
print on his friends.

It was at Christie's, in 1906, that he bought Titian's "Portrait of a Man in a Red Cap." This account of it was later given in the *Morning Post :* "In May, 1906, it appeared at Messrs. Christies' as a 'Portrait of Lorenzo Dei Medici by Titian,' and starting at twenty guineas it was run up to two thousand one hundred guineas, at which figure Sir Hugh Lane acquired it. Exactly thirty years earlier the portrait had been bought in at Christie's for ninety-one guineas. . . . Our information is that at some time after 1876 it was sold in the provinces for a less sum than that at which it was bought in. In 1906 there was a thick coating of dirt and varnish on the picture through which the handiwork of a great master did not emerge to the satisfaction of many experts. Some adhered to the attribution to Giorgione suggested earlier, some regarded it as a Francesco Vecellio influenced by Giorgione; others as a Moretto affected by that master. On this point opinions generally changed when the work was cleaned and shown in the Grafton galleries at the National Loan Exhibition in 1909. Mr. Charles Ricketts has publicly recanted an adverse judgment and claimed it as a genuine Titian."

This is what Mr. Ricketts has written of it: "This picture passed through Messrs. Christies' hands in a darkened and dirty condition. I then imagined this beautiful Giorgionesque painting to be an early work by Francesco Vecellio, basing my impression on the colour and on the evidence of Francesco's knowledge of Titian's technical methods. The picture has since been cleaned. When I saw it again the scales fell from my eyes, to use a consecrated expression. How was it possible that I could have mistaken this master-piece for the work of a second-rate man ? How was it that the shape of the eyelids, the construction of the chin, had escaped me ? The background, formerly brown, had become a luminous warm grey, the glove and fur, which I had thought indifferent, revealed the tender pigment of the master ; the painting of the linen in ' pàte sur pàte ' was a practice of Titian's. The work stood out, not as a mere interesting problem, but a masterpiece superior in preservation to the Cobham ' Ariosto,' contemporary with, or slightly later than, the beautiful portrait at Temple Newsam."

Hugh had never any doubts about it, he was certain it was by Titian. It was bought from him by Mr. Grenfell for £25,000.

Another great picture that he owned for a while, and that he cared for most of all those he sold, was Titian's portrait of Philip II. of Spain. One evening he had promised to come to the theatre with me ; I had been given a box and we were to see Miss Marie Tempest in some new play. But when I came in to dress for dinner he met me at the foot of the staircase, very pale, and said, " I can't come—haven't you seen the evening papers ? " I had not then noticed the placards, " Great Titian gone to America. Eighty-thousand pound picture sold." He said men from the newspapers were arriving constantly to question him about it and he must stay and see them ; people seemed angry at the picture having been allowed to go out of the country. It was

the great portrait of Philip II. that had gone.
It had been bought as a gift by Mrs. Emery for
the Gallery at Cincinnati.

It had been in the collection of Professor von
Lembach who had bought it from its original
owners the Giustianini family. Hugh said to some
one writing of it, " I've been on the track of this
great painting for years. I first saw it in Germany
when I was a youth of nineteen, and I was fasci-
nated by the wonderful workmanship. No other
picture has affected me so strongly." Mr. Charles
Ricketts writes to me of it : " When in the
Lembach collection this picture was overlaid by
the work of other hands ancient and modern. I
think the open princely crown—now revealed by
the removal of a velvet cap—proves it to have
been the rapid sketch done at Augsburg from
which Titian painted his superb full-length
portraits of Philip II. in the Prado and at Naples.
The handling is looser than in these two highly
finished works and I believe it to be to some
extent still unfinished, as it resembles in many
points of handling the group of ' Paul III., Ottavia,
and Cardinal Farnese ' at Naples."

It was after the death of Professor Lembach
that it came through other hands to Hugh. It
had then the cap upon the head, but he was
convinced there must be a crown underneath, and
with that certainty of insight that did away with
any credit or blame for courage or rashness, he
cleaned away the paint and found the crown. It
was no wonder if he had remembered that great
portrait for years, one it is difficult to forget.
But after he had become Director of the Dublin

National Gallery he saw the notice of a sale of furniture in a house in Limerick, which he had visited in his early boyhood, and he remembered a picture of Still Life he had seen there, and sent an order to buy it, and placed it in the Gallery.

It happened when I was giving some lectures on a National Theatre in the United States that I spoke at Cincinnati. I was pleading for what I called "parochialism," the building and endowment of a theatre in each State, in each city; and I said I believed this would come, because the sense of citizenship was so strong in America. And then I told of the great Titian, and of that evening when it had become known it had been taken away from the Chelsea house; taken, I said, "because someone living in far-off Cincinnati had not thought the best too good, the greatest too great, to bring to her own place and her own city." Only after I had finished speaking I learned that the giver of the picture was there in the Hall, and she came and spoke to me and seemed pleased. I told this to Hugh when I saw him again, just before he set out for that last voyage; and he was happy that a generosity akin to his own had thus been recognised. After his death I met friends to whom he had told the story in his enthusiastic way.

Mr. Duncan tells me: "I was with him one day in an old furniture shop in Dublin, and I said, as we looked at some fine old pieces, 'Buying and selling these must be a pleasant trade.' But he said, 'Buying, yes, like buying pictures; but selling is the very devil.' And he went on to say, 'I never sell a picture till I am driven to it. And if

I sell it to some millionaire it is lost, I don't see it
again, it may not give any very great pleasure to
him and it is lost to everyone else.   But if I give
a picture to a gallery, that is really good business.
It is as much mine as ever, I still possess it, I can
see it when I like and everyone else can see it
too, so there's no waste in the matter.   I hate
waste.'   That was his temptation, to give away
was to possess."

CHAPTER XV

THE DUBLIN NATIONAL GALLERY

Hugh told me one evening in London that he had spent the day at the National Gallery because he had been asked, on behalf of some in authority, if he would, when the place fell vacant, be willing to become its Director. "But, I felt," he said, "as I went through the rooms that they were so well arranged and catalogued, the pictures so well cared for, that there would be but little for me to do. I made up my mind I would rather go to Dublin."

I was very glad he said this, for I had feared he might have been tempted to forsake Dublin, where some hostility yet lurked and muttered, and stay in the brilliant hospitality, the gracious geniality of the society around him in London. He hated the railway journey, the early rising or the night crossing, he could not sleep in the train, and he had long abandoned those Castle festivities that had served his purpose for a while.

I did not know our National Gallery well, I went into it but seldom, I had been but little in Dublin until my theatre work began, and that once having begun held me to the Abbey. My husband had taken me there one Sunday long ago, soon after my marriage, that I might see the people coming in, and that many of them were working men with their wives and children ; for he was proud of having fought in Parliament for that Sunday opening, and proud that it had been accepted in Ireland long before London museums and galleries had unlocked their Sabbath door. Although a trustee of the Trafalgar Square National Gallery he had never lost interest in the one on Leinster Lawn.

That Dublin Gallery had been founded and built in the last century, soon after the great Exhibition of 1851. Mulvany, the painter of the portrait of O'Connell, now in the Gallery, was its first Director ; then for twenty-three years Henry Doyle. A note in the Catalogue of 1914 says of him truly that " by his sound judgment, pure taste, and wide knowledge he made the collection under his charge one of great interest." He had much charm of manner, though he was more staid in appearance than his brilliant brother " Dicky," whose name is kept before us every week in the " D " and the dicky-bird in the corner of the cover of *Punch*, and who was as whimsical in conversation as in design. Lord Houghton told me of hearing him say one day at the Garrick, when advised to give up his quill pen in favour of a steel one, " Would you have me take the bread out of the mouth of the poor goose ? " Henry Doyle had stayed with us at Coole, and was often at our house when he came to London, where I know the National Gallery Trustees of the time looked on him with favour as a desirable successor to Sir Frederic Burton, then growing old. But he died suddenly in 1892, and left Ireland with no successor at hand. My husband was written to for advice, but was lying in the illness from which I yet thought he might recover ; so hoping that I might some day be able to tell him what I had done in his name, I took the letter and the bundle of applications to Sir Frederic Burton and asked whom he would recommend. He would not hear of any of those who had offered themselves, and said he only knew two men well fitted for the office, Mr. Claude Phillips and Mr. Walter Armstrong. I think Mr. Phillips was unwilling to leave London, but I sent on Mr. Armstrong's name to the Dublin Trustees, or, as they are called, Governors, and he was appointed Director, and held the office until 1914. So there was to me a sort of traditional interest as well as the personal one when I found his successor might perhaps be Hugh Lane.

Bernard Shaw, arguing against me for argument's sake, that pictures ought to be kept in a place where the greatest numbers see them, confessed that his own interest in art is due to the days he spent as a boy going idly through that gallery ; and this had but given me a new argumènt, for one had already been that Foley had become a sculptor through wandering as a poor boy among the collection of casts given to the city of Cork ; given by George the Fourth, who, receiving during his visit to Ireland at the same time news of the arrival of that collection as a gift from some Italian Government, and of a deputation of Cork Aldermen, had bestowed the one upon the other. Yet who would have prophèsied the creation of a sculptor as an outcome of that royal after-dinner mood ?

Hugh had already taken his place on the Board in 1903. He says in a letter to Lord Gough : " I have just been appointed to be a ' Governor and Guardian ' of the National Gallery of Ireland, in place of the late Lord de Vesci. This was a great surprise, as I was supposed to be at war with the Director, Sir W. Armstrong, and at the same time, having no ' influence ' or official position I could only have been appointed on my merit." It amused me to hear later that one of the Governors of that time had resigned rather than " sit with a man who sells pictures."

When Sir Walter Armstrong's time was near its end Hugh was asked by some of the Governors to apply to be made Director in his place. He had already written to a friend : " The Directorship of the Dublin National Gallery used to be the great longing of my life, it is only serious ill-health and perhaps the realising of how little interest is taken in art in Dublin, that makes me dread a fresh task. Still, I would like to leave my mark there, and as old pictures are the only things in the world that I know anything about, I feel that in two or three years (if I live so long) I may be able to do some little good. Of course I would spend the salary on the collection—probably a great deal more— and though I feel bound to add to the Modern Gallery, collecting old pictures is my real pleasure in life. . . . I have always contended over here, in reference to the London National Gallery, that if a Director has not a special ' flair,' he is not wanted, and his salary can be added to the purchase fund.

There is always a secretary or registrar to do the practical managing of the Gallery, and Trustees to see that the accounts are paid. *Anyone* can go to a first-class firm and buy an annual picture of good pedigree that will not disgrace a Gallery." One evening in December, 1913, just before he left Lindsey House for his first visit to America, he asked me to write to Dr. Mahaffy, the Chairman of the Board, begging him to give any help he could during the time he was away. "Tell him," he said, "that if I am appointed to the National Gallery I will make it my adopted child."

Some were against his appointment, because they only thought of him as a dealer, and some because he would not promise to live in Dublin. He was not likely to neglect Dublin, but he believed he would serve the Gallery better by staying within reach of Christie's.

And as to dealing, he made a promise to give the first offer of any picture he might buy in each year to the Gallery at cost price, if it was within the limit of its means.

I was able to write to him in January, 1914: " I have been working about the National Gallery, and as far as I can ascertain a good majority of the Trustees are safe for Hugh Lane."

But on February 2, I wrote to Yeats: " To-morrow may bring another blow, for the election of the National Gallery Director comes on. I had a letter from Colonel Poë saying Hugh hadn't applied, and that it would probably go to Strickland, and that there was a good deal of feeling against the dealing; but by the same post one from Bailey, saying he thought most of the

Trustees were for him. Then I wrote to Mahaffy to ask if I should cable to Hugh to send in an application, and he answered that he considered the letter Hugh had written him as an application, and would rule it so at the meeting, and that he thinks he has a good chance. But I don't feel hopeful, there seems misfortune over us just now." For there were still men in Dublin who believed in some hidden covetousness, and some who twitted him with his trade.

And at the election when his name was put up by Dr. Mahaffy, one of the Governors, a Mr. Kennedy, objected, pointing out a rule that no Governor could become Director. Hugh, with his usual carelessness as to the forms of business, had never looked into the rules. Dr. Mahaffy at once adjourned the meeting to give him time to resign. It was supposed that this objection had been made to give Mr. Strickland, the only other candidate, the place, and there was some anger about this. But Miss Purser tells me, " when Kennedy was lying a long time in his last illness I used to go and see him, and once he spoke of the matter, and said he had only made the objection because Mahaffy had offended him, he thought him too dictatorial in the Chair, and was glad of the opportunity to snub him, and this with no intention of helping any other candidate."

But on the 26th Hugh was elected by ten votes to five, and I wrote to Yeats again : " I awoke this morning more happy and satisfied than for a long time—almost radiant—because of Hugh's election to the Directorship yesterday. It seems as if that barren tide may have turned, and that the worst hour is over. There is one of our 'best men' employed anyhow. And though you have not been chosen yet" (he was a candidate for a professorship of literature) "you are working as though you had been called to employment (and, indeed, so am I), and I don't think our work can go to loss. I am quite satisfied now about the Modern Gallery; that is, satisfied that Hugh will be very generous, and that the matter is out of our hands." And Yeats answered: "I am greatly cheered by the news of Lane's appointment, it will improve the whole position in Ireland."

Hugh himself was less elated. He wrote: "I am feeling very depressed at my new responsibilities, but I am sure that once I get started it will become absorbing."

And when he took up his duties he was not free from discouragement. For one disappointment, the rooms had just been decorated in a way he disliked, and, of course, the Treasury could not be asked for money to undo what had been done. He gave up his search for a country house and seemed more content, and wrote in April: "I have begun rehanging and repainting (at my own expense) some of the smaller rooms. I have discovered a good picture by N. Poussin at the Castle, which had been lent by the National Gallery some years ago, so that I have demanded its return! Mr. Bailey has been most helpful. . . ." But a little time later, in May, I heard from him from London: "I have had to give up the Butes, and am going to Dublin on Saturday next to make preparation for the

Board Meeting. I have received a very rude letter from the Treasury (evidently inspired from Dublin) saying that they could not accept me as a civil servant, but that I can draw my salary, which they consider excessive, considering that I am only giving a part of my time. Besides giving up my salary I have just bought a great bargain for the Gallery. I gave pictures to the value of at least £18,000 at last meeting, and I was going to give an important Gainsborough landscape and some good pictures to fill important gaps in the collection at next week's meeting, but I feel rather angry at the moment. I've a good mind to write to Mr. Birrell and demand a ' decoration ' to confound my enemies and complete my costume for future functions, or to resign my post." I am glad to say he gave the Gainsborough landscape, and glad he did not carry out either of these momentary threats.

And in the autumn Yeats wrote from Dublin : " I went yesterday morning to the National Gallery and found Hugh there. I think he is getting more content as he is planning to get Lutyens over to see how the building could be improved. He seems to have added a great many very fine pictures." For, as one of the Governors said to me, " He was giving all the time."

The other day, at Mespil House, Miss Purser showed me in every room something she owed to Hugh, by a gift, as the Chinese figures and over-mantel, or by advice or choice ; all had helped to make her house beautiful.

I asked her if he had been impatient at the National Gallery Board, and she said he was very courteous there, did not, she thinks, assert himself enough, though at one's own house he would criticise and say, " upright bricks are not the right pattern for a wallpaper." But he would not have liked her wallpapers whatever their pattern, she says, because they were chosen by him who had chosen also the decorations for the rooms of the National Gallery.

Some of his best friends and supporters were Governors, Sir W. Hutcheson Poë and Lord Mayo and Miss Purser and W. F. Bailey. Dr. Mahaffy, though a friend, was at times a rough one, and I heard that at one meeting he rather curtly refused to allow a picture by Devis to be bought, that Hugh had bought at Christie's. He said the drawing was bad, and Hugh had accepted the judgment quietly. One is glad to know it was sold later at a much higher price than he had given, and at which he had offered it. He had been anxious to have a little room of the " English conversation school," that is why he had wanted the Devis; there was already the little Hogarth and some others, and one he had just given. At another time he was going to read a very interesting note about the fine portrait of Gainsborough's brother, " Scheming Jack," which he had just given to the Gallery, but Dr. Mahaffy, wanting to catch a train, said : " We'll take it as read " ; and broke up the meeting.

Yet there was a real friendliness between them. Mahaffy had, when he was made Provost, asked him to arrange for the cleaning of the pictures in the Provost's House, and an estimate was made which was accepted. Miss Purser tells me, " I went to the National Gallery one day and found him with his sleeves rolled up, in an overall, cleaning some of them himself.   Afterwards he came to me and said he had saved £40 on the estimate by doing a large part of the work himself, and he wanted me to arrange through my brother Lewis, who was Bursar of Trinity, that this forty pounds should not be given back to the College funds, but should be spent on lights—some special electric fittings—for the Provost's drawing-room, that he thought would suit its stateliness.   I didn't think this could be done, I thought the authorities would say the estimate had been too high, and would just keep the money.   But he in his urgent way insisted.   He could not see any justice in that ' I saved the money by doing the work myself because I wanted to see those lights put up on that fine room.' "

After his death she told this to Mahaffy, and he said he would like indeed to have whatever Hugh had recommended, if they could find out where the fittings were to be had.   And by inquiry in London they found those he had set his heart on, and these were put up in the house which I grieve to think the Provost did not long live to enjoy.

Mr. Thomas Bodkin, one of its Governors, has been good enough to write—a welcome enrichment of this chapter—this account of the Dublin National Gallery : " It now consists of over six hundred pictures, about six hundred drawings and watercolours, and a collection of engraved portraits and busts, which latter are mainly of local interest.   It is without question the second Gallery in importance in the three kingdoms. It was opened in 1864.

"Its most remarkable feature prior to Sir Hugh Lane's Directorship was its group of paintings of the Dutch and Flemish schools. This comprised not only adequate but exceedingly fine, examples of the art of Rembrandt, Franz Hals, Jan Steen, the two Ruisdaels, De Hoogh, Cuyp, and Rubens. The best Dutch critics are familiar with these pictures ; and references to them may be found scattered in such books as Dr. Bode's ' Dutch and Flemish Masters.' But the very existence of the Gallery is scarcely adverted to in England. The minor Dutch and Flemish masters, such as Bega, Codde, Van de Capelle, Claesz, Duyster, Van Delen, Dusart, Berchem, Eeckhout, Karel du Jardin, Duck, De Jongh, Van Goyen, De Keyser, De Heem, Van der Helst, Hondecoeter, Van Huysum, Wouter Knijf, Govert Flinck, Judith Leyster, Jordaens, Nicholas Maas, Jan Molenaer, Adrian van Ostade, Gerard Terborch, Palamedesz, Paul Potter, Pourbus, Van Rossum, Ravestyn, William Romeyn, Schalcken, Sorgh, Storck, William van de Velde, and Cornelius Troost are also amply well represented.

" The outstanding pictures in the Italian school are Andrea Mantegna's ' Judith with the head of Holofernes,' of which Mr. Berenson says : ' The Dublin Judith is one of the masterpieces of Italian art, as composition, as arrangement, as modelling, as movement only to be surpassed by Mantegna himself.' This picture is a companion to the ' Samson and Delilah ' in the National Gallery of London, and to ' The Judgment of Solomon ' in the Louvre. The three were apparently painted on the same piece of linen, and folded in the same way across the centre ; the trace of the fold still remains on each. The Dublin ' Fra Angelico ' is almost as famous as the Mantegna. It is a small panel, supposed by most authorities to be a portion of the predella of the altarpiece in the Saint's own Convent of San Marco at Florence. Of almost equal interest is the extraordinarily fine portrait of a musician, now generally attributed to Sandro Botticelli, formerly variously ascribed to Raffaellino Del Garbo, Ercole Roberti or Francesco Cossa.

" The Italian section of the Gallery contains several other items of almost unique interest. Chief among these is the superb altarpiece by Zenobio de Machiavelli. It is undoubtedly the best of the three or four known examples of this master's work. Remarkable, too, in their way, are the two pictures by Alesandro Oliverio. These two works are the only known pictures by him which now exist. The portrait of a man which is inscribed ' Alesander Oliverius v,' was formerly ascribed to no less a person than Leonardo Da Vinci. The Palmizano (signed in full) is also a striking example of the art of a master who ranks high among the quattrocentisti.

" Neither the English, the French, nor the Spanish school was well represented in the Gallery before Lane took up office. Yet, in the English section were such magnificent works as Reynolds' portrait group of ' George, the Second Earl Temple, his wife and son, and servant ' ; Raeburn's ' David, Eleventh Earl of Buchan ' ; Hogarth's portrait group of ' George the Second, his Queen, son, grandson, and others ' (this was Whistler's favourite picture of the Gallery); and Gains-borough's ' Hugh, Duke of Northumberland.'

" The French section contained an excellent Watteau purchased with the help of a donation from the National Arts Collection Fund.

" The Spanish room contained a fine portrait ' Josua Van Belle' by Murillo, two remarkable pictures of saints by Ribera, a good, small, Goya, and an indifferent one from the same hand.

" Between the years 1904 and 1915 Sir Hugh Lane, by his judicious additions to the Gallery, more than doubled its interest and importance. He made efforts to fill every gap in the collection, to make every group of painters representative, to give the whole a unity and significance which it had not hitherto possessed. His first gift to the Gallery was the striking portrait of John Hoppner, by himself, which he presented in 1904 when he had become one of its Trustees, or Governors. He gave twenty other pictures in his lifetime ; and on his death forty-one were selected from those which he possessed and had bequeathed to his country. He supplemented the Italian school with the superb portrait of Baldassare Castiglione, by Titian ; with the portrait of Cardinal Antonio Ciocchi del Monte Sansovino, by Sebastiano del Piombo ; with a portrait of a gentleman (as fine as most Van Dyeks) by Bernardo Strozzi (Il Prete Genovese) ; with a gorgeously caparisoned lady by Veronese ; and with a ' Diana and Endymion,' which, if not altogether by Tintoretto, was certainly painted in part by the Master and pervaded wholly by his influence.

" The Gallery, before-Lane's advent, contained a charming group of pictures of the silver period

A SPANISH GIRL.

By Goya

of Italian painting by Tiepolo, Canale, Belotto, and Panini. Lane crowned this group with his great decorative composition by Giovanni Batista Piazetta, Tiepolo's son-in-law.

" To the meagre group of Spanish pictures he added the astonishingly impressive El Greco— 'St. Francis in ecstacy,' formerly in the collection of the Conte de Quinto ; and the portrait of a Spanish girl, by Goya, traditionally known as 'La Moue,' which he bought at the Rouart sale in 1912. I have his own catalogue of this sale, which records that he paid no less than £5680 for this small picture, which was only valued by the experts at £3000. The French Press at the time made a great stir about this purchase, and I remember sending Lane an article on his prowess, which appeared, I think, in the *Echo de Paris*, and was entitled ' La folie des Enchères.'

" To the English school in the Irish National Gallery, Lane added the two great Gainsborough portraits of Mrs. King and Anne Houghton, afterwards Duchess of Cumberland ; the Gainsborough ' Landscape with Cattle,' from the Grenfell collection ; Romney's ' Portrait of a Lady ' (the one he discovered under the pseudo Lawrence. A reproduction of the picture before it was cleaned appears in the margin of the Medici print which was afterwards done from it) ; two Hogarth groups of the MacKinnon family and the Western family ; the Constable portrait of a child in a landscape ; the magnificent Lawrence from the Vere Foster collection, of Lady Elizabeth Foster, afterwards Duchess of Devonshire, as fine an example of the pathetic fallacy as exists in paint ; the

Reynolds portrait of Mrs. Frances Fortescue ; the Romney portrait of his wife ; the Gainsborough portrait of his brother ; and several others.

" He practically created a French room in the Gallery, giving no fewer than four Poussins, two Chardins, the great Claude from the Choiseul collection, and ' The Broken Doll,' not to be sur- passed in its degree by any other picture of the size by Greuze.

" The Gallery, though containing a Rembrandt interior, a Rembrandt landscape, and Rembrandt portraits of an old man and a young man, con- tained no Rembrandt portrait of a woman.   Lane remedied this deficiency with a most famous picture, which was formerly in the collections of Count Pourtalès, Prince Demidoff, and many others.   To the Dutch and Flemish school he also added a large and excellent Van Goyen—' The Winter. Palace of the King of Bohemia '—more prosaically described in the catalogue as ' A view of Rhein-on-the-Ems ' ; a boy, by Sir Anthony Van Dyck, and an elderly woman by Ferdinand Bol."

It was at the National Gallery I last saw Hugh. I had arrived on Easter Monday, 1915, from America, and I did not hear until the next day that he was in Dublin. I had a note from him : " Dear Aunt Augusta, what a pleasant surprise ! I have just received Yeats' card telling me that you are here. I wonder if you can possibly manage to look in at the National Gallery between 11 a.m. and 2 p.m. I am very busy hanging an exhibition of the Provost's pictures at the Gallery. We have a Board meeting at 2.30, I have another engagement

at 4. On Thursday I leave for London, on Friday
for New York ! All news when we meet. If you
cannot turn up I will call at Bailey's between
6 and 7."

I had some work that kept me at the Theatre,
but he came to dinner, and the next afternoon I
spent with him at the National Gallery, but Yeats
being with us we had no intimate talk. He took
us through the rooms to show me all he had done
and all he had given in those thirteen months. He
was proud of his work and well pleased. I said to
Mr. Bailey, to whose house I returned, that I had no
more anxiety about the French pictures. I felt certain by seeing Hugh's renewed devotion to his work
in Ireland that he would bring them back to us.

His life's desire had been accomplished ; he
had charge of a great Gallery already enriched by
his bounty ; his heart was in it, and in that other
Gallery he had created. I said to him as he gave
us tea in the Directors' room, with its look of
dignity, its mahogany bookcases, and its books, "I
am glad to see you in your right setting at last."

I like to remember him there, in authority, in
love with his work, in harmony with all that was
about him.

There are others who remember him in the
same way. The other day Oliver Gogarty quoted to
Yeats some lines from a poem of Lionel Johnson's,
saying, "You will know who these lines describe—

> "'Magnificence and Grace,
> Excellent courtesy ;
> A brightness on the face,
> Airs of high memory,' "

and Yeats had nodded "Yes," so well they fitted
Hugh.

CHAPTER XVI

His first serious anxiety about money came towards the end. Though I hold to it that the keeping back of that Rembrandt was all for Ireland's good, its sale to the Cape Town Gallery would have brought in ready money, whereas he had to pay out money for the pictures he bought in its place. Then he bought many pictures at the Grenfell sale, and as we know for him to bid was to send up prices. Some spoke after his death as if he had but thought of his own profit in doing this, but I knew it was not so by what he had said to me at the time; and Alec Martin also had told me he had crippled himself for the sake of his friends. It had troubled him that they should be forced to sell at a time when the trade in pictures had languished as it were under the shadow of the brooding war; for there was misgiving in the minds of those who best knew of the nations' unrest, and how the armies, trained and over-trained, had become like a nut over-ripe, that must be loosed with the first stir in the air.

So I was happy when meeting with Mrs. Grenfell I found she had nothing but kind memories of Hugh, as she told me how good he had been at that troublesome time, and of his generosity through it all. For I knew that it was

his buying so largely at that sale that had left him
with heavy bills to meet when war was indeed
declared. A year or two earlier this would have
meant nothing to him, when, as Alec Martin says,
" he had but to walk into Bond Street and sell a
picture to get what money he would." But the
war had crippled him, " the worst season on record,"
he wrote to Mr. Bodkin, " and the dealers against
my things." His creditors wanted their money.
" The hounds are after me," he said in his depression to Gerald Kelly. He wrote me a very
sad letter on the last day of 1914, saying : " I
suppose that it is always what one cares for most
that gives us most trouble and anxiety. In my
case it is the probable losing of all my pictures,
which I must do unless I find a large sum by the
1st of April. I feel, however, that one's troubles
ought not to count at this time, considering what
those have to suffer at the front. . . . Best of
wishes to you all for the New Year."

He had been used to take money troubles
lightly. Mr. Duncan says he told him once he
had to raise £30,000 by a certain date, " and I was
appalled, it seemed such a colossal sum, and he
had failed so far in getting it. He was amused
when he saw my despair. He took my arm and
said, ' Don't worry, it will be all right. You've
got it rather out of proportion. Think of a char-
woman trying to raise thirty shillings and you'll get
the idea.' "

But now, in war time, when he asked his bank
to advance the money he needed it was doubtful.
I went to see its manager, Mr. Meagher, in the City
the other day, an old and good friend of Hugh's,

and one I had often met at Lindsey House, and I asked him about these difficulties. He said it was £30,000 Hugh had owed for the Grenfell pictures. Agnew had them in his care, and at last it was decided that if the money were not forthcoming next day they would have to be sold.

Hugh owed the Bank already £30,000, and there would have been no trouble about it, or a further advance at any other time, but the war and the fall in pictures had made bankers nervous. But on that very last day Mr. Meagher, saying he himself, had he the money, would not hesitate to trust Hugh with it, persuaded the Directors to lend it. He took this news to Hugh in the evening, there was no telephone to Lindsey House—Hugh used to say that he wouldn't have one because people so often said to him, "If you were on the telephone I would have asked you to lunch." He found him just sitting down to eat his dinner, a piece of cake and two oranges. Anxiety had left him no stomach for more. He took the news quietly, and celebrated it by taking him to dine at the Good Intent, "a very pleasant evening." And then when Mr. Meagher said he must take out some insurance policies, he began to cavil and grumble at the cost.

His immediate anxiety was thus quieted, but there was still £60,000 of debt. He had undertaken to go to America to appraise for Lloyds some pictures damaged in a burning ship, and he kept to this promise, though it had been in part to look at the market there and free himself through it that he had accepted the commission.

As he was at Liverpool leaving for America

further relief came.   He had a cable telling him
that the Titian " Man in a Red Cap," and Holbein
" Thomas Cromwell," had been sold in America.
He was free again.   The first use he made of his
freedom was to cable to Christie's making an offer
of £10,000 for a portrait to be painted by Sargent
for the benefit of the Red Cross.

A letter from New York, and that only reached
me after his death, though written on April 28,
said : " It is beginning to be very pleasant here.
I am quite sorry to be leaving next Saturday.   I
was fortunate in selling my Holbein and Red
Cap Titian the day before I sailed—by cable,
through an agent, and only found out on my
arrival that it was to Mr. Frick.   Unfortunately
he got them at nearly cost price.   I am happy at
getting the Titian installed in such a famous
collection.   Quinn has twice dined with me here,
and he took me a delightful motor ride on Sunday,
and also to a play.   The exciting air of New York
made a wreck of me for the first week, but now
I feel better than I have done for years !   All
other news when we meet."

On May 5 I was at Coole with my son.
Bernard Shaw and his wife were with us, and
Augustus John.   I was to leave the next day to
take charge of the Abbey Plays, which were just
being taken to London ; I looked forward to seeing
Hugh there very soon.   But at midday I had a
cable from New York, from John Quinn, saying he
had heard of the sinking of the *Lusitania*, and
hoped Hugh Lane was safe.   I enclosed it in a
letter to Yeats, saying : " I had enclosed this
morning.   The postman had brought a rumour,

and then there was a wire saying the *Lusitania* was lost, but this was the first I heard of Hugh being on board. I have wired to Ruth for news, but no answer so far, and I am almost without hope, for I am sure he would have sent me a message if he had come to land—though it is possible he might be wounded or unconscious. I had a terrible feeling of depression all yesterday and last night. I thought it must be the dislike of leaving home and going to London, and put off going till to-morrow night. Now I think it was presentiment. It is too dreadful to think of. . . ."

The rest may be told in this letter from his sister, who, when the news reached her, had gone over to Queenstown. She wrote to Alec Martin, Hugh's devoted friend, who had gone to see him off from Liverpool three weeks before:

" There is no hope of finding him alive now. . . . It is not even certain his dear body can be found, as there are currents running off shore round this coast.

" The Mr. L. I saw yesterday had been raving for two days from the shock, but was quite calm when I spoke to him ; he had sometimes played Bridge with Hugh. My uncle motored us down to Queenstown in the afternoon to inquire for Lady Allan, whom Mr. L. told me Hugh had played Bridge with the night before. She saw me, though badly hurt, very bruised, and they think a slight fracture of the thigh. Hugh came up to her when she was standing ready, holding her two young daughters by the hand. He had no life-belt on. There was only a small one to be had. He then said (he was pale, but quite calm) he would try and find the Pearsons in case he could help them. He walked towards the bow of the ship, and that was the last she saw of him. Mrs. Pearson's body has not been found yet." He had said also, "This is a sad end for us all."

Mr. J. B. Yeats has written to me of him: "I don't think there is anything so fine in life as a man sufficient unto himself, or so rare. It is what is called a 'personality.' Hugh Lane was a man sufficient unto himself, and that self—what was it? A strange combination of extreme sensitiveness with an absolute intrepidity. Indeed, he was so sensitive that it was to me a constant surprise that he could not be frightened. Given these conditions of fearlessness and sensitiveness there had resulted such a plenitude of resource that I verily believe what he most enjoyed was a desperate situation. Remembering this, I have speculated in my mind as to what he must have thought, or did, during those last few moments of his life when he stood on the deck of the *Lusitania*. Of two things only am I sure—that he was not angry, and that he was not afraid. Yet, because of the sensitiveness of his mind he would miss nothing of the dreadful inevitableness. I suppose that all his thoughts went away from himself to what was before his eyes—the women and the children especially. . . ."

Mrs. Hindé was told afterwards by a steward who had been on board that he had seen Sir Hugh Lane at the last, helping women and children to get into the boats. I cannot be certain this is true, but I am certain he met the end in a way that was in tune with the undaunted courage, the passionate generosity, of his dedicated life.

CHAPTER XVII

THE CODICIL OF FORGIVENESS

WHEN I had to write about the rebuffs Hugh had to suffer from Dublin I felt very sad at having to show to the outside world these "wounds with which he had been wounded in the house of his friends." And yet I could not tell the story of his passionate pilgrimage without telling of the thorns and thickets he had to go through. I have also told, and found the telling difficult, of the impatience and excitability that at some times made these difficulties harder for his helpers and friends.

But all the time I had thought that it would be with positive joy I would tell how the ungraciousness shown him in Ireland had been outdone by that shown to him later in London.

And yet I have only pain now in the telling. Personal sorrow and the advance of years and the grittiness of official discourtesy have done away with any joy of battle. And if " to understand all is to forgive all," then also what we do not understand we must forgive.

About the time (September 15, 1911) Hugh had

taken away his group of French pictures, his conditional gift, from Dublin, he wrote to me: "My operation is to take place in about a week's time, and then I am supposed to go back to the 'rest cure' for two months. Some days I feel that I won't be alive then, on others I think that I don't require any rest. The Doctors say that I can never be really rid of neurasthenia, I have left it too long. But they say by living a quiet life without worry (!) that I shall feel much better. As soon as I can get my affairs in order, establish the Gallery and make my will, I shall not much care what happens."

His will, made in anger that autumn (October 11), I have already given.

But his anger had soon begun to slacken. Only a month later Yeats wrote to me in a letter dictated to Mr. Ezra Pound: "November 5, 1913. I saw Lane last night. He says you may write to your subscribers that we hope to carry through the Gallery project after the change in the Irish Government, though we have been defeated for the moment through passing conditions of political and economic strife. At first he said that you could write that the collection would be kept together, but afterwards said, 'No, that statement might get back to Dublin.' He doesn't want the National Memorial" (I had made some proposal of one) "because he says his supporters are all tired. He thinks the whole thing should be allowed to rest for the present. He says he wants time to recover his own enthusiasm. He then said: 'But you may be very sure I have no desire to leave the present Dublin collection to represent me.' * His plan is to found an International Gallery in London, to use his French pictures for it ; but only if sufficient endowments are forthcoming to make a really great gallery. If he can do this he is convinced that his prestige will be so great that it will be impossible for Dublin to refuse his next offer. He will make a completely new collection for Dublin. He says he is tired of the old one, and knows much more now. He needed no urging, and is, I really think, as determined about Ireland as we are ourselves. He evidently intends to take the Dublin National Gallery post, though he professes to have lost all desire for it. He has re-made his will. He had left everything to the Modern Gallery, but has now left his money to the Irish National Gallery and his (French) pictures to England. Belfast has no chance of getting anything from him. They refused a painting of a mother and child because they couldn't see a wedding ring (the hands were rather roughly finished)."

I wrote in answer : " I had been anxiously watching for your letter, and now it has come and is the greatest relief. I feel Hugh is behaving so well, that is the great thing. He is extraordinarily generous and forgiving. . . . I don't like the idea of any pictures going to London, but if Hugh comes to the National Gallery all that may change. I am glad he is going away for a time

---

* He wrote to me a few days later (November 12, 1913) : " You give me much too much credit for my intentions toward Dublin. But I am simply ashamed to have my name associated with a bad collection, and would like to make it really good of a kind. I don't think that I will ever bring back the same pictures, as I could best work up a fresh interest (to myself as well as Dublin) by making a fresh collection."

to get his nerves right and forget some of the annoyances."

And I wrote to Hugh: "I have heard from Yeats of his talk with you, and I am very happy about it. All I want to be able to say to my American people is that there is hope in the future —it seemed so ignominious to say we had quite failed. And of course for the sake of my descendants I am glad to think there is a chance of a fine Gallery for Ireland. And I am best pleased of all at being more than ever proud of you! I am afraid at moments my own indignation and temper would have made me sell the pictures at Christie's to show Dublin what it had lost, but you have kept your generosity and nobility in spite of all. Of course I shall feel jealous if London gets any pictures, but perhaps ' the longest way round is the shortest way home,' and that it is ' reculer pour mieux sauter.' With love (and pride), Yr. aff. A. G."

And two months later (January 17, 1914) there is other evidence, in an American paper, the *Art News*, that his forgiveness had begun: "As to Sir Hugh Lane, he says the Municipal Art Gallery is now in temporary quarters in Harcourt Street, and he has been agitating to secure a permanent building, and hopes that when Home Rule comes he will get one. He thinks Municipalities rather slow to appreciate the educational value of fine paintings."

As to the story of his troubles with the London National Gallery, Yeats, summing up the case after a controversy, in the *Observer* of January 21, 1917, says: " On July 27th, 1913, Lane wrote to

Sir Charles Holroyd: ' These pictures are complementary to the collection I have already given them (the Dublin Corporation), and the other pictures given and subscribed for by others. I think if they were hung in the National Gallery or the Tate Gallery it might encourage the Corporation to fulfil my conditions.'

" A little later, when it had become probable that the Dublin Corporation would refuse the building upon the Bridge over the Liffey, that he had asked for, he got a letter from one of the London Trustees asking if there was any chance of the National Gallery receiving a gift of the pictures ' or would the loan, if accepted, be a loan in reality for the aid of Dublin.' A gift of the pictures to London would have implied the foundation of some kind of International Gallery to contain them, for neither the National Gallery nor the Tate can, by their constitution, permanently exhibit modern Continental works of art.

" It must have been about this date (I have no means of fixing the exact date) that Lord Curzon suggested to him the foundation of such a gallery." (Hugh wrote to me on July 31, 1913: " I am busy taking down my ' conditional gift.' It is my last trump card. . . . I have had a good many letters from Directors of English and Scotch galleries asking for the loan of my pictures—Aitken, Sir C. Holroyd. Lord Curzon came to see me—pressed me to give them to London if they got a new building. I refused, but offered to lend them to the National Gallery. This they are considering. If it comes off it may help to bring the Corporation to its senses.") " There was always someone at his elbow to suggest that he should give to England—so rich in pictures—what he had promised to Ireland in her poverty. He replied on August 8: ' As I still hope that my work in Dublin will not prove a failure, I cannot think of giving them to any other gallery at present. But the gallery that, not having such, refused the loan of them for one or two years, would appear to be quite unworthy of them as a gift. I confess to being quite out of sympathy with the English National Gallery.'

" On August 12 the Secretary of the National Gallery replied, unconditionally accepting the loan of the pictures. A few days later came the Dublin refusal, and its refusal was aggravated by a disgraceful Press attack. In a cautious interview in the *Manchester Guardian*, Lane spoke of a possible international Gallery. He took his French pictures from Dublin, sent them to the National Gallery, where they are still in the cellars, and changed his will. He had left everything he possessed to the Dublin Municipal Gallery, but now, with the exception of these pictures left to London, he gave all to the Dublin National Gallery. Dublin was still, it is plain, his chief interest.

" Yet in letters to Lady Gregory, who always pleaded for Ireland and the work there, he spoke of Ireland with great bitterness. We were all very angry, less indeed with the Corporation than the newspapers, and some of us thought that only the sale of the pictures in the open market would prove their value. I myself printed as a pamphlet, ' Poems written in Discouragement 1912-1913,' and certainly those poems are as bitter as the letters Mr. MacColl has quoted. That is the manner of our intemperate Irish nature (and I think the Elizabethan English were as volatile); we are quick to speak against our countrymen, but slow to give up our work. I once said to John Synge, ' Do you write out of love or hate of Ireland ? ' and he replied, ' I have often asked myself that question '; and yet no success outside Ireland seemed of interest to him. Sir Hugh Lane wrote and felt bitterly, and yet when the feeling was at its height, while the Dublin slanders were sounding in his ears, he made a will leaving all he possessed except the French pictures, to a Dublin gallery. A few days after writing Ireland had so completely ' disillusioned ' him that he could not even bear ' to hear of his early happy days in Galway,' he had bequeathed to Dublin an in- comparable treasure.

" Now a wonderful thing happened which certainly did not incline his mind to London. The Trustees, after they had accepted his loan un- conditionally, after they had hung his pictures, after he had announced in Dublin (he was still thinking of Dublin) the day when they were to be first shown to the public, decided to make con- ditions. They would only hang a small collection chosen by themselves ; fifteen pictures which they considered well worthy of temporary exhibition in the National collection, and they would not hang even these fifteen unless he promised to bequeath them to the Gallery in his will. The selection was capricious or careless ; it rejected, for instance, Daumier's ' Don Quixote,' according to the mind of some of us a master work surpassing all the rest in beauty. Sir Hugh Lane, though his new will was only some three months old, refused both conditions. It became exceedingly difficult to get any reparation made to him for the Dublin Press attack; all his enemies were heartened. The rumour ran, ' The National Gallery in London has refused the Lane pictures because they are not good enough.' He considered himself abominably treated, and remained so far as I know of this mind to the end."

In his answer to that letter of the Trustees, which had met him on his return from New York, he says (February 12, 1914): " Its contents were an unpleasant surprise for me, rendered no more agreeable by its singularly ungracious tone. . . . The loan of pictures was proposed not by me, but by Lord Curzon and others connected with the National Gallery who persuaded me to make a formal offer. In that letter I submitted a list of the pictures from the Dublin collection that I had in mind, pictures most of them known to Sir Charles Holroyd and familiar to other students of painting. My letter was duly considered by the Board, and my offer formally accepted by your letter of August 12th on their behalf. . . . The collection had been accepted, arranged, publicly announced, and a date fixed for its opening. I am now informed that the Board have reversed the decision communicated to me, that they have made a selection of fifteen pictures out of thirty-five (about), and that they will be good enough to accept those as a loan on condition I pledge myself ultimately to present or bequeath them,"

In a later letter he says: "I cannot even return the pictures to Dublin without removing the slur that has been cast upon them."

The fifteen pictures chosen for exhibition from the thirty-nine were: "The Present," Alfred Stevens; "Summer Morning," "Papal Palace, Avignon," and "Italian Peasant," Corot; "Fontainebleau," Barye; "Duc d'Orleans," Ingres; "Study of a Woman," Madrazo; "Eva Gonzales," and "Concert aux Tuileries," Manet; "Skating in Holland," Jongkind; "En Voyage," Mancini; "La Plage," Degas; "The Law Courts," Forain; "Still Life," Bonvin; "The Toilet," Puvis de Chavannes.

Among those left out were Monet's "Vetheuil"; Daubigny's "Portrait of Daumier"; three landscapes by Courbet; Rousseau's "Moonlight"; Daumier's "Don Quixote and Sancho Panza"; Renoir's "Les Parapluies"; and "The Beheading of John the Baptist," by Puvis de Chavannes.

Hugh had said in his letter of February 12, to the Trustees: "I would never have dreamed of submitting my pictures for selection to members of the Board. I took for granted the Director was their adviser in matters of art. If that were not so I should have been ready to refer the matter to any other expert agreed upon between the Board and myself."

This authoritative opinion was not long in coming to him, for he wrote to me from London later in February: "I am rather enjoying myself with the National Gallery here. After sending me a list of the pictures that they would kindly hang, if I promised to give them later, they asked

MacColl and Sargent to make a written report. They are both very hard to please about pictures, but they have sent in very good reports, particularly praising most of the pictures that the Trustees left out. I have written to them rather strongly."

He wrote to me a little later: " The National Gallery here is coming to its senses, and is likely to offer the Tate for the showing of my pictures. They are also taking immediate steps to found a Gallery for foreign contemporary art ! "

Yet in spite of Mr. Sargent and Mr. MacColl's reports, " that are quite satisfactory from my point of view," the pictures were sent back to the cellars where they remained until 1917. They were only brought out and exhibited after we had publicly asked that according to Hugh Lane's direction as written in his codicil they should be returned to Dublin.

I do not think that this discourtesy was the cause of his revoking his bequest ; that was rather through his continued interest in his own country. Yet it was surely a good reason for such revoking.

I was myself at Lindsey House at the time these pictures were hung ready for exhibition in a room of the National Gallery, and with Ruth Shine I went to see them on Sir Charles Holroyd's invitation. He asked for a list of friends we might like to have invited to the private view. I was puzzled at missing so many of what we had considered the best pictures, but diffidence in the presence of exact knowledge did not allow me to venture any questions.

I read the other day in an article on Renoir

in a New York magazine: "When in 1917 'Les Parapluies' was placed in the National Gallery some hundred English artists and amateurs seized the opportunity of sending the Master a testimony of their admiration. In this they said: 'Dès l'instant où votre tableau s'est trouvé installé parmi les chefs-d'œuvre des maitres anciens, nous avons eu la joie de constater qu'un de nos contemporains avait pris place d'emblée parmi les grands maitres de la tradition Européenne.'"

Yet in 1914 that picture had not been even thought worthy of hanging with other modern pictures. It had been one of those left in a cellar by those in authority at the National Gallery.

I quote again from Yeats: "His interest in Dublin was returning; he had become Director of the National Gallery there. Dublin became as little distasteful to him as any place can be to a man whose nerves are kept on edge by bad health and the desire to achieve more than the public opinion of the time permits. He took a keener interest in the Municipal Gallery and began to give it gifts, adding to it, for instance, a fine bust by Rodin. After all, Dublin had founded a gallery for him, and exhibited his French pictures for years, and that gallery was well attended, and among the rest by working people. His most vehement years had been expended in its service; it could but remain his chief work, his monument to future generations, and lacking important pictures that he had gathered for it, that noble monument would lack a limb. Was it not more natural to wish to leave behind him a small perfect thing with the pattern of his own mind than to be

LES PARAPLUIES. ·

By Renoir.

half remembered for a bequest soon lost in the growing richness of a London Gallery ? More than all the rest, he was Irish, and of a family that had already in their passion and in their thought given great gifts to Ireland."

It was on February 3, 1915, that he wrote, with his own hand and signature, what has been called " The Codicil of Forgiveness."

Some ten days after the sinking of the *Lusitania*, Hugh Lane's executors were at Lindsey House, and with his sister looked in all places where he had kept papers, for he had, before sailing for America, spoken of making a will to take the place of the one he had dictated to his sister in 1913, and which was acted upon in the end as no later one was found.

I was tired and sad, and went to lie down in my old room upstairs. My mind was upon that will he had made in anger, and I longed that another might be found in which, as I believed, those harsh words about Dublin would have been left out, and the pictures restored, as I felt certain Hugh had intended to restore them. After a while I felt a sudden conviction that had he made such a will, it might be found in the desk of his room at the Dublin National Gallery. I had only been once in it, and had not taken notice of a desk, but I went down at once to Ruth Shine and found her alone, the others having gone. I told her this, and though she did not think it likely there would be anything there I urged her to write at once to Dublin to have the desk searched. She wrote to Mr. Duncan, who took the letter to Mr.

Strickland, Hugh's Registrar, who afterwards became Director for a short while in his place. Mr. Strickland found no will there, but found a sealed envelope addressed to Mrs. Shine. It contained a codicil written in Hugh's own handwriting and signed by him, signed (or initialled) three times. I give a facsimile of it.

There was no doubt in his sister's mind or mine that he had written it believing it to be legal, and that in addressing it to her who had the keeping of his will, he had intended it to be carried out. But she had at once noticed that the signature had not been witnessed, and that it was therefore not valid in English law, although it would be valid in Scotland, or in the trenches.

I did not know if the codicil could yet be accepted as legal. But I rejoiced that Hugh had shown this great forgiveness of those in Dublin who had roughly driven away his offered gift, and that he was in full reconcilement with his country when he died.

His signature has never been questioned, but because of the lack of a witness to it, the pictures with which it is concerned have become the property of the London National Gallery.

Memorials asking that Hugh Lane's last wishes as expressed in his codicil may be carried out, as well as a resolution to the same effect passed at a great meeting held at the Dublin Mansion House in 1918, have been laid before the Trustees by me as the Trustee he had named ; by the Lord Mayor and Corporation of Dublin ; by representatives of the Learned and Educational Societies of Dublin, including the Vice-Chancellor of the University of

3rd Feb. 1915

This is a codicil to
my last will. To the
effect that the group
of pictures now at
London National Gallery
I had bequeathed to the
institution. I leave
to the City of
providing that a suit
building is provided
them within 5 years
of death. The group of
... I have lent to

Belfast) given to the Municipal Gallery in Harcourt St. If a Building is provided within 5 years the whole collection will be housed together. The sole Trustee in this question — to be my Aunt Lady Gregg. She is to appoint any additional trustees she may think fit.

I also wish that the pictures are on loan of the (National Gallery of Ireland

... ...

Hugh Lane

I would like my friend
Tom Bodkin to ... ...
to help in the obtaining
of these and failing his
... ... for Dublin.
... within 5 years a ...
... ...
the ... of ... ...
the ... ...
... to be used ... the ...
... to fulfill the purpose
of ... Hugh Lane

3rd Feb. 1915

Dublin, the President of the National University, the Chief Commissioner of the Board of National Education, the Archbishop of Dublin (representing the Royal Irish Academy), the Presidents of the Royal Hibernian Academy, the Royal Institute of Architects, the Royal Society of Antiquarians, the Royal College of Physicians, the Director of the National Gallery, and the Principal of Alexandra College; by English artists who had already given of their work to the Dublin Gallery— among them Max Beerbohm, George Clauson, Augustus John, William Nicholson, Briton Riviere, William Rothenstein, Charles Shannon, William Strang, and Wilson Steer. And an appeal has been made to the Prime Minister by Irish artists and writers, including Sir William Barrett, John Eglinton, Mark Fisher, Katherine Tynan, Nathaniel Hone, Douglas Hyde, Sir John Lavery, George Morrow, Standish O'Grady, Sir William Orpen, George Russell (A. E.), Dora Sigerson Shorter, James Stephens, Bernard Shaw, Jack B. Yeats, and W. B. Yeats.

Although several among the Trustees have recognised that this is a matter where a greater thing than legality is concerned, they do not as a whole feel at liberty to give up a bequest that has become their legal property, except through legislation that will set them free from possible reproach from any who may put the legal before the moral claim. We have, therefore, appealed to Parliament to pass a Bill legalising this codicil, as it had already done in the case of wills signed without a witness by soldiers who lost their lives in the War.

As to the moral claim, those who knew Hugh best have no doubt as to what his intention was "at the time he wrote the codicil, and up to the time of his death." His sister, who had no great mind to see Dublin's ungraciousness to him so easily forgiven, yet says in her statutory declaration, " I have no doubt whatever that he considered the codicil legal."

Mr. Alec Martin, who " would have preferred to have seen the pictures placed in London," declares that on the way to Liverpool, where he went to see the last of Hugh as he set out for that journey from which he was not to return, " he spoke of Ireland and of his recent visit to Dublin with the greatest affection, and he gave me to understand that his mind was made up that it should be after all the destination of his pictures."

Mr. John Quinn, the distinguished lawyer and art collector, writing from New York, tells how Hugh on that last visit had given him to understand Dublin should be the destination of his pictures, "as he had always wanted them to go there "; Mr. S. O'Kelly, an Alderman of Dublin, told at the Mansion House meeting that having seen Hugh at a picture gallery in New York, and asked him if he would return the pictures to Dublin, he answered, "They will all be in Dublin yet." And that was but a day or two before he sailed in the *Lusitania*.

These are his last recorded words on the matter.

And this is the record of his last day in Ireland in that 1915 Easter week.

He had been urged with insistence in London

to promise his collection should remain there if London should outstrip Dublin in the promise or foundation of a gallery, and this idea as we know had for a short time tempted him. But as if to secure himself against further importunity we see in the sworn statement of Mrs. Duncan, the Curator of the Harcourt Street Gallery, that on that last day, that was but two days before he sailed from Liverpool, he being in the Harcourt Street Gallery, said he wished to bring back the pictures to Dublin, and would be content if the Corporation reaffirmed their already expressed intention of building a gallery (and this has since been done). "For," he said, "I wish to bring the pictures back to Dublin as soon as possible; they could hang here pending the building of any gallery the Corporation may decide upon."

It does not seem as if evidence could be any stronger. Yet five years have passed away since his death. Chief Secretaries have one after another promised sympathy and help; the last, Mr. Macpherson, has given it, carrying the needed Bill before the Cabinet, believing as he said to me after he had examined all the evidence "absolutely convinced Hugh Lane intended that codicil to be carried out at the time he wrote it and at the time of his death." But Parliament has been occupied with many things, some it may be of less lasting importance than this; and Ireland is out of fashion, and the London Trustees still hold to their legal right.

And yet they have been set what I must think a fine example by the Trustees of the Irish National Gallery, the residuary legatees of Hugh Lane's will.

For that promise of ten thousand pounds to the Red Cross Fund for a picture by Mr. Sargent might well have been contested in law, and advice was not wanting that this should be done. But those legatees, knowing Hugh personally as they did, were certain it was his wish that his splendid promise should be fulfilled, and so carried out that wish, to their own loss except in honour.

I write this in May, 1920, just five years after Hugh's death. I have, I will not say wasted, but spent unceasingly time and energy and strength that might have been better used than in refuting quibbles, striving to carry out the trust that he placed in me. I have written the story in full from month to month through those years, but this is not the place to give it. I have knocked at many doors. Some helpers, among them John Redmond and W. F. Bailey and Robert Ross, have died ; some, like that good friend Mr. Birrell, are out of office. Yeats is in America. But when one helper fails another comes. Those who are for us are stronger than those who are against us. I have never given up assurance, because as I have felt and said from the beginning, we have "the Cloud of Witnesses" on our side.

CHAPTER XVIII

MEDITATIONS AND MEMORIES

FEBRUARY 18, 1920. I went to London last September, having found that the writing of this story of Hugh's life must be done by me or left undone. And finding also that through some untoward mistrust or misunderstanding, the letters and documents from which a part of it should have been told were withheld from me, I turned to find in place of them some chronicle in the memory of his friends, so each afternoon I went out from the little house in Chelsea that had been my son's to look for any of these who might have come back from their summering. But they were few, for the sun was yet warm and the branches of the trees were full of leaves. Yet some I found, and these were kind, and searched their minds for such things as they could remember of him. And when I returned home in the evening I would write down my day's gains, what I had gathered through a memory that had been trained through much gathering of folk-lore. And this seemed akin to folk-lore, the tradition coming through many memories, and that come together makes a whole. Some of what I reaped I have already given, and some I am giving here.

Of the artists I looked for, Sir William Orpen

was away, still painting that great hall at Versailles
where the Peace Conference had held its meetings.
But he was back before I left London in November,
and on, I think, my last evening in London I
dined with him in the Corner House, that is only
two doors from mine. Lady Orpen and her
daughter were there, and one or two guests, and
through dinner time we talked of the war and of
France. But later, in the drawing-room, he said:
" Of course Hugh and I came near to quarrelling
sometimes—he said things that hurt, and I would
say, ' This brings us very near to a break,' and then
he would burst out laughing. He was the most
forgiving man I ever knew. You know how they
treated him in Dublin, they could not believe he
could be so generous without a motive—they said
he wanted them to build a gallery for rubbish he
couldn't sell. It was the same here. Wertheimer
said to me, ' I know now the sort of man he was,
I used not to know it, I used to think it was
humbug when he talked about buying pictures
to give to a gallery. I never thought then it was
true.' "

Then he told me what I have already recorded,
of Hugh's early ignorance of French pictures, and
he went on, "I will tell you a story about him
though it may seem to go against myself. We
went together to Spain. He had no money then,
and I had no money. But when we got to Madrid
I wanted to be enjoying myself and have a good
time. But he would scold me and say, ' How can
you waste money on dinners when there are such
beautiful things to buy ? ' He would hardly eat
enough, he would keep bread and fruit from his

lunch and make it do for his dinner. I didn't like his wanting me to live like that, I was cross. We used to go into antiquity shops together, and in one I saw that pair of figures, Adam and Eve, you see them on the chimney-piece [he took down two fine old pieces of wood carving]. I said, ' Those are what I would like to have, I like them better than anything I have seen.' But they were £20, that would have been a big sum to either of us in those days. Well, we went on in the same way, he going hungry and grumbling at me, and I getting crosser and crosser, so that when he left— he was going on to Rome—I wouldn't go to the station to see him off. And when I went up to my room after he had gone I saw on my bed those two figures. He had bought them without telling me, and left them there as a gift. That is just what he was, giving everything away, denying himself. He thought anything spent on himself was waste. He had a great power of enjoyment for all that, he saw the humour in everything. That kept him from rancour."

October 6. This evening I went in to Mr. Steer's house where Hugh had so often been. The artist had painted there a portrait of her who had given Hugh that short dream " that had been so delightful in the beginning," but as it faded he and his criticisms had been less helpful and the sitter had come less frequently, and in the end the picture itself had vanished away.

He is glad he does not know those who now inhabit Lindsey House, he likes to think of it always as he knew it. He had signed the request to the London Trustees asking for the return of the French pictures; he knew that Hugh had always kept to that one idea, that one purpose in his mind. He thinks that " as to portraits we are happy in having as well as the Sargent the Mancini. He is sitting alert, on the edge of the chair, as he used to do, though it cannot be compared with the Mancini portrait of you—that wonderful thing." He had thought when he saw the Kelly portrait of Hugh unfinished that the head was very fine, though not the composition. But the El Greco Hugh gave as his first gift to the Dublin National Gallery may also count as one, " a wonderful likeness."

Mr. Steer harbours a little regret in his memory. He recalls a day when Hugh came in and he offered him lunch, sending down for a cottage pie he had used but a part of. But it had been eaten downstairs, and Hugh had only bread and cheese. He had not minded, " he never cared what he had "— it was his host whose hospitality was wounded. It is just such a consuming thought, " a worm that dieth not," that regret for a lost opportunity, that grips a liberal housewife in the night time.

I spoke of Yeats' line in a Cuchulain play, " his life as a bird's flight from tree to tree," as appropriate to Hugh's swift, soaring transit. But he said the lines I had sent him awhile ago from another play were yet closer; he had quoted them to Mr. MacColl, who had thought of putting them on the first page of the Memoir if he had written it:—

" the laughing lip
That shall not turn from laughing whatever rise or fall,
The heart that knows no bitterness although betrayed by all.
The hand that loves to scatter, the life like a gambler's throw."

And strangely enough I had not thought of these of late, while he had kept them all the time in his mind.

On one of those autumn evenings Mr. Charles Ricketts came to see me bringing a sheaf of beautiful lilies, perhaps in memory of the day when Hugh had called on him and Shannon, and although or because they were out had filled the vases in their rooms with flowers. " He was almost criminally generous," he said, " but almost criminally penurious to himself." He remembers him once at the door of Christie's; rain had just come on, but he would not hear of taking a cab.— " Don't you know what I've just given for that picture, how can I afford a cab ? " He told me of a tragedy at an American house where Hugh had been invited to come from New York and see some pictures, and while finding them admirable he, as usual saying out his conviction, said that the best would be better seen with some change of light or position. The owner did not take the proposal well, he was not used to have his judgment questioned, he had already said his collection was as good as any to be found in Europe, and Hugh's spirit had, I imagine, already burned within him. But the host turned his back, would not speak further to his guest. He could not lessen his ungraciousness even through the meal to which he had been invited, " and it seemed a very long time," said Hugh, " till I could escape to the train."

And some days later I was at tea with Mr. Ricketts and Mr. Charles Shannon. I had indeed invited myself, for I felt a longing to sit in spacious rooms looking at beautiful things. They showed me a table in the studio where we were sitting, a long marble one against the wall, and said it had been in the centre of the room, and Hugh had told them they ought to change its place, and they had cried out against this. But lately they had been making some changes, and when all was arranged they suddenly remembered that this table was now standing exactly where Hugh had seen it as its right and inevitable place in his mind's eye.

October 28. I was with Sir John Lavery this afternoon, and spoke of his kindness in helping Hugh when the Modern Gallery was first spoken of. He had forgotten this and said: " After his death, when I knew what sort of man he was, I felt sorry I had not done more for him." But I knew he had done a great deal for him when he was but little known, giving his own name to the appeal for a Dublin Gallery, and going to plead with Whistler on its behalf, and that with such success that Whistler promised to give a picture " to show his sympathy with Irishmen in the endeavour."

I think he was pleased at having this brought to mind, and he told me that Belfast, where he had been the other day, is now asking for a modern gallery " because the students say if they want to see fine work they have to go to London—or Dublin ! " He showed me a report of some advice he had given there at a meeting : " Artists might arrange good exhibitions, but unless they had the support of the people they could not go on, or unless they had a power like that of the late Sir Hugh Lane behind them, one of the greatest experts on modern masters, who, in spite of the greatest difficulties raised by those he worked for, had left them one of the greatest heritages that any city could possess." Yet his gentleness could not leave even these words unsoftened, and he had spoken of the needs and poverty of Dublin at that ungracious time. He had said also that " but for a technicality omitted in his last will, which enabled the National Gallery of London to take possession of the French pictures Sir Hugh Lane had collected for Dublin, the Municipal Gallery would have been second to no other gallery of modern pictures in Europe." And he had spoken at another gathering of Hugh's " untiring zeal." One of our obdurate opponents is coming to dine with him to-night, and he will tell him that no one who understood how Hugh's life had been given up to that one aim could imagine he had not meant his wish for the return of the pictures to be accomplished. Also, he is going to paint one of them, and, as I said, a portrait painter is a dangerous man for his sitter to offend.

October 30. I have been to see Gerald Kelly. He had a Spanish friend there who sat and listened as he walked up and down the studio talking. And then he got out the portrait he had made of Hugh, tragic with its melancholy eyes. He says a young doctor, a friend of his, had often gone to see Hugh though not professionally, and had believed his life would be but a short one. Hugh, when he said good-bye to Kelly before sailing for America, had said he was going into danger. " And

I saw he was a frightened man." He had asked
Kelly to come with him to the Grenfell sale, and
to sit beside him while it went on: "But you
talk too much, you mustn't talk unless I speak to
you." When it was over he went away without
saying good-bye, but explained next day that he
had been very tired.

"He wore a great coat while I painted that
portrait rather than light a fire—'such extravagance'—amongst those pictures he had paid vast
sums for. That was his way, a bun and a glass
of milk for lunch, saving everything to buy pictures
for Dublin. I believe he would have killed his
whole family, his grandmother—though perhaps
not his aunt—he was very fond of you—but
certainly he would have killed me and all his
friends for the sake of that Dublin Gallery. He
was so excited when he thought he would get his
beautiful Bridge building, and he was never so
cast down in his life as when he failed. No wonder,
it was a splendid thought.

"He helped Orpen, and he was the first to
give John a commission, and he did a great deal
for Alfred Hayward. And as for me, within a
week of my coming as a young man from Paris he
came to Camberwell, and there were four pictures
in the studio. He bought the 'Mrs. Harrison'
for Dublin, and then 'this must go to such an
exhibition, and this to such another.' And they
were all sold. Then he would get me portraits,
bringing me through a line of duchesses at his
parties and saying to some unfortunate woman,
'Here is Mr. Kelly who is going to paint you.'
There was Lady X. The day she promised to

sit I saw him when she was leaving take down a jade figure and give it to her—I suppose it was worth £40. He bribed her. It was a bribe."

" But he was angry with me for going to Spain. He would say, ' I don't mind your going abroad to idle as much as you like, I mind your going to paint there. If you can't find anything worth painting near your own door you are no painter.' He was very quick to point out anything wrong in a picture, but he had no idea how it should be put right. There was one I was pleased with and had taken great trouble with, and he said, ' It is a cigarette paper ! ' I was very angry, he often made me angry. I have often worked at that picture, but I have never been able to get it right. Of course he made me angry sometimes . . .

" With all his kindness he was hard, because he couldn't understand temperament—he couldn't understand that one's mistakes may be worth something to one. He could not bear bad taste. I have seen him pull down the curtains from a window in a friend's drawing-room, saying, ' You really must not have these in your house.' He would come in among apathetic people and take them by the hair of the head as it were, and fill them with enthusiasm for some ideal that perhaps he did not himself understand.

" He gave me advice as to painting. He said, ' Don't try to improve your faults, try to increase your good qualities. Hard work is necessary because it will give you power.' He was like no one else—he was unearthly."

Someone else said, " He seemed to me

whenever I saw him like a drawing in pastel, something free from heaviness, he gave an impression of something fugitive."

And a friend in Dublin, writing about the Gallery, says: "It has become more personal to me since the last time (as I heard it was) that Sir Hugh was in the Abbey. I did not know his appearance, but remarked to my friend with me that there was something very unusual and beautiful about the personality of the young man in the seat right in front of me, ' he did not seem to belong to this world,' and soon after, he turned round and I saw his wonderful eyes, I could never forget them. I asked an attendant who he was, and she told me, but my friend and I (she, too, is like me, somewhat psychic) came away from the theatre very sad, for we both *knew* that we would never see that beautiful face again. I do not think anyone ever made such an impression on me."

I am afraid he angered more people than Gerald Kelly by his over-candid words. I wrote to ask one of my nieces about some story I had heard through her of a Frenchman who had written to ask Hugh to take his son as an apprentice that he might learn the secret of discovering masterpieces. She had forgotten it, but wrote: "One thing I remember, when Lady Z. said, ' Mr. Lane, *do* tell me what you think of my drawing-room'; Hugh: ' Do you really wish me to tell you what I think ? ' ' Oh, do, please ! ' ' It is like a Bazaar.' " Mrs. Grosvenor, when I told her this, said it was with difficulty she had kept him from telling some friends of hers whose house she brought him to that their room was of the Bazaar type. He did tell them what he thought of some of their pictures. Yet he spent hours on his knees cleaning for them some that he thought worth it.

And Mr. Duncan says: "I remember our going together to lunch with Lady ——. She kept talking about two pictures by Leader on the wall, asking him if he thought they looked well there, or if he would advise any other place. He hated Leader, and when at last he gave his opinion it was 'hang them behind the coal-box.' But he knew her well, and she was very fond of him and didn't mind."

I came again to London in March, hurrying my visit that I might see Mr. Solomon. He said how much Hugh had done for him, "he put me in touch with influences that will last through my lifetime. I was young and raw—a barbarian— when he came out to help Lady Phillips about the Johannesburg Gallery, but he believed in me, and when he found I wanted to work, to do the best with my life, he helped me in every way. He made all the plans for me to come to Europe for three years. He told me how I must save money for it. 'You spend too much on food,' he said, 'going to your clubs. Come with me to-morrow and I will show you how to lunch.' So he took me to a little shop next day, and we each had a glass of ginger-beer and a bun. But a friend of mine said to me, 'It is all very well for him, with his lean body he looks as if he had never eaten anything more substantial than a bun, but you are of a substantial build, it is not enough to keep you going. And the ginger-beer is bad and the bun is worse, and all the nourishment you get out of them both is the little bit of sugar that sweetens them.'

" This passion for economy was very strong in him. He used to say that unless you economise on the unessentials, upon which most people were inclined to waste, you would never be able to own the essentials, which to him meant beautiful pictures and objects of art.

" But when I was staying with him at Lindsey House I wanted to buy a present for my mother, and I consulted him. And one day as we were walking we stopped to look in at a little jeweller's shop in the King's Road, and saw in it a pendant, a beautiful thing, old German work with enamel. He said, ' That is what you must give your mother,' and I said it was beautiful, but I was sure beyond my means. We went in and asked the price, and it was ten pounds. I had very little money at that time, I was earning about ten pounds a month, and I said I couldn't think of it ; but he insisted, he made me buy it. And I am always so glad he did when I see my mother wearing it. He used to say, ' If you see a thing you are certain you like, do not hesitate, don't go home to think about it, buy it at once. You may be sure the first thought is right.'

" But he thought I spent too much on meals when I was in London. He said, ' A young artist like you should never depend on getting a good dinner unless you are invited out.'

" He and I were left alone at the Villa Arcadia

in Johannesburg for a while. Sir Lionel and Lady
Phillips had gone to Cape Town for the opening of
the first Parliament of the Union of South Africa.
He saw my interest in art and architecture, and
that drew us together. He used to ride in the
morning, it was the only thing that could get him
out of bed before breakfast—and at sunset. He
loved riding passionately, rapid riding ; he always
would race ahead and with so much pace that at
the end of his visit his horse was a crock. It
seemed to me extraordinary, this recklessness and
longing for rapidity on horseback in so frail a body.
In motoring here it was just the same, he would
have the chauffeur go at top speed, though all the
time he sat up straight, and one could feel he was
nervous.

" With all his kindness and humour he had a
very penetrating way of discovering the weak-
nesses of friends and acquaintances, and he would
point these out with a sort of rapier-like thrust
if he were annoyed. He of course offended people
sometimes by plain speaking. There was a
magnate out there who had filled his house with
huge sentimental pictures. He often invited Sir
Hugh to come and see them, but he never would,
having heard what they were. But then he heard
that this magnate was likely to help (as he afterwards did) the Johannesburg Gallery, and fearing
his help would take the form of a present of
something from this collection he went to see it.
He looked at the pictures, and when his host
asked what he thought of them he said, ' Do you
really want to know ? ' ' Yes, of course.' ' Well,
I think they are worse than oleographs.' ' Oh,

you may not approve of them, but why worse ? '
' Because they are bigger ! '

"But he told me he was obliged to speak
frankly in matters connected with pictures, because
he had very often, when he had not said how bad
he thought them, found he had been quoted as
having approved.

"Before I came to stay with him in London I
had lived as it were by a miracle through an
accident in Italy.   I had fallen over a steep
precipice at Frascati, and lay there for many hours.
When I was rescued and found to be alive it was
declared to be a miracle.   The Italian papers were
full of it.   I stayed at Lindsey House while I
was recovering from it, and he would insist on my
telling the story to people who came in, he wanted
to interest them, to make them friendly to me.
George Moore was one of them, and when Sir Hugh
sent me down with him afterwards to let him out
he said on the staircase, ' That is a wonderful
adventure you told of.   Of course you had made
it all up ! '   I was amused, but when I told Sir
Hugh he was quite vexed and said, ' I wish you
had brought all those Italian news-cuttings.'

"I was surprised to find how little he read.
He used to say ' nothing but news-cuttings.'   Yet
authors were always presenting him with their
books, and I used to be amused by his tact and
humour in evading the reading of them.   He had
an almost uncanny remembrance for these gifts,
and I remember many occasions when an author
coming to dine at Lindsey House, his book would
be put out on a table in the drawing-room, and
with a ' See, this is a pleasure I am reserving for

myself,' Sir Hugh would sail round any awkward questions that might be asked. I used to remonstrate with him sometimes, but he always pointed out to me that life would be so much easier if we all thought a little more of the other fellow's feelings and vanity, and harmlessly played up to it. He would not give in to this amiable insincerity though, if he thought it might hurt the work he cared for.

"When I was last in London I went to see the firm that had carried out Lutyens' designs in the Lindsey House garden, and one of them said, ' Sir Hugh was a very remarkable client. When we sent in our account he came to pay it with some Old Masters under his arm.' They seemed very well content.

"When he was giving me advice once he said, ' And you must learn to play a chatty game of Bridge. That will help you along.' But I found it didn't, and that he himself talked more than people liked at Bridge.

"My mother, who admired him as the most courteous of gentlemen, wrote one day of his kindness to me, and said she must put his name in her will. But he said quite seriously, ' Don't let her do that. I feel that if I knew my name was in anyone's will I should die.' He noticed omens very much, and days of ill-luck. But he had always courage to venture into anything he believed in. He held that when he was on the edge of a crisis something always turned up to carry him through.

"When I was going to marry and set up for myself many of my friends thought I was rash and

PORTRAIT OF CARDINAL ANTONIO CIOCCHI.

By Sebastian del Piombo

foolish. But he wrote, 'If two people love each other, Providence will look after the well-matched pair.'

"He was always an influence for good, inspiring one to do more, admiring and encouraging any talent, endeavouring to find opportunity for its display. I could tell much more of his kindness and encouragement to me, but that is not what you want."

It was what I wanted, but Mr. Solomon in his hurried visit, filled with business, had already been most generous of his time. He showed me then his design for the great University, and when, finding it so beautiful, I said Hugh would have been so glad to see it, he said, "Yes, that is my great regret. He saw something in me. I should have liked him to see this."

I wrote one afternoon: "I have been sitting in a beautiful drawing-room in an old Georgian house, where he used to say he liked to go and spend a restful hour; I could understand that, for art is held in honour there, and colours are harmonious. And like every house he had much frequented there remained gifts that are cherished for their own beauty as well as for his memory's sake. 'His coming in was like the sun shining,' one said. 'There is but little pleasure in setting out new treasures when we know we cannot call him to admire.' And another said, 'There were some houses we could not bring him to, the owners would have been angry. He could not keep from telling out what he thought. There was that Lazlo portrait of their daughter those poor Z.'s had paid so much for; they would have his

s

opinion on the best place for it, and he said, 'The best place would be in the dark.'

"And one, still young in married life, went on to laugh and tell how when her own portrait was being painted and he found her sitting in some diaphanous dress, he had water-lilies brought in to deck her in the likeness of a Naiad. But when meal-time came, and she, young and hungry from the long sitting, ate heartily, he was sad and grumbled at her for not keeping up the illusion of that ethereal part. 'He was wonderful in his influence,' she said. He had so filled her with the desire to excel that she had left him and other friends with whom she had been motoring towards Italy, and turned back to Munich to work at what she had a gift for, that was singing. 'He had a way of making every one do their best with whatever talent they possessed. He always hated waste.'"

Mrs. Nicholson had been of that motor party with Hugh in Italy, and said how wonderfully he enjoyed it—loved every moment of it and made the most of all. One evening at a small town where they stopped he said they must go to a circus, and they found one in a tent—he always liked a circus. And he would find treasures in unexpected corners, even in Johannesburg he had found a fine pendant made from an old Dutch earring, and had given it to her.

He had made her work also at her gift of painting (perhaps her marriage was the result!), and not waste it. "No waste," he would say. All the coffee brought them after lunch should be drunk, and he would gather up the fruit they had not eaten and give it to poor children. Once Lady

Phillips, teasing him, had motored to Florence especially that they might buy him the rarest fruits at some renowned shop. He had accepted it, but at a railway crossing there were children watching them while they waited, and all that expensive fruit had gone to them, such an emptying of Ceres' basket !

Another friend, Mrs. Reeves, has told me of her first meeting with Hugh when he had come to dinner in the country, and at dinner she had told him that she had possessed and had sold to her brother Holman Hunt's " Pot of Basil," and he said at once, " They ought to have that at Johannesburg ! " But that could not be.

He had often stayed with them after that. " I think he was a little puzzled, did not quite know me. One evening I went to the piano and sang some little German songs, and after a time he started up and said, ' Now I know where your force comes from. You have force, and I didn't know its root. You must work at singing, you must go to the best masters.' He did make me go and work, and helped me to find who could teach me best, but now I have given it up. I don't know how to express it—that vision he had—this was a glimpse of it."

I said I thought it was a perception of the essential in people as well as art, and that when he found it he insisted it should be made the most of. " No waste ! " That was the feeling that was behind his economies in small things that his friends laughed at. But as one of those friends, Mrs. Hinde, said to me, " His economies were all upon himself, he made fun of them. He would have tea if he was alone at any little shop he passed, but if he took one to have tea it would be at Rumpelmayer's. He would make a joke of his economies. He took us to dinner one evening, Lutyens was there and Mrs. Fry, and he declared that if we had a sweet we mustn't have a savoury, and if we had a savoury we mustn't have a sweet."

She told me also that Agnew had said to her: "We had quarrels. He would come here in anger and he would call me a thief, and I would call him a liar. And yet I loved the man. Now that he and Morgan are gone, I feel my interest has died away. They were the two who bought pictures because they loved them."

One October evening when I came in late for tea I thought that this had been a lost day, for I had seen no one who had known Hugh. But as I was pouring out tea Miss Swan came to the door, and I very happily brought her in. And among other things we talked of the "little economies." She told me how one night at the Reeves', playing bridge, someone had said, "Let us go to Monte Carlo," and they did go there, within a few days, Hugh among them. He had been there in other years and brought them to his old hotel. I asked if it was a good one or chosen for economy, but she said, "Very good," but that Hugh, leaving before them, cried out, "When 1 am gone I know you will all waste your money eating things in the restaurant!"

He had taken her and Ruth to keep Bank Holiday just after the war had begun, motoring to

Boxhill with lunch, eating it where they had the finest view; and when they came back they stopped for dinner at a little restaurant in the King's Road. She had wanted to act hostess there, but he would not allow her, said, "This is my treat, but you may take us to the cinema that is opposite." "So I took the best seats for them there, at about sixpence each, but he looked at the boxes and said, 'They are a shilling—but we'll take one after the war.'

"At the Collin's little church there was a shabby curtain, baize, with holes in it, and he said he would make a present of a new one. And when he came again it had been chosen, but not by him, gorgeous with crimson and gold, and it had cost £16. He made loud lamentations, saying he had expected it would cost but twelve and sixpence, or possibly up to thirty shillings, the baize, and that a housemaid would have sewed the seams. But then he took comfort in the thought that its richness would earn him a high place in heaven. But in the evening and after he had seen soiled hands of villagers pushing it aside, he was sad again and said: 'I'm afraid it is the intention that counts in Heaven, and that I will only get credit for the twelve and sixpence, and all the rest of the money will go to waste!' She had asked him why he did not throw up the Dublin Gallery with all its annoyances and he said, 'What should I do then? That would be waste of my life.' And one evening at dinner he had taken jade ornaments from his pocket and given one to every guest. 'Two hands scattering and one hand saving.'"
I may so quote an old Kiltartan saying.

I have compared him already to the old poet
Raftery, whose coming "'made a wedding where
there was no wedding," and who left something
to be remembered by, if only a word of praise,
in many a house. And I thought of this when
one Sunday in Connemara I went a long way to a
poor little empty church, and was glad I did so.
For the preacher came to speak to me afterwards
and told me that Hugh, like me a guest at some
house a good way off, had once come to service there.
And again at his son's, a clergyman's, marriage
he had met Hugh, where the finest of the wedding
gifts was a picture of great beauty given by him.

For Mrs. Grenfell's marriage at the Royal
Hospital, Dublin, when her father was Com-
mander-in-Chief, Hugh had decorated the Chapel
with laurel wreaths, he himself making them, and
orange trees—or bay trees hung with oranges—
to be a fit setting for so beautiful a bride. And it
happened this year, 1919, that when the younger
sister's marriage came it was at the Chapel of the
Royal Hospital, Chelsea, where their father was
now Governor, and where no wedding had taken
place since that of Napoleon's Gaoler a hundred
years ago. I took my little grandchildren to see
the marriage procession, and there was again a
beautiful bride, and it pleased me to know that the
London chapel was dressed with laurels and golden
fruit according to Hugh's old design.

One evening I went to the Royal Hospital and
found Lady Lyttelton and Hermione at tea.
When I told them what I was writing Lady
Lyttelton told me it was Hugh who had saved the
old oak panelling there. It had been in part

broken away and in part covered with canvas and wallpaper, and she, when she came there, had lamented this, but was a new-comer, and " treading on eggshells," and could not assert herself too vehemently against the representative of the Office of Works who said the panelling was past repair, and nothing could be done but to pull down what was left or put over it canvas or wallpaper. She was coming down one day in despair, having given up the argument, when she saw Hugh Lane at the foot of the staircase and told him her trouble, and he went up to see the official, and spent an hour with him. Next day Lady Lyttelton had a letter from the Office of Works saying it was believed the panelling could be saved after all. And so it was, and not only that, but a little room long covered with laburnum-yellow paper was found to be also oak panelled, and that also was uncovered and saved. Hugh had appealed to the official's ambition, told him of the lasting reputation he would leave if he succeeded in saving this ancient and beautiful decoration.

At the Royal Hospital in Dublin he had begged her to take down an engraving by Leader of " Light in the Evening." But she said it had been a wedding present. But one day when she came in she found he had come in and taken it down and another with it, and had put in their place some French engravings she still possesses. She spoke of his enjoyment of little things, and said the saying of some writer fitted him, " He had a genius for festivity."

He did enjoy and bring enjoyment with him

motoring with him one day to some place in Kent, where he had an appointment with a " faith-healer " or Christian Scientist. " He left me for an hour at the door, and when he came out told what the process had been—' he took me into a sort of church and asked questions, and told me there was nothing the matter. Then he took me to a room and made me lie down on a sofa and bring my mind to repose while he counted twenty-five minutes ; and then he told me to lie quite still with my eyes closed till the end of the hour.' ' And did you lie still ? ' I asked. ' No, after a while I got up and walked about looking at his beastly pictures and china, and when I heard him coming I lay down again.'

" He was so kind teaching me what he could. One day in London I said I had never seen the Dulwich Gallery, and he said I must not miss it, he would take me there. And though he had been going to keep an appointment that morning, he put it off and motored me to Dulwich and spent the morning showing me the pictures.

" We were motoring to Brighton one day, and after we had passed through Lewes he said, ' I'm sure we shall not get a cup of tea at Brighton as cheap or as good as at Lewes,' and we turned back and had it there."

November 16. I went by train to Dundrum though the rain had come on, it seemed as if it would be a soft wet afternoon in our Kiltartan way. But as I walked up the bare steep road the wind rose, I was almost driven back, the ribs of my umbrella were forced backwards, the silk was torn. It was too late to turn back, and I am glad of that, for when I came to the little Cuala workshop I found shelter and peace ; the girls were working at their embroidery in one room, in another they were printing cards for Christmas. A little blot came upon each, they were trying to discover from what fault in the type. And when we went on to Gurteen Dhas I found warmth and welcome, my hostesses gave me tea by a bright fire. Many of their father's sketches were on the walls, and among them they showed me one of Hugh, and they talked of him for a while.

I said he seemed never to have even walked through a room without making some difference in it. "Yes," one of them said, " even at the Abbey I remember him standing on the steps inside the auditorium and saying, ' I don't feel I am looking my best,' there was a very white light, and even beautiful people were looking haggard, and he asked to see the electrician, and they put in a kinder lighting, amber, and we all rejoiced. But now the white lighting has been brought back again." So I promised to have it changed.

Then they reminded each other of a party given at the Club in Lincoln Place, and how at the last he had come in and changed the whole appearance of the table, piling wonderful fruit in its centre. He was vexed because beautiful Miss E. went out to sit on the balcony with some young men. " She ought to have stayed in here," he said. He lamented the loss of so much beauty to the room. " He made us all feel at our best because he appreciated it. He came to a little party we gave here, and when he was going he said,

'I wish I had you in Dublin, I would make you give one every week.'"

One of them said, "I was at the opening of the Harcourt Street Gallery, and the room where the speeches were to be was so crowded that the architect was in a panic, he thought the old floor would give way. But Sir Hugh went about quickly getting people into the other room without giving the real reason, saying, 'Only the deadheads will stay in here!' or some such thing. I did not hear the speaking, he had sent me to the upper room, I forget what he said, but I know I felt as if I had been paid a compliment.

"Do you remember Sara Allgood being asked to recite at the supper you gave on the night of the opening of the Gallery? She stood up and looked straight at him, and said in her beautiful voice, just as she used to do on the stage, the lines from *Cathleen ni Houlihan*, but putting 'he' for 'they':—

> 'He shall be remembered for ever
> He shall be alive for ever
> The people shall hear him for ever!'"

I had forgotten that, I am glad she brought it back to mind.

January 8, 1920. I came back to Dublin to see *The Golden Apple*. Kerrigan came to the Green Room to-day, back from America, and not ill-content with Ireland. All other countries are, he says, in the same state of unrest, but with money as the motive; in Ireland there is the idealism of Nationality.

When I spoke of Hugh he said, "He used to

come in like a breeze of wind. There seemed always something boyish about him."

Later looking for Miss Mitchell I found A. E. alone in the big room at Plunkett House, and we talked for a while. He thought I might write the book all the better for the want of the documents, and reminded me that when Standish O'Grady was writing his "History of Ireland for Boys," he had deliberately gone to some place where there were no books, and written it there from memory.

He remembered going through the National Gallery with some critics, and how they had judged the pictures by "cracks or technical points," and that Hugh, who was one of them, said, "If a picture is beautiful it is certain it was not painted by a second-rate man." And that he seemed to know the picture's worth by instinct rather than by science.

Later when we were at tea at the little room, "The Sod of Turf," and Miss Mitchell and James Stephens and his wife had joined us, he said that Hugh had told him of a visit to Belfast where some one had asked him to come and see a "splendid picture," a sunset on the Rhine (a dreadful thing), and had told him its history to prove how splendid it was. He had bought it in Germany, and some years afterwards a friend at Hamburg had written to tell him of a fine picture to be sold—a great bargain, he could have it for £12. He bought it, and when it came found it was identical with this. He found that one man had gone on painting these replicas, and after his death the demand had continued, so that another, finding it so popular, had taken up the trade and gone on painting replicas. " So you see what a fine picture it must be ! "

I told of the " Mother and Child " Belfast had refused to hang because the Mother was without a wedding ring, and Stephens said, " Let us make a legend of Belfast—put it away as if in a distant age."

Stephens said some pictures stored in the National Gallery were being sent back to the Castle, and that to-day he had told one of the porters that he should go there and see after them. But he had been reluctant and said at last : " I might be shot by the sentry." This at 11 o'clock a.m.

He said Hugh's death was a great misfortune in his life, for these last four years in the National Gallery that have been so irksome would have been a delight, " No one has ever showed me a picture, he would have showed them to me." But by ill chance he had never met him at all.

He, like A. E., longs to be free from' bonds, but the war stopped the sale of his books, and he must keep to the National Gallery to pay his way. But he is writing still.

A. E. said an Alderman had offered Hugh a bust of himself, stating as reason for its acceptance that " it was real marble."

I asked him about Alderman Thomas Kelly, now in gaol, who supported Hugh so well. He says he was the only pacifist in *Dail Eireann*, was always standing up against violence, and now the Government have seized him and put him in prison.

December 17.   The other day when I heard of the death of the American millionaire Frick, and

of the great collection of pictures he had left to
New York, I felt a sort of jealousy for Hugh, his
gift seemed for the moment to be thrown into
shadow. But that thought lasted but for a
moment ; there are in what the one has given to
Dublin and the other to New York, and each gave
of his best treasures, examples of the highest
attainment of some among the greatest masters.
And then, thinking of the many millions Frick
had owned, I found it harder to drive out a regret
that Hugh had not made a fortune great enough to
allow him to build a gallery at his own cost and
according to his desire. And, indeed, in now
writing, this regret returns, and I suffer in thinking
of the unfulfilled dream, the anguish of longing to
carry out that " harmony of purpose," that fitting
home for the pictures he had gathered with such
joyous intention.

I had written one Sunday evening, in London :
" To-day I went to service in the Old Chelsea
Church. It was there that Hugh's friends had
come to the service in his memory, when all hope
of his having been saved had died away. Hymns
that he had liked had been sung there :—

'Peace, perfect peace—our future all unknown—
Jesus we know, and He is on the throne.

'Peace, perfect peace—death shadowing us and ours—
Jesus hath vanquished death and all its powers.'

And the flowers heaped about the altar were as
beautiful as he could himself have chosen, for they
were placed there, like the tablet put up to his
memory in a distant Irish Church, 'by his sorrowful
sister, Ruth Shine ' ; and many of his friends were

there. . . . That gathering was in my memory to-day, and I remembered also Sundays when Hugh had sat there, his morning pallor after those difficult nights made still more ghostly by the green-dyed window-panes. And with this vision, as it seemed, more distinct to me than the figures of living worshippers, I heard the words read of one of the psalms for the day : ' I will not suffer mine eyes to sleep nor mine eyelids to slumber, neither the temples of my head to take any rest until I find out a habitation for the mighty God of Jacob.' And it seemed to me that Hugh's lifelong dream of that shining treasury he so passionately coveted to create was not far away from that of the Jewish King. And I can surely witness how from first to last, when all went well, or when discouraged and foiled and out of heart, he never, when there was any work to be done towards it, suffered ' the temples of his head to take any rest.' "

I am glad that on Hugh's last visit to New York he and Mr. Frick, these two good lovers of pictures, had met ; and I was pleased when Mrs. Hinde told me she had been lately in the house of the great American collector, and he had said to her as they looked at I know not what picture, " Some say I ought to change that picture to another place, but I will never move it because it was hung there by Hugh Lane."

January 1, 1920. This morning, being away from home and idle, and no newspaper having come, I took up a volume of Lodge's Portraits and read the memoir of one whose name was to me unknown, Sir Hugh Middleton. But the historian, after an apology for the lack of " lively occurrences " and " decorative materials," claims that he had well earned the epithet " illustrious " through " superlative public beneficence and the contrivance and execution of a design worthy of the mind."

It is likely this design and its accomplishment in the reign of James the First are better known to others, for it was surely a worthy one, " the better supply of water to London through the means of that artificial stream so well known by the name of ' The New River ' " ; and I, no great Londoner, had never heard, or heard so as to note, whence that clear and sparkling water comes, save that science or superstition has at times attributed its brightness to the properties of ancient and dissolving bones ; and so this benefactor's name had been a stranger.

But I knew well what had been the achievement of the illustrious person on another page I turned to, by no chance but of purpose, it having of late been in my mind. For Yeats, newly settled in Oxford and offering me a welcome to his house, had more than once spoken of the great ease and delight of reading in the Bodleian Library. And so I was glad to learn something of the Elizabethan diplomatist who threw up his Embassy and gave his life and wealth to " the noble design of restoring or rather founding the public Library at Oxford."

And in reading one of his letters I could not but think of Hugh, and indeed this passage of it might well have been written by him : " And as for myself I am wholly uncertain how far I shall proceed in my expense about the work, having hitherto made no determinate design, but purposing to do as my ability shall afford, which may increase or diminish, and as God shall spare my life, though unto myself I do resolve in a general project to do more than I am willing to publish to the world."

At midday when the newspapers came to hand they told the grievous (but happily false) news of Horace Plunkett's death. . . . After a while my meditation turned to the work of these two my countrymen, and I wondered whose name would longest endure, his who brought the helpful Danish methods to our farms and dairies, as Middleton had brought spring water from the Welsh well-heads to Islington; or his whose Gallery is of the kindred of the great Library. Both have made a noble use of their life, both are like Hyde and A. E. and Yeats and Synge and others whose names I have written in this book, and some, our fellow-workers, whose names are "in the book of the people," of those who, in Lord Rosebery's fine words, "form the pedigree of nations, and whose achievements are their country's title-deeds of honour."

A POSTSCRIPT

AFTER Hugh's death some of his friends arranged that a memoir should be written that would give some account of what he was and what he had done. I was told of this, and while refusing a request to write it I helped to gain Mr. MacColl's consent to do so. In talking of this he said, as I have already told, he had first been interested in Hugh by "finding he was making people do what I had been for years begging them in vain to do, buy the work of living men"; but that he knew nothing of his early life. To make a beginning easier for him I wrote some of the notes on "Causes," which I have now used. He withdrew his consent later in the heat of a newspaper argument as to Hugh's intention in the codicil to his will, and the work abandoned by him was given to Mr. Martin Wood, together with the documents that had been entrusted for the purpose to Mr. MacColl.

I had again at that time been urged to take up the task, but had refused. I had written to Yeats in December, 1916: "As to Hugh's Life, I should not feel it right to undertake it now, and doubt if I could in the future. I am really suffering from the long strain of anxiety about Robert, and his ever-increasing danger. He is kept very hard at work now leading patrols and his squadron in these air-fights, his promised leave has been twice withdrawn, and there is no doubt the German machines are ahead of ours. I try to do what work comes my way as well as I can, and not to be a nuisance, but my mind is not free for a new task. I sometimes awake feeling as if some part of me was crying in another place. And all the war seems horrible and interminable.

"I think in any case I should have found it hard to write about Hugh till the picture question is settled—it is a constant irritant. My hope is that if any scheme of Home Rule is carried through this may be pressed at the same time. . . ."

I, however, undertook the work later, in the autumn of 1919, after a failure in Mr. Wood's health, followed by his death.

As to the papers given to Mr. MacColl and then to Mr. Wood, and containing, as well as letters written by Hugh to me and to some near friends, "fourteen or fifteen newscutting books; ten or twelve envelopes of letters from individuals; diaries; bundles of letters to do with various collections"; by some mistake or misunderstanding they did not come to me until I had all but finished these pages. That is my apology for making them so personal as to seem egotistic, my own memory being the nearest attainable document.

This is my apology to the many I have troubled and importuned, asking for recollection of a phrase, a movement, a moment of gaiety or anger, to help the portrait's shadows or its lights.

These hold my lasting gratitude ; for all I have written of Hugh seems now as nothing beside the record that has come out of the memory of his friends.

APPENDIX I

WHEN Hugh Lane's will was read, it was found that, after disposing of his modern pictures, he had left the residue of his property—which included Lindsey House, Chelsea, and his collection of old masters there—to the National Gallery of Ireland. He directed that the pictures and objects of art in his house in London were to be sold, and that " the revenue " was " to be spent in buying pictures of deceased painters of established merit." The Board of Governors and Guardians of the National Gallery of Ireland, however, decided to apply to the Courts for permission to retain forty-one of the more important of the works by old masters owned by him at the time of his death.

Of the sixty-two pictures from his collection, now in the Irish National Gallery, forty-one were thus chosen, and twenty-one had been given during his lifetime. They are as follows :—

LIST OF PICTURES GIVEN AND BEQUEATHED TO THE NATIONAL GALLERY OF IRELAND.

BRITISH SCHOOLS.

Chinnery (G.R.H.A.), Portrait of a Mandarin.
Linnell (John), Portrait of a Lady.
Romney (George), Portrait of a Lady.
——, Portrait of Mrs. Edward Taylor.
——, Portrait of the Artist's Wife.
Hoppner (John), Portrait of the Artist.
Doughty (William), Portrait of Miss Sisson.

Lawrence (Sir Thomas), Lady Elizabeth Foster (afterwards Duchess of Devonshire).

Reynolds (Sir Joshua), Portrait of Mrs. Francis Fortescue.

Hogarth (William), The Mackinnon Family.

——, The Western Family.

Hunt (William Henry), Portrait of the Artist's Mother.

Gainsborough (Thomas), Portrait of John Gainsborough.

——, The Gamekeeper.

——, Portrait of Mrs. King, *née* Spence.

——, Portrait of General James Johnston.

——, Portrait of Mrs. Horton (afterwards Anne, Duchess of Cumberland).

——, A Landscape with Cattle.

Collins (William), Portrait of the Artist's Mother.

Slaughter (S.), A Lady and Child.

Constable (John), Portrait of a Child with a Dog.

Wilkie (Sir David), Portrait of a Lady in White.

Stubbs (George), Sportsmen at Rest.

ITALIAN AND SPANISH SCHOOLS.

Florentine School, The Battle of Anghiari, A.D. 1440.

——, The Taking of Pisa, A.D. 1406.

Bordone (Paris), St. George and the Dragon.

School of Tintoretto, Diana and Endymion.

Greco, El (Domenico Theotocopuli), St. Francis in Ecstasy.

Magnasco (Alessandro), Landscape.

Strozzi (Bernardo), Portrait of a Gentleman.

Ilanos y Valdés (Sebastian de), The Madonna with the Rosary.

Vecelli (Tiziano), called Titian, Portrait of Baldassare Castiglione.

Luciani (Sebastiano), called Sebastiano del Piombo, Portrait of the Cardinal Antonio Ciocchi del Monte Sansovino.

Bassano, Il (Jacopo da Ponte), Portrait of a Man.

De Espinosa (Jacinto J.), Jael and Sisera.

Piazzetta (Giovanni Battista), A Decorative Group.

Veronese (Paolo Caliari, called Il Veronese), Portrait of a Lady.

Goya (F.), A Spanish Woman.

FRENCH, FLEMISH, AND DUTCH SCHOOLS.

Vallain (Nanine), Portrait of Letitia Bonaparte.

Gellee (Claude, called Claude Lorrain), Juno confiding Io to the care of Argus.

Jamesone (George), ascribed to, Portrait of Lady Alexander.

Desportes (Alexander François), Group of Dead Game.
Chardin (Jean Baptiste Simon), The Young Governess.
——, Still Life.
Poussin (Nicholas), The Youthful Romulus.
——, Bacchante and Satyr.
——, Pluto and Proserpine.
——, The Marriage of Thetis and Peleus.
School of Watteau, A Musical Party.
Horemans (Jan), Interior of a Kitchen.
——, Interior.
Lancret (N.), Mischief.
Greuze (J. B.), The Broken Doll.
School of the Master of the Holzhausen Portraits, Portrait of a Man
Witte (Emanuel de), Interior of Antwerp Cathedral.
Cuyp (J. G.), The Violinist.
Horstok (J. P.), Portrait of a Man.
Goyen (Jan Van), A View of Rhein-on-the-Ems.
Rembrandt Van Rijn, Portrait of a Young Woman.
Dyck (Sir Anthony Van), A Boy Standing on a Terrace.
Bol (Ferdinand), Portrait of a Lady.
Beerstraaten (Jan), A Winter Scene.
Snyders (F.), A Breakfast.
Early Flemish School, The Adoration of the Magi

APPENDIX II

GIFTS AND BEQUESTS TO THE DUBLIN MUNICIPAL ART GALLERY

Bayes (W.), The Bathers.
Boudin (E.), At the Seaside.
Bough (Sam.), A Wet Day, Kileburn Castle.
Burne-Jones (Sir E.), The Sleeping Princess.
Charles, (J.), A Country Road, November.
——, Landscape.
——, In the Orchard.
——, Return from the First Communion.
——, Winter Landscape.
Chinnery (G.), Oriental Group.
Conder (C.), A Stormy Day, Brighton.
Connard (P.), Flowers.
Corot (J. B.), Evening Landscape.
Crowley (H.), The Grandmother.
Fisher (Mark), The Bathers.
Granet (F. M.), Interior of a Monastery.
Greaves (W.), Old Battersea Bridge.
Gregory (E. J.), View of the Mall.
——, Piccadilly.
Gregory (R.), Coole Lake.
Harrison (S. C.), Portrait of Mr. and Mrs. T. Haslam
Hayes (E.), Coast Scene.
Holloway (C. E.), Tilbury Fort.
Hone (N.), The Donegal Coast.
——, A Grey Day, Malahide.
——, View of Howth, with Cattle Grazing.
——, View on the Nile.
——, Malahide Sands, Stormy Weather.
Hurlestone (W. Y.), A Spanish Jade.
Ingres (J. A. D.), Portrait of Vincent Léon Pallière.
Jacquand (C.), At the Bedside.

John (A.), Decorative Group.

——, Portrait of a Lady.

——, Portrait of Miss Iris Tree.

——, A Boy in Brown.

Kelly (G. F.), Portrait of Mrs. Harrison.

Knight (Buxton), Peele Harbour.

——, View in Wales.

Knight (Laura), The Cottager's Family.

Maclaren (D.), Celtic Legends.

Mancini (A.), Portrait of Sir Hugh Lane.

——, Portrait of Mrs. Shine.

——, Portrait of a Lady.

——, Portrait of a Man.

——, Portrait of Lady Gregory.

Markievicz (Dunin), Portrait of George Russell (A. E.).

——, Study of Trees.

Millais (Sir J.), The Return of the Dove to the Ark.

Moore (Albert), Azaleas.

Muirhead (D.), Harvest Time.

Nicholson (W.), Souvenir de Marie.

O'Brien (D.), Portrait of Alderman Cotton, M.P.

——, Landscape Study.

O'Meara (F.), Towards the Night and Winter.

Orchardson (Sir W. Q.), Imogen in the Cave of Belarius.

Orpen (Sir W.), China and Japan, Reflections.

——, A Breezy Day, Howth.

——, Portrait of the Rt. Hon. Sir T. W. Russell, Bt.

——, Portrait of Lord MacDonnell.

——, Portrait of William O'Brien, M.P.

——, Portrait of Michael Davitt.

——, Portrait of Nathaniel Hone, R.H.A.

——, Portrait of Sir J. P. Mahaffy, D.D., K.C.V.O.

——, Portrait of Captain Shawe Taylor.

Osborne (W.), The Fishmarket.

——, Tea in the Garden.

——, Mother and Child.

Potter (F. H.), Study of a Child.

Previati (G.), Funeral of a Virgin.

Robinson (F. Cayley), The Landing of St. Patrick

Russell (George), (A. E.), The Winged Horse.

——, Children at Play.

——, The Woodcutters.

——, The Log Carriers.

——, On the Roof Top.   Moonlight.

Russell (George), (A. E.), The Stone Carriers.

——, Is not this Great Babylon that I have built ?

Sargent (J. S.), Portrait of Sir Hugh Lane.

——, Portrait of Lady Charles Beresford.

——, Statue of Vertunnus at Frascati.

Sickert (W.), The Old Church, Dieppe.

Shannon (C.), The Bunch of Grapes.

Solomon (S.), The Finding of Moses.

Spencer Stanhope (R.), Venus.

Steer (P. Wilson), The Bend of the Severn.

——, The Estuary, Porchester.

——, Evening.

——, The Blue Girl.

——, Iron Bridge, Salop.

Stevens (J.), The Lacemaker.

Swynnerton (A. L.), The Young Mother.

Symons (W. Xtn.), The Convalescent Connoisseur.

. Unknown, Portrait of G. F. Watts.

Ward (James), Sheep Dipping.

Watts (G. F.), Portrait of Mrs. Louis Huth.

——, Head of a Girl.

Whistler (J. McN.), The Artist's Studio.

Yeats (J. B.), Portrait of the Rt. Hon. Sir Horace Plunkett, K.C.V O.

——, Portrait of Edward Dowden.

——, Portrait of John M. Synge.

——, Portrait of W. B. Yeats.

——, Portrait of W. G. Fay.

Yeats (Jack), The Maggie Man.

DRAWINGS AND WATERCOLOURS.

Beerbohm (Max), Mr. W. B. Yeats introducing Mr. George Moore to the Queen of the Fairies.

Bonvin (F. S.), In Church, Vaugirard. `

Boudin (E.), The Market Place.

Burne-Jones (Sir E.), Two Designs for Stained Glass.

Callow (W.), Southampton.

Chavannes (Puvis de), Study of a Man.

——, Seated Figure.

Conder (C.), The Bather.

——, The Finding of Don Juan.

——, The Bather's Repose.

——, Behind the Scenes.

Corot (J. B.), Landscape with Figures.
Daumier (H.), In the Omnibus.
Duff (James), The Sheepfold.
Fisher (Mark), Boat House, Bourne End.
——, The Back of the Mill.
——, Arcachon.
Helleu (P.), A Lady Resting.
——, Study of Children's Heads.
James (F.), Lilies.
——, Geraniums.
——, White Stocks.
——, Primulas.
John (A.), Study of a Girl.
——, Study of a Girl.
——, The Artist's Wife.
——, Portrait of Mrs. Shine.
——, Studies of Children's Heads.
Lamb (H.), Head of a Girl.
Leighton (Lord), Studies of Boys.
——, Study of a Draped Figure.
——, Study of a Nude Figure.
MacNair (F.), The Birth of the Rose.
MacNair (J. H.), Tamlaine.
Mancini (A.), Portrait of Mr. Alabaster.
——, Portrait of the Artist.
——, The Mantilla.
——, Four Studies.
Maris (W. the Younger), The Straw Hat.
Millet (J. F.), Studies for " The Bather."
Orpen (R. C.), Fishing Smacks, St. Ives.
Orpen (Sir W.), The Gipsy.
——, The Artist's Wife.
——, Family Group, after Ingres.
——, Five Pen and Ink Drawings.
——, Five Watercolours.
Pearce (C. M.), The Vestibule.
——, The Court of the Palace.
School of Burne-Jones, Death of a Saint.
Scott (G.), The Advance Guard.
Segantini (G.), The Sheepfold.
——, The Shepherd Asleep.
Solomon (S.), The Bride.
——, The Bridegroom.
——, The Greek Festival.

Solomon (S.), The Acolyte.
——, Illustration to the Song of Solomon.
Steer (P. Wilson), Porchester Castle.
——, Portsdown Hill.
——, A Stormy Day.
——, With the Tide.
Tonks (H.), Les Sylphides.
Tyrwhill (U.), Four Flower Pieces
Walker (J. C.), At Sea.
Wolfing (E.), Nude Figure.
Yeats (Jack), An Old Slave.
——, On the Lake.

ETCHINGS, LITHOGRAPHS, AND WOODCUTS.

Conder (C.), Le peau de Chagrin.
Daviel (L.), Study of a Baby (after A. John).
Legros (A.), The Frugal Meal.
——, The Fisherman.
——, The Woodcutters.
——, The Pear Tree.
Sherborn (C. W.), Etching.

SCULPTURE.

Aronson (N.), Count Tolstoi.
Barye (A. L.), A Lion.
        (Lent by the National Gallery of Ireland.)
——, A Lioness.
        (Lent by the National Gallery of Ireland.)
Carpeaux, The Empress Eugénie.
        (Lent by the National Gallery of Ireland.)
Dalou, Study of a Woman.
        (Lent by the National Gallery of Ireland.)
——, Head of a Girl.
        (Lent by the National Gallery of Ireland.)
Epstein (J.), Lady Gregory.
Furse (J. H. M.), Horses Fighting.
Maillel (A.), Three Statuettes.
        (Lent by the National Gallery of Ireland.)
Rodin (A.), The Age of Bronze.
——, Frère et Soeur.
        (Lent by the National Gallery of Ireland.)

Rodin (A.), L'Homme au Nez Cassé.

> (Lent by the National Gallery of Ireland.)

——, Le Prêtre.

> (Lent by the National Gallery of Ireland.)

Stevens (A.), Truth and Falsehood.

> (Lent by the National Gallery of Ireland.)

——, Courage and Cowardice.

> (Lent by the National Gallery of Ireland.)

APPENDIX III

PICTURES NOW IN POSSESSION OF THE LONDON NATIONAL GALLERY

PICTURES now in possession of the London National Gallery; the bequest revoked in favour of Dublin in the Codicil, of which a facsimile has been given:—

Monet (Claude), Vetheuil : Sunshine and Snow.
Renoir, Les Parapluies.
Manet (Edouard), Le Concert aux Tuileries.
——, Portrait of Mademoiselle Eva Gonzales.
Pissarro (C.), Printemps, vue de Louvecienne.
Vuillard (E.), The Mantelpiece.
Boudin (E.), Le Rivage, entrée de Tourgeville.
Degas, La Plage.
Morisot (B.), Jour d'Eté.
Ingres, Duc d'Orléans.
Forain, In the Law Courts.
Mancini (Antonio), Portrait of Marquis del Grille.
——, En Voyage.
——, Aurelia.
——, La Douane.
Brown (John Devis), The Mountebank.
Madrazo (R.), Portrait Study of a Woman.
Daubigny (Chas. H.), Portrait of Honoré Daumier.
Barye (Ant. Louis), Forest at Fontainebleau.
Corot (J. B.), Avignon : Ancient Palace of the Popes.
——, Landscape : A Summer Morning.
Fromentin (Eugène), The Slave.
Courbet (G.), The Snow Storm.
——, The Pool.
——, In the Forest.
Diaz, (N.), The Offspring of Love.
Jerôme (Jean Leon), Portrait of a Naval Officer,

Fantin-Latour (J. H. J.), Still Life.
Ronvin (François), Still Life.
Rousseau (Theodore), Moonlight.
Chavannes (Puvis de), The Toilet.
——, Decollation de St. Jean Baptiste.
Monticelli (A.), The Hayfield.
Daumier (Honoré), Don Quixote and Sancho Panza.
Maris (James), Feeding the Bird.
Stevens (Alfred), The Present.
Corot (J. B. C.), An Italian Peasant Woman.
Yongkind (J. B.), Skating in Holland.
Courbet (G.), The Artist.

APPENDIX IV

STATUTORY DECLARATIONS

STATUTORY declarations made with regard to Hugh Lane's intention that his codicil should have the weight of law, by his sister Mrs. Shine, his friend Mr. Alec Martin, and Mrs. Duncan, Curator of the Dublin Municipal Gallery :—

I, RUTH SHINE of Lindsey House, 100 Cheyne Walk, London, S.W., Widow, do solemnly and sincerely declare as follows :—

The late Sir Hugh Lane was a brother of mine and he is hereinafter referred to as " my brother."

In January 1915 my brother spoke to me of making another will. He went to Dublin, however, without having done so. It was there (on February 3rd) that he wrote and signed his codicil and locked it in his desk at the National Gallery in a sealed envelope addressed to me ; it was very clearly and carefully written and I have no doubt whatever that he considered it legal.

My brother had no business habits in the ordinary sense of the word and was ignorant of legal technicalities. He dictated both his wills to me, the first leaving all to the Modern Art Gallery in Dublin and the second leaving all to the National Gallery of Dublin with the exception of the French pictures left to London. But for my persistence neither would have been witnessed ; even when he dictated the second will he had forgotten all I had told him about that necessity. So little

286

am I surprised at there being no witnesses to the codicil that my surprise is altogether that he should have written it so carefully. He must have made rough drafts, as he composed letters with great difficulty, and the codicil was so well written.

I think from my knowledge of him that if he thought of a witness at all he would perhaps have considered that a codicil to an already witnessed will needed no further formality. When he sealed up the envelope he was going on a dangerous journey to America, and was so much impressed by that danger that at first he had refused to go at all unless those, who had invited him for business reasons, would insure his life for £50,000 to clear his Estate of certain liabilities, and he thought he was going not in seven or eight weeks as it happened but in two or three.

I have approached this subject without any bias in favour of Dublin but as his sister anxious that his intentions should be carried out, and I make this declaration conscientiously believing the same to be true and by virtue of the Provisions of the Statutory Declaration Act 1835.

RUTH SHINE.

Declared at Markham House, King's Road, Chelsea, in the County of London, this 13th day of February 1917

Before me

G. F. WILKINS.

A Commissioner for Oaths.

I, ELLEN DUNCAN, Curator of the Dublin Municipal Gallery of Modern Art, 17 Harcourt Street in the City of Dublin, aged 21 years and upwards make oath and say as follows :—

1. For fifteen years I was acquainted with the late

Sir Hugh Lane, who was a close personal friend of my husband and myself.

2. Sir Hugh Lane was Honorary Director of the Municipal Gallery of Modern Art until his death. I was Curator from October 1914. Whenever he came to Dublin he spent a good deal of time in the Gallery and took a keen interest in its working and obtained some gifts for it, the last being a bust by Rodin.

3. I last saw Sir Hugh Lane on the last day of his stay in Dublin before he sailed for America. He came to the gallery that day and had a conversation with me about his collection of continental pictures which were then stored in the London National Gallery. He said that he wished to bring these pictures to Dublin. He said that with regard to the building of a new gallery he did not wish to insist now upon any special plan but would be content if the Corporation reaffirmed their already expressed intention of building a gallery. He asked me whether I thought I could get the Corporation to give some assurance to this effect. The words he used were, " I do not wish to appear to have ' climbed down ' about a new gallery building, but I do not wish to revive any of the old controversies. I wish to bring the pictures back to Dublin as soon as possible, and they might be rehung here pending the building of any gallery the Corporation may decide upon."

4. The impression I gathered from the conversation aforesaid was that Sir Hugh Lane had definitely made up his mind to adhere to his original intention with regard to these pictures which he bought for the Dublin Municipal Gallery of Modern Art. He expressed himself as indignant at the way in which these pictures had been treated by the London National Gallery, with the result that the public had no opportunity of seeing them.

ELLEN DUNCAN.

Sworn this 12th day of February 1917 at City Hall in the City of Dublin before me a Commissioner to administer oaths for the Supreme Court of Judicature in Ireland and I know deponent.

HENRY LEMASS,

Commr. for Oaths.

I, ALEXANDER MARTIN, of 37, Vicarage Road, East Sheen, do solemnly and sincerely declare as follows :—

I have been asked to state in a word my impression of Sir Hugh Lane's wishes regarding these Pictures, in so far as I gathered it in conversation with him when I accompanied him to Liverpool.* I am pleased to accede to this request, and I should like to preface it with the remark that it was the more strongly fixed in my mind because his wishes as he expressed them were not those with which I had most sympathy Personally, I should have preferred to have seen the Pictures placed in London rather than in Dublin. From earlier conversations I was aware, of course, of Sir Hugh Lane's deep interest in Ireland, and was not, therefore, at all surprised when on this occasion he spoke of it, and of his recent visit to Dublin, with the greatest affection. He spoke to me also of the Modern Gallery, referring again to the ambition he had entertained when collecting the Pictures of seeing them housed in Dublin, and he gave me to understand that his mind was made up that it should after all be the destination of his Pictures, and I make this declaration conscientiously believing the same to be true, and by virtue of the Provisions of the Statutory Declaration Act, 1835.

Signed : ALEXANDER MARTIN.

* Where Sir Hugh Lane was to sail for America.—A. G.

Declared at No. 15 Duke Street, St. James's, in the County of Middlesex, this 27 day of February 1917. Before me,

A. FAIRLIE ALLINGHAM.

(*A Commissioner of Oaths.*)

PRINTED BY WILLIAM CLOWES AND SONS, LIMITED, LONDON AND BECCLES, ENGLAND.

The OLD STORIES of IRELAND.

Works Treating of Gaelic Legends.

Edited and Translated by LADY GREGORY.

CUCHULAIN OF MUIRTHEMNE.

The Story of the Men of the Red Branch of Ulster. With a Preface by W. B. Yeats. *4th Edition.*

"In his interesting preface, Mr. W. B. Yeats expresses his opinion that it is the best book that has come from Ireland in recent years. In this we heartily concur. For the first time we have a thoroughly literary version of the 'Tain' and its cycle of tales, which may be compared, without the least misgiving, to Lady Charlotte Guest s version of the 'Mabinogian.'"—*The Times.*

GODS AND FIGHTING MEN.

The Story of the Tuatha de Danaan and of the Fianna of Ireland. With a Preface by W. B. Yeats. *5th Impression.*

"Lady Gregory has added another leaf to the crown of laurel she is winning by her studies in ancient Gaelic folklore and legend. Her 'Gods and Fighting Men' is as naïvely delightful, as mentally refreshing and invigorating as her previous books. . . . She is at heart a poet, and the limitless wealth of imagination of the Irish mind, its quaintness and simplicity, its gravity and peculiar humour, have passed into her possession and. inspired her pen to fine issues."—*Yorkshire Post.*

A BOOK OF SAINTS AND WONDERS:

According to the Old Writings and the Memory of the People of Ireland. *3rd Impression.*

"A delightful volume of stories. . . . The book imparts a fresh literary charm to the fine old times about Saint Bridget, about Columcille, about Saint Patrick, about the Voyagers Maeldune and Brendan, and about many other legendary wonder-workers and uncanny adventures. For an Irish youngster, or, indeed, for anyone interested, to have the old Irish tales simply, faithfully, and sympathetically told, it would be hard indeed to find a better book."—*The Scotsman.*

THE GOLDEN APPLE.

A Play for Kiltartan Children in three Acts. By Lady Gregory. With Coloured Illustrations by Margaret Gregory.

This play deals with the adventures of the King of Ireland's son, who goes in search of the Golden Apple of Healing. The scenes are. laid in the Witch's Garden, the Giant's House, the Wood of Wonders, and the King of Ireland's Room. It is both humorous and lyrical and should please children and their elders alike. The coloured illustrations are by the same hand as' those in "The Kiltartan Wonder-Book," and have the same old fairy-tale air as the play itself.

JOHN MURRAY, ALBEMARLE STREET, W. 1.

WORKS BY ARTHUR C. BENSON

THE HOUSE OF QUIET. An Autobiography. *21st Impression.*

THE THREAD OF GOLD. *16th Impression.*

FROM A COLLEGE WINDOW. *20th Impression.*

THE UPTON LETTERS. *18th Impression.*

THE SILENT ISLE. *4th Impression.*

ALONG THE ROAD.

THE ALTAR FIRE. *5th Impression.*

BESIDE STILL WATERS. *4th Impression.*

AT LARGE. *2nd Impression.*

RUSKIN : A Study in Personality.

JOYOUS GARD.

THE ORCHARD PAVILION.

FATHER PAYNE.

THE CHILD OF THE DAWN.

THE LEAVES OF THE TREE : Studies in Biography. *2nd Edition.*

THE GATE OF DEATH. A Diary. *3rd Edition.*

THY ROD AND THY STAFF. *3rd Impression.*

WHERE NO FEAR WAS.

ESCAPE, and other Essays.

WATERSPRINGS. A Novel. *3rd Impression.*

PAUL THE MINSTREL, and other Stories. With a new Preface.

HUGH : MEMOIRS OF A BROTHER. With Portraits and Illustrations.

LIFE AND LETTERS OF MAGGIE BENSON. With Portraits and Illustrations.

THE LETTERS OF QUEEN VICTORIA. A Selection from Her Majesty's Correspondence between the years 1837 and 1861. Edited by ARTHUR C. BENSON and VISCOUNT ESHER. With 16 Portraits. 3 vols.

POEMS : Selections from the Poetry of Charlotte, Emily, Anne, and Branwell Bronte. Edited, with an Introduction, by ARTHUR C. BENSON. With Portraits.

WORKS OF ROBERT BROWNING

POETICAL WORKS

COMPLETE EDITION. Edited and Annotated by the RT. HON. AUGUSTINE BIRRELL, K.C., and SIR FREDERIC G. KENYON, K.C.B. 2 volumes, with a Portrait in each.

INDIA PAPER EDITION. In 1 volume.
In 2 volumes.

POCKET EDITION. In 8 volumes (size $4\frac{1}{8}$ by $6\frac{1}{4}$ inches), printed upon India Paper, with a Portrait in each volume. Bound in Cloth or in Leather. The 8 volumes in gold lettered case, in Cloth.

UNIFORM EDITION. Containing Portraits and Illustrations. 17 volumes.

SELECTIONS. Crown 8vo. and Pocket Edition.

THE BROWNING LOVE LETTERS. THE LETTERS OF ROBERT BROWNING AND ELIZABETH BARRETT BROWNING. 2 volumes. Also New Edition on Thin Paper, 2 volumes.

LIFE AND LETTERS OF ROBERT BROWNING. By MRS. SUTHERLAND ORR. Edited, with a Preface by SIR FREDERIC G. KENYON, K.C.B. With Portraits.

BROWNING : How to Know Him. By W. L. PHELPS.

THE BROWNINGS FOR THE YOUNG. Edited by SIR FREDERIC G. KENYON, K.C.B.

WORKS OF ELIZABETH BARRETT BROWNING

POETICAL WORKS

COMPLETE in 1 volume, with Portrait.

UNIFORM EDITION. In 6 volumes.

POCKET EDITION. In 3 volumes. Printed upon India Paper, with a Portrait in each. Cloth and Leather.

POEMS. Cloth and Leather.

THE LETTERS OF ELIZABETH BARRETT BROWNING. Edited, with Biographical Additions by SIR FREDERIC G. KENYON, K.C.B. With Portraits. 2 volumes.

ELIZABETH BARRETT BROWNING IN HER LETTERS. By PERCY LUBBOCK. With Portrait.

Life and Works of
CHARLES DARWIN

THE ORIGIN OF SPECIES BY MEANS OF
NATURAL SELECTION.

THE DESCENT OF MAN AND SELECTION
IN RELATION TO SEX. With Illustrations.

VARIATION OF ANIMALS AND PLANTS
UNDER DOMESTICATION. Woodcuts. 2 vols.

EXPRESSION OF THE EMOTIONS IN MAN
AND ANIMALS. With Illustrations.

VARIOUS CONTRIVANCES BY WHICH OR-
CHIDS ARE FERTILIZED BY INSECTS. Woodcuts.

MOVEMENTS AND HABITS OF CLIMBING
PLANTS. Woodcuts.

INSECTIVOROUS PLANTS.

FORMATION OF VEGETABLE MOULD
THROUGH THE ACTION OF WORMS. Illustrated.

JOURNAL OF A NATURALIST DURING A
VOYAGE ROUND THE WORLD IN H.M.S. "BEAGLE." With
16 full-page Plates.

CHARLES DARWIN:
His Life told in an Autobiographical Chapter, and in a Selected Series
of his published Letters. Edited by his Son, SIR FRANCIS DARWIN.

CROSS AND SELF-FERTILIZATION IN THE
VEGETABLE KINGDOM.

DIFFERENT FORMS OF FLOWERS ON
PLANTS OF THE SAME SPECIES.

MORE LETTERS OF CHARLES DARWIN:
A Record of his Work in a Series of hitherto Unpublished Letters.
Edited by FRANCIS DARWIN and A. C. SEWARD. With Portraits. 2 vols.
Demy 8vo.

THE
CORNHILL
MAGAZINE

1s. 6d. net

MONTHLY

Edited by LEONARD HUXLEY, LL.D.

"Can a magazine have a soul? In turning over the pages of the hundred volumes of the 'Cornhill,' I have been on the search, and I believe I have found it. . . . The range of subjects is very wide, the methods of treatment are infinitely various. Politics and public affairs have for the most part been avoided, though the fringe of them is often touched. . . . The 'note' of the 'Cornhill' is the literary note, in the widest sense of the term; its soul is the spirit of that humane culture, as Matthew Arnold describes it in the pages, reprinted from the 'Cornhill,' of 'Culture and Anarchy.'"

—SIR E. T. COOK.

OPINIONS OF LIBRARIANS.

"I find upon inquiry at our five Libraries that the 'Cornhill' is well read, and certainly it appeals to a section of readers who can appreciate better literary fare than is offered in most of the modern monthlies. May I take this opportunity of expressing my own admiration for the high literary tone which you preserve in the 'Cornhill.'"

"My Committee are of opinion that there is room for one of its kind. (Personally, I think there is only one of the 'Cornhill' kind, and that is the 'Cornhill' itself.) I may say at once that the 'Cornhill' exactly meets the wants of a select body of readers."

"It is one of the few magazines of which a complete set is kept in stock for the benefit of borrowers."

OPINIONS OF THE PRESS.

"'Cornhill' is in a class by itself and is full of the most entertaining reading with real literary flavour."—*Liverpool Courier.*

"The counsel of perfection is to purchase the 'Cornhill,' that you may not only enjoy its contents but keep them to show a friend."

—*Guardian.*

"Those of us who are not in the habit of reading the magazine will be well advised to repair the omission."—*Oxford Magazine.*

THE CORNHILL *can be obtained of all Booksellers and Newsagents, price* 1s. 6d. *net monthly. The Subscription for a year, including postage, is* 20s. 6d.

LB

SD - #0061 - 241022 - C0 - 229/152/18 - PB - 9781330553695 - Gloss Lamination